Basic HUMAN *Anatomy*

Laboratory and Study Guide

A215

Fall 2017
Anatomy Faculty & Staff
Medical Sciences
Indiana University

Name _______________________________

Email _______________________________

Phone _______________________________

Lab Section _______________________________

*A215: Basic Human Anatomy
Laboratory and Study Guide*

Fall 2017
Anatomy Faculty & Staff
Medical Sciences
Indiana University

Printed in the United States of America
10 9 8 7 6 5 4 3 2 1
ISBN: 978-1-61740-475-7

Van-Griner Publishing
Cincinnati, Ohio
www.van-griner.com

CEO: Mike Griner
President: Dreis Van Landuyt
Project Manager: Maria Walterbusch
Customer Care Lead: Julie Reichert

O'Loughlin 475-7 Sp17
183646
Copyright © 2018

Acknowledgements

We express our appreciation to former A215 students, Associate Instructors and U.T.A.s, too numerous to mention, for their patience with shortcomings in this laboratory guide and for suggestions which have contributed to its improvement. Special thanks to Diane Richardson for her help in its preparation. Thanks also to Jennifer Morris for several figures and to Sue Childress for her assistance with the former histology appendix. We thank Mr. Jim Heersma, Lab Director, for his special assistance and direction with all aspects of this laboratory guide, and Mr. Jim Knowlton, Associate Lab Director, for vital contributions to the preparation of recent editions. Finally, we thank Dr. John Watkins for his approval and support of this project.

Contributing Editors
Valerie Dean O'Loughlin
Professor of Anatomy and
Director of Undergraduate Studies
Medical Sciences
Indiana University

George S. Dougherty
Lecturer
Medical Sciences
Indiana University

Polly Husmann
Assistant Professor of Anatomy
Medical Sciences
Indiana University

Guidelines

Missed Exams

If you expect to miss, or have missed, a scheduled exam, no matter what the reason, you must contact the lecturer (for lecture exams) or the lab director (for lab exams) *as soon as possible* at the number or email on the current course syllabus or via the

Anatomy office = 812-855-0616

The syllabus also specifies policies concerning the rescheduling of exams due to conflict or emergency.

Cheating

University policies expressed in Student and Academic Handbooks will be followed. It is each student's responsibility to avoid any form of cheating, including the appearance of cheating or providing the opportunity for others to cheat. Penalties include the lowering of the student's grade and sending a report to the Dean of Students for possible further action.

Withdrawals and Incompletes

We will adhere to university policies. W's and I's can be granted only by a course director.

Important details:
- Check the current course syllabus or Schedule of Classes for the last day to withdraw with an automatic grade of W.
- Any student with a grade of I on record for A215 may remove that grade only by arrangement with the current course director; re-registration for A215 by any such student to remove an I is invalid.

Whom to contact when about what ("chain of command"):

See **Associate Instructors** (A.I.s) about:
- questions over lab material
- questions over lecture material
- lab exam questions or scoring

Contact the **Lab Director** about:
- missed labs or lab exams
- posted exam scores and grades
- unresolved lab problems or questions
- questions over lab material

Contact the **Course Director** about:
- missed lecture exams
- unresolved problems
- questions about lecture material
- lecture exam questions
- withdrawals and incompletes

Table of Contents

A215 Laboratory Introduction

In the laboratory section of Anatomy A215, you will study examples or models of many of the anatomical structures covered in your lectures and reading. Seeing these structures and their spatial relations will help immensely in learning their names and understanding their functional relations. Your success in doing so will be evaluated by laboratory practical examinations which stress recognition and identification, but your understanding of the questions will depend heavily on your understanding of the material.

Two Associate Instructors (A.I.s) will supervise your lab section. Their purpose is to help you learn by demonstrating and explaining material and answering your questions about it. In addition, you will have an Undergraduate Teaching Assistant (U.T.A.) to assist you further.

This course utilizes two demonstration cadavers. We refer to the cadavers as DONORS because these individuals donated their bodies for educational purposes. Please treat the donors with the same respect you would treat a living individual.

This lab guide presents, **in bold**, all the **terms** you must know for lab exams (**potential answers**), and the LAB MATERIALS, in CAPITAL LETTERS, which demonstrate them (and could be used on an exam). Always use the lab guide in conjunction with your text which usually has illustrations and explanations of the structures being studied. The referenced figures are all from the 5th edition of McKinley/O'Loughlin/Pennefather-O'Brien (*Human Anatomy*) except as noted.

Some Suggestions on Studying (how to do your best!):

1. If you *prepare for labs*, you will be better able to observe material and make discoveries, to clarify questions, and to enjoy the experience. Therefore, *before coming to lab:*

    a. *always read over the scheduled lab guide section(s)* to be familiar with the procedures, goals, and terminology, and to use your time in lab to the fullest. Also, whenever possible,

    b. preview and/or print related lab introductions/images on the course website,

    c. read textbook assignments which relate to lab material and review your notes of lectures which pertain to the lab.

2. Plan to *use the entire lab period.* If you feel you have covered the day's material, and your A.I.s and U.T.A. agree (ask them to quiz you), then review it and earlier material until the end of the period. All materials will be in lab until the exam covering them, but *review time before each exam will be very limited.*

3. *Use all reference materials in the lab.* Specific figures in the *Clemente Atlas of Gross Anatomy* (1987 ed.) and the *Sobotta (Hammersen) Atlas of Histology* (1985 ed.) will be referred to in this lab guide.

4. *Identification keys for models* used in lab are included at the end of the corresponding lab guide chapter. These are most helpful when used along with definitions in the lab guide and text and with figures in the text and atlases. *Do not rely on the keys alone!!!* In addition, you can review several models using the "Virtual Lab" on the course website.

5. Learning, both in and outside lab, is often easier and more productive if you *work in pairs or small groups* where you can help and challenge each other. Questions which remain unanswered can then be brought to an instructor.

6. There is no such thing as a dumb question, but be sure you have *first checked any textbook, virtual lab, virtual microscope or atlas references* for an answer.

7. Taking notes and making sketches can give you something to refer back to, especially when you aren't in lab.

8. While studying in lab or reviewing outside, *practice writing the required terms* down, just as you will have to do in answering lab exam questions.

9. As soon as possible *after lab, go over your lab guide and notes* while you can still visualize the material. Be sure you have achieved the objectives of the lab; if not, seek assistance immediately. A small gap in your understanding now may become an insurmountable barrier later.

ONE General Method to HELP Review and Prepare for Lab Exams

1. Reread *everything* in the assigned lab guide sections or chapters you are reviewing.

2. List *all* the **bold-print** terms, either on paper (with 2–3 blank lines between) or on flash cards.

3. With lab guide and books closed, go through your list/cards, *writing* definitions and complete descriptions of each term (including everywhere in lab it is seen). Skip any you can't recall.

4. Look up and complete definitions and descriptions for any terms of which you were unsure.

5. Reorganize your list/cards into groups with identical or very similar descriptions.

6. Within each group, ask yourself what distinguishes each term from the others. If you can't recall, look it up. If you can't find the answer, ask one of your instructors as soon as possible.

Laboratory Policies and Regulations

Each of you should have an equal opportunity to study lab materials, but this is possible only if each of you cooperates in following certain procedures. Therefore, you should be aware of all these *laboratory policies and regulations:*

1. Unless prior arrangements have been made with the Lab Director or Assistant Lab Director, you may attend only the lab section to which you are assigned. You may enter no more than 5 minutes before your lab period begins; you will have to be out of the lab by 5 minutes after your lab period ends.

2. *No teaching materials may be taken from the laboratory.* They will be inventoried after each lab period; anything missing will be dealt with as a theft.

3. *Handle all materials with great care.* Many, such as parts of the skeleton and some models, are fragile. (Because our demonstration donors, in particular, are readily damaged, only A.I.s will be allowed to handle them.)

4. After using teaching materials, *return them to their place* in lab for use by others.

5. Always *carefully reassemble models* having more than one part when you finish studying them so others can use them.

6. *Never use pens or pencils as pointers* in examining lab materials. Pointers will be provided to prevent accidental damage. Above all, please *do not deliberately draw or mark on anything in the lab* that is not yours.

7. In general, two of you will share the use of one computer during most lab sessions. *Be sure, if you are the last to use it during a given session, to log off* (but *not* turn off) your computer *before leaving.*

8. For the most part, you will use microscopes and slides only indirectly in this lab via the Virtual Microscope. Occasionally, however, we may set up actual slides on microscopes in lab as demonstrations. Therefore, to assist you in both understanding what you see on the Virtual Microscope and your limited use of actual microscopes, we include a detailed guide in the "Use of the Microscope" section (see page 4).

9. If any lab material is damaged while you are using it, please report it to your A.I. or the lab director right away so it can be repaired or replaced as soon as possible!

10. *Do not leave waste* of any kind on lab tables or seats or in the drawers at your lab stations. Appropriate receptacles are readily available, including for a variety of recyclable materials.

11. To help us learn who you are, a seating chart will be made up for each section early in the term. Thereafter, *each student will be responsible for the condition of his or her lab station at the end of each lab period.*

12. For several reasons, *no visitors or guests* will be allowed in the lab unless specific prior permission has been given by the lab director.

13. As in other classrooms, *you must turn of your cell phone before entering the lab* and *you many not use it while present.* Furthermore, *taking of photographs, of any sort by any means, is not permitted in the lab.*

14. Each time you come to lab, take with you to your lab station only material you will need there. Leave book bags, tote bags, etc., on the shelves provided for that purpose at the back of the lab. There are coat hooks along the same wall.

15. Be sure you take with you when you leave all personal belongings you brought with you to lab. In addition, *put your name in your lab guide and any other hard-copy references you bring to lab;* if you do leave them somewhere, your chances of getting them back will be much better.

Use of the Microscope

1. Familiarize yourself with the parts of your microscope (see page 5), their roles and operation.

2. Keep the dust cover in your drawer when using the microscope.

3. Turn your microscope lamp on and adjust it to a medium-to-bright intensity. The iris diaphragm should be about two-thirds open. The condenser lens beneath the stage should be raised almost up to it and left in this position.

4. Lens paper is in your drawer if a lens or slide requires cleaning.

5. *Begin with the stage at its lowest position. Then, position the lowest power objective lens* (usually the shortest) *under the microscope barrel.* It should click into position. The magnification of each lens is printed on its side: 4×, 10×, 40× (you should **not** use the 100× objective lens in this class if there is one on your microscope).

6. *Examine the tissue on a microscope slide with the unaided eye.* You may recognize its structure and be able to locate a particular part you want to examine microscopically. Place the slide in the clamp on the stage with its coverslip up, then adjust its position until the area of interest is centered under the objective lens.

7. Watching from the side, use the coarse focus adjustment knob, turning it forward to move the slide as close to the low power objective as possible.

8. Looking through the eyepiece(s), slowly reverse the coarse adjustment until the tissue comes into focus. If nothing becomes visible, reposition the slide according to step 6 and repeat the procedure.

9. To examine a tissue under higher magnification, focus under lower power as above, then move the next higher power objective into position. If the tissue is not then in focus, slowly turn the fine adjustment knob *backward* until it is. If this does not work, *watch from the side* and slowly bring the slide as close as possible to the objective, then look through the eyepiece and again focus backward. *Never focus forward* unless you are watching to be sure the slide has not reached the objective. Breaking this rule could break both slides and lenses.

10. If ever the above procedure does not work, seek help from your A.I. or U.T.A.

11. Each microscope has a pointer in the right eyepiece to let you indicate a particular structure in the field being viewed. To do this *adjust the slide position; do not rotate the eyepiece.* Also, please do not rotate the eyepiece assembly on the microscope.

12. IMPORTANT: Throughout this course, be sure, *when examining organs, tissues or structures microscopically, to use all available magnifications* (4×, 10×, and 40× objectives). Any magnification at which features studied are recognizable could be used on an exam question.

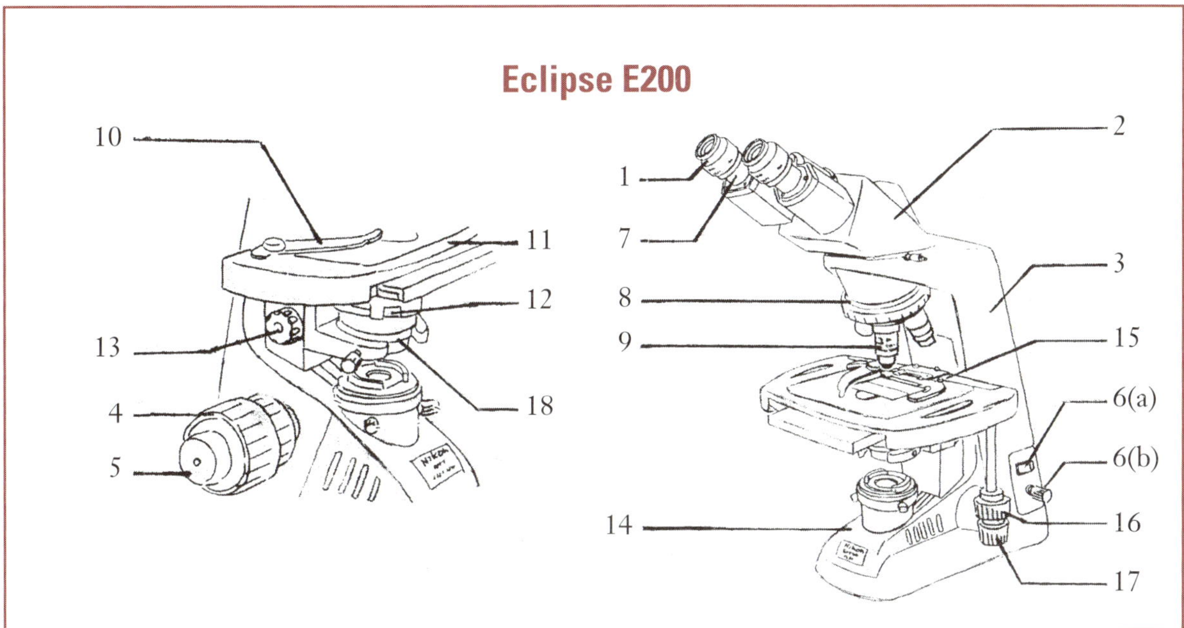

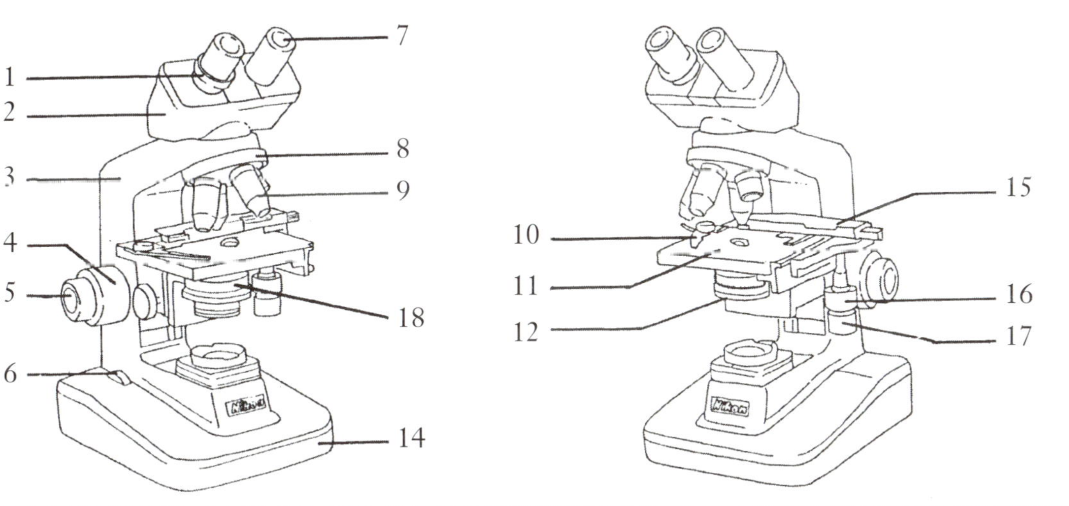

Microscopes

Key

1. diopter ring
2. binocular eyepiece
3. arm
4. coarse focus knob
5. fine focus knob
6. (a) power switch
   (b) brightness control
7. eyepiece
8. revolving nosepiece
9. objective
10. slide holder
11. stage
12. diaphragm control lever
13. condenser focus knob
14. microscope base
15. mechanical stage
16. stage Y axis travel knob (forward and backward)
17. stage X axis travel knob (lateral)
18. condenser

The Cell & Cell Division

I. Introduction

II. The Cell
    A. Structure
    B. Electron Micrographs

III. Electron Micrographs

IV. Cell Division
    A. Mitosis
    B. Meiosis

I. Introduction

When studying microscopic anatomy, several important points must be kept in mind:

A. Since there are many ways to prepare tissues for microscopic examination, tissue components do not always look the same from one preparation to another. You will notice, for example, a great deal of variation in the colors of a preparation depending on the stains used.

B. When viewing the projected slides or pictures, it is important to realize that the magnification may vary from one preparation to the next. Thus, a single blood cell may appear as a small "dot" in one slide at low magnification or, at higher magnification, may fill the entire field of view. It is important that you always consider the entire "field" in view *before* you concentrate on a more specific area or single cell.

C. Use your lecture notes and text (the references in parentheses, unless otherwise noted) to explain and reinforce the microscopic anatomy you see in lab.

D. Go to the following URL:

http://www.indiana.edu/~anat215/virtualscope2/start.htm

and read the "Use of the Virtual Microscope" section before using the VIRTUAL MICROSCOPE. Throughout the lab guide, the virtual microscope slides to be observed will be in capital letters.

II. The Cell

(pp. 24–45)

A. Cells are traditionally divided into three parts, the **cytoplasm**, the **plasma membrane** (or **cell membrane**) and the **nucleus** (Fig. 2.3). The **cytoplasm** includes everything between the plasma membrane and the nuclear envelope. The **nucleus** is the nuclear envelope and its contents. Using the virtual microscope and the SLIDES OF BLOOD and SPINAL CORD, find examples of these.

    1. In BLOOD, examine white blood cells, each having a darkly stained **nucleus**. (Fig. 21.2, p. 635; Table 21.3, p. 643).

    2. In a SPINAL CORD cross section (there may be two or three sections on the slide), examine the large, irregularly shaped motor neuron cell bodies found in the anterior horn (Fig. 14.3, p. 415; Sobotta, Fig. 199). The round **nucleus** in these cells is lighter staining than the **cytoplasm**; identify also the **nucleolus**, a spherical dark-staining body within the nucleus.

B. In order to fully distinguish the structures within the cell, ELECTRON MICROGRAPHS (EMs) must be used. The following structures should be identified on the "EMs" in lab (*NOTE*: section III below specifies which structures to identify on each EM) (see also Table 2.2):

    1. The **plasma membrane** (or **cell membrane**) (Fig. 2.3, 2.4).

    2. Within the cytoplasm, the following organelles:

        a. **mitochondria**: usually ovoid with a double membrane. The outer membrane completely surrounds the mitochondrion and the inner membrane has folds called cristae extending inward (Fig. 2.3, 2.12).

        b. the endoplasmic reticulum is an extensive intracellular double-membrane network throughout the cytoplasm. There are two types (Fig. 2.3, 2.8):

            i. **rough** (or granular) **endoplasmic reticulum,** having small dense bodies, ribosomes, on the surface.

            ii. smooth (or agranular) endoplasmic reticulum, having a smooth surface, without ribosomes.

        c. the **Golgi apparatus** (or **Golgi complex**): consisting of short, smooth membranous sacs (cisternae) "stacked" upon one another, and small vesicles (Fig. 2.3, 2.9).

        d. **centrioles**: occurring in pairs, each centriole is made up of nine triplets of microtubules (Fig. 2.3, 2.15).

        e. **ribosomes**: small particles found either in clusters within the cytoplasm (free ribosomes) or attached to the endoplasmic reticulum (fixed ribosomes) (Fig. 2.3, 2.8, 2.13).

    3. The **nucleus** (Fig. 2.3, 2.17).

    4. Specializations of the **plasma membrane**:

        a. **cilia** (singular: **cilium**): motile eyelash-like processes which project out from the plasma membrane (Fig. 2.3, 2.16; Table 4.2 d, e, pp. 87, 88; Sobotta, Figs. 97–98).

        b. **microvilli**: much smaller, non-motile, finger-like processes, uniform in size and shape and, most often, evenly distributed over the cell's apical surface (Fig. 2.3; Fig. 26.15, p. 792; Sobotta, Fig. 94).

III. Electron Micrographs

from Toner and Carr: "Cell Structure" (see references) used in lab.

PLATE #	STRUCTURES ILLUSTRATED
1	plasma membrane (or cell membrane), rough endoplasmic reticulum, mitochondria, nucleus, free ribosomes (Fig. 2.3)
7	rough endoplasmic reticulum (Fig. 2.8)
10	Golgi apparatus (Fig. 2.9)
11	mitochondrion (Fig. 2.12)
12	centriole (Fig. 2.15)
25	microvilli (Fig. 26.15, p. 792)
43, 44	cilia (Fig. 2.16)

IV. Cell Division

(pp. 46–49)

A. Mitosis is a continuous process but has named stages. We will illustrate cells passing through these stages by using projected slides. You should then find examples of four stages on the VIRTUAL MICROSCOPE SLIDE OF ROOT TIPS (Fig. 2.20; Sobotta, Fig. 73).

    1. **Prophase**: look for the chromosomes appearing as threads within the nucleus.

    2. **Metaphase**: you should be able to see the chromosomes lined up in the center of the cell; the nuclear envelope has disassembled.

    3. **Anaphase**: the chromosomes have been pulled apart; they appear as strands moving toward the opposite poles of the cell.

    4. **Telophase**: the chromosomes have reached and are clumped together at the poles. The cell itself appears to be pulled apart.

B. Meiosis occurs in the sex cells and is a reduction division. The stages of meiosis are the same as for mitosis but are repeated in two successive events. Therefore, understanding the stages of mitosis will help in understanding meiosis. We will not demonstrate meiosis in the lab, but the topic will be covered in lecture.

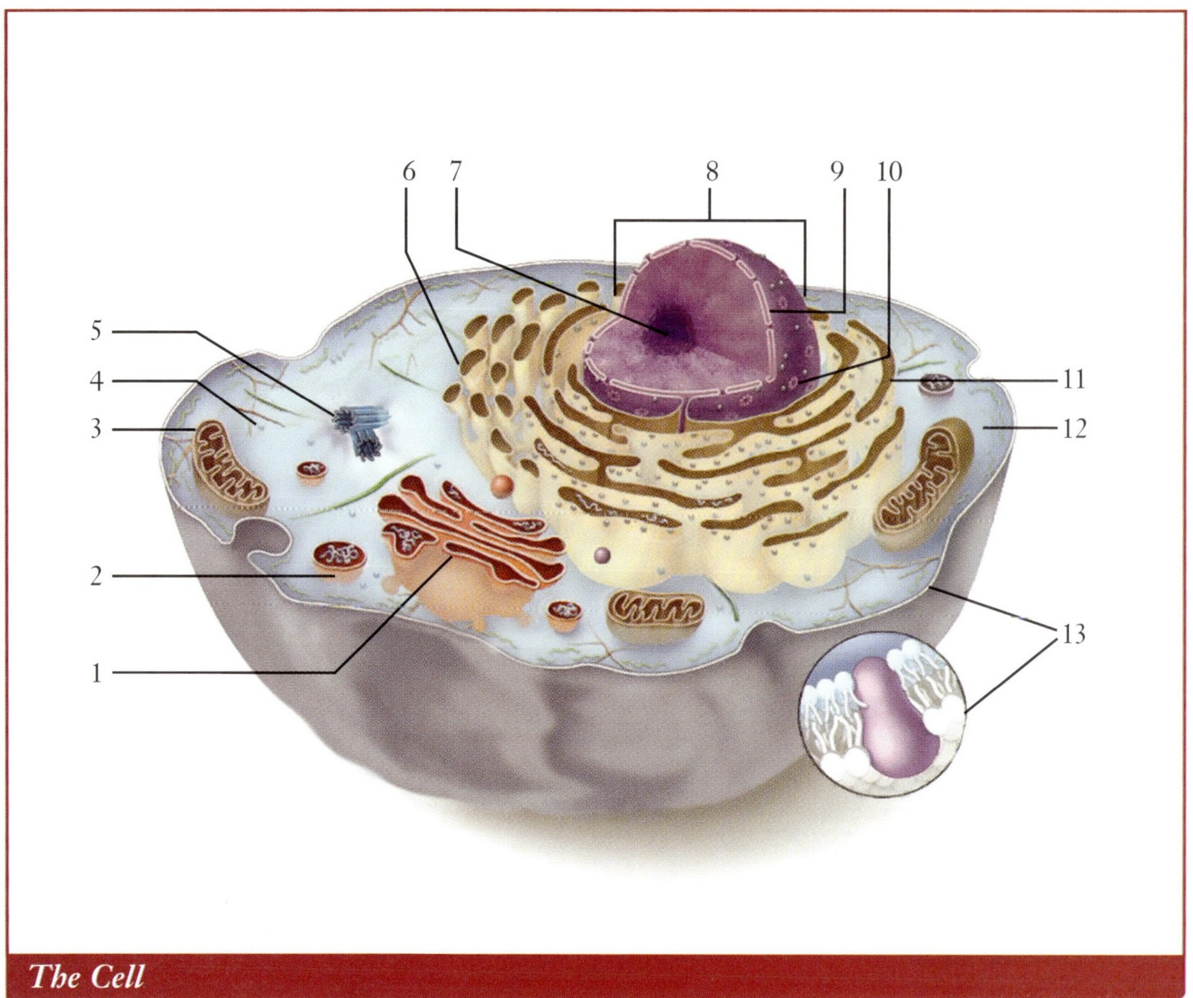

The Cell

Key

1. Golgi apparatus
2. lysosome
3. mitochondrion
4. free ribosome
5. centriole
6. smooth endoplasmic reticulum
7. nucleolus
8. nucleus
9. nuclear envelope
10. nuclear pore
11. rough endoplasmic reticulum
12. cytoplasm
13. plasma membrane

2

CHAPTER

Tissues: Epithelial, Connective

I. Introduction

(pp. 81–82, 95–96)

A. Tissues are groups of similar cells specialized for the performance of a common function. There are four principal types of tissues, each functionally and morphologically distinct from the others.

    1. Epithelial: covering surfaces and having one side free and the other attached to underlying supportive tissue.

    2. Connective: often packed between and around other tissues; in general, they support structures but may also have special functions.

    3. Muscular: specialized for contraction.

    4. Nervous: specialized for impulse conduction, integration, and storage of information.

B. This chapter examines epithelial and connective tissues. (Muscle and nervous tissues will be studied with their respective systems.) We will use several VIRTUAL MICROSCOPE SLIDES, so review the procedures described in the Introduction. (All references listed are from McKinley/O'Loughlin/Pennefather-O'Brien, unless otherwise noted.)

II. Epithelia

(pp. 81–95)

A. Epithelia form layers covering surfaces or lining cavities; they often fold inward to form glands. They may consist of a single layer of cells (simple) or more than one layer (stratified). Epithelia are anchored to the underlying connective tissue via a thin basement membrane. The side of an epithelial layer opposite the basement membrane is called its apical (or free) surface.

B. Simple Epithelia: There are four specific types of simple epithelia distinguished by the shape of the cells; use the virtual microscope slides (designated by capital letters) to find examples of these.

    1. **Simple squamous epithelium**: KIDNEY. In the darker outer region of the kidney find small round structures scattered through out the slide. Magnify one and note that the circular clear space around it is lined by very flat cells, each with a dark flattened nucleus (Table 4.2a). The nucleus may be all of the cell you can see. Also in this region, note the many sections of tubules lined by simple cuboidal epithelium, described below.

    2. **Simple cuboidal epithelium**: KIDNEY. The darker outer region of the kidney also has many sections of highly coiled tubules cut at different angles. Most of these are lined by a layer of cells about as high as they are wide. If the nucleus is visible, it will be centrally located (Table 4.2b; Sobotta, Fig. 78). The lighter-stained, deeper region of the kidney is composed of many small, straighter tubules. Many are lined by a simple cuboidal epithelium but with somewhat flatter cells. Also, some tubules in this region are lined by a simple squamous epithelium.

    3. (Nonciliated) **simple columnar epithelium**: SMALL INTESTINE. In this cross-section of the intestine, the inner cavity (where food would be digested) is lined by a single layer of cells; each cell is like a tall column with an elongated nucleus near its base (Table 4.2c).

    4. **Pseudostratified** (ciliated) **columnar epithelium**: TRACHEA. In cross-section, the inner or concave surface (the air passage) is lined by an epithelium that appears to have more than one layer of nuclei, but is simple because all cells touch the basement membrane even if they do not all reach the apical surface (Table 4.2e; Sobotta, Fig. 86). Cilia should be visible on the apical surface.

C. Stratified Epithelia: There are always two or more cell layers and only the cells of the deepest layer contact the basement membrane. Use the virtual microscope to see examples of two specific types of stratified epithelia.

    1. (Keratinized) **stratified squamous epithelium**: SKIN. The darker-stained surface of this section consists of an epithelium having many layers of cells, those nearer the basement membrane appearing darker and more rounded, those nearer the free surface appearing lighter, flattened and indistinct (Table 4.3a). The basement membrane is wavy or rolling, not parallel to the apical surface.

2. **Transitional epithelium**: URETER. This long tube's inner space is lined by a darker stained epithelium having a small number of layers of cells. This epithelium takes on two appearances: surface cells may appear cuboidal or dome-shaped when the epithelium is non-stretched; when it is stretched laterally, however, surface cells appear flatter (Table 4.3e; Sobotta, Fig. 90). The basement membrane nearly parallels the apical surface.

D. Surface Specializations of Epithelia *(p. 43)*

1. **Cilia**: on the slide of TRACHEA, these hair-like projections can be faintly seen on the apical (free) surface of the pseudostratified columnar epithelium (Table 4.2e; Sobotta, Fig. 92).

2. Microvilli: the slide of SMALL INTESTINE may show evidence of microvilli, appearing as a very thin brush border on the apical surface of the simple columnar epithelium (Table 4.2c; Sobotta, Fig. 91).

E. Glands, some terminology and examples

1. Glands which release their products for diffusion into nearby blood vessels are termed endocrine glands, and are found in various locations throughout the body. They play important roles in regulating normal body function and will be discussed and illustrated later in the course.

2. Glands which release secretions into a duct or onto a surface are termed exocrine glands.

3. Both endocrine and exocrine glands develop from epithelial tissue, but exocrine glands retain their connection to the epithelial surface, usually in the form of a duct.

4. Exocrine glands are variable in their size and the arrangement of their cells.

    a. **goblet cells** are unicellular glands, i.e., each gland consists of a single secretory cell. Examples of this type of cell may be observed on the SMALL INTESTINE slide (Table 4.2c , Fig. 4.4; Sobotta, Fig. 100) interspersed throughout the corresponding epithelium studied above. Goblet cells secrete mucus directly onto the apical surface and thus may be identified as having a globular, usually light-staining area just below the apical surface.

    b. to see the more elaborate arrangement of some multicellular exocrine glands, examine Fig. 4.6 and Sobotta, Fig. 99. Several examples will be identified in other chapters.

III. Connective Tissues

(pp. 95–108)

A. All connective tissues consist of three basic components: cells, fibers, and ground substance. The proportions and nature of these three components vary in the different connective tissues depending on their location and function.

B. Connective tissues may be placed in several different classes:

1. Four to be studied in lab (among those called connective tissues proper) are important as packing, binding, and supporting tissue of the body. You should be able to recognize the following specific types of connective tissues proper on the VIRTUAL MICROSCOPE SLIDES. Usually the nucleus of a cell is darkly stained but its cytoplasm may not be clearly distinguishable from that of nearby cells or ground substance.

   a. loose connective tissues (including two to be studied in lab):

      i. **areolar connective** tissue (often called simply "loose connective" tissue): AREOLAR CONNECTIVE TISSUE. Notice the loose arrangement of the fibers (Table 4.7a; Sobotta, Fig. 116).

      ii. **adipose** connective tissue: MESENTERY. This tissue contains large numbers of fat cells (adipocytes) that will appear as large, pale cells with the nucleus pushed off to one edge (if visible). (Table 4.7b; Sobotta, Fig. 127).

      iii. reticular connective tissue: the fibers in this connective tissue are extremely fine and have a net-like arrangement (Table 4.7c; Sobotta, Fig. 119).

   b. dense connective tissues (including two types to be studied in lab):

      i. **dense irregular connective** tissue: SKIN. Examine the dark pink tissue deep to the darker epithelium at the free surface. Notice how the collagen fiber bundles are arranged randomly (Table 4.8b; Sobotta, Fig. 118).

      ii. **dense regular connective** tissue: WHITE FIBROUS TISSUE. The fibers in this connective tissue are largely parallel (Table 4.8a).

      iii. elastic connective tissue: This tissue is characterized by large numbers of elastic fibers which must be specially stained to be seen. Use your text to see examples of this connective tissue (Table 4.8c; Sobotta, Fig. 266, 269).

2. Other connective tissues are classified by the presence of a particular component or a modification of one of the basic components. These specialized connective tissues will be studied later in the course.

    a. cartilage: (Table 4.9). To be studied in Chapter 4.

    b. bone: (Table 4.10). To be studied in Chapter 4.

    c. blood: (Table 4.11; Sobotta, Figs. 229–35). To be studied in Chapter 7.

IV. Study Tips for this Chapter

A. Make sure you look at every VIRTUAL MICROSCOPE SLIDE listed in this chapter, and be able to identify every type of tissue listed. If you are having problems with the identification, ask for help!

B. In lab, have your lab partner "quiz" you on the slides. Your lab partner can set up a virtual microscope slide, hide the label, and then you try to identify the tissue or structure that the pointer is on. Reverse roles: YOU set up a slide to quiz your lab partner. Both you and your lab partner will be better able to identify the structures on the slides.

C. At home, make a list of all of the different kinds of tissues you examined and write out the characteristics of each. By writing the names of the tissues in a list, you will better remember the names.

D. Draw simple pictures of each type of epithelium (similar to the "Epithelial Types" figures on the next page). The act of drawing the pictures will help you better remember the characteristics of each type of tissue.

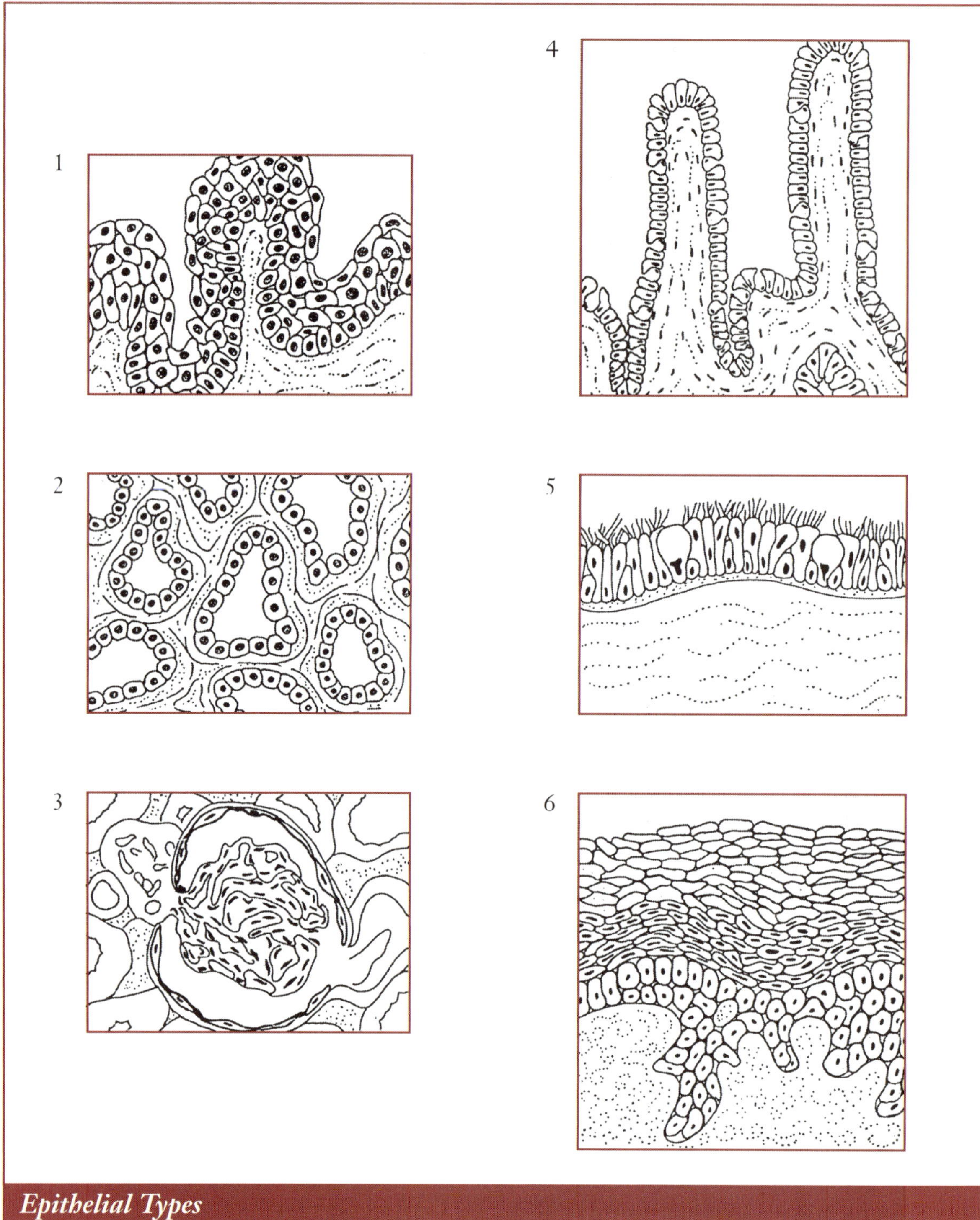

Epithelial Types

Key

1. transitional
2. simple cuboidal
3. simple squamous
4. simple columnar
5. pseudostratified ciliated columnar
6. stratified squamous

Integumentary System

I. Introduction

II. Structure of the Integument
    A. Epidermis
    B. Dermis
    C. Subcutaneous Layer
    D. Epithelial Specializations of the Integument

III. Study Tips for this Chapter

IV. Integumentary System Model Key

I. Introduction
(pp. 119–120)

A. The **integument**, commonly called **skin**, forms the outer covering of the body. The functions of the skin include protection, prevention of water loss, temperature regulation, metabolic regulation, immune defense, sensory reception, and excretion by means of secretion.

B. The skin consists of several layers: a surface epithelial layer called the **epidermis** composed of 4–5 specific layers; and an underlying connective tissue layer termed the **dermis** with 2 specific layers. The **subcutaneous layer** (also known as the *hypodermis* or *superficial fascia*), is a connective tissue layer attaching skin to structures beneath it. Thus, skin is considered an organ, and is the largest organ of the body.

C. The structure of the skin will be shown using projected slides, VIRTUAL MICROSCOPE SLIDES and MODELS.

II. Structure of the Integument
(pp. 121–134)

A. Epidermis (Figs. 5.1–5.3, Table 5.2; Sobotta, Fig. 472) microscope slides of THICK SKIN and THIN SKIN, and the SKIN MODEL.

    1. **Epidermis** consists of keratinized stratified squamous epithelium, a specific type of tissue. It is considerably thicker in areas of the body exposed to friction, such as the palms of the hands and soles of the feet.

2. On the THICK SKIN SLIDE(S) and on the SKIN MODEL, the **epidermis** is divided into specific layers based on staining changes as cells are moved toward the surface. These specific layers, called strata (singular: stratum), are listed from superficial to deep:

   a. **stratum corneum**: this is the most superficial stratum and composed of 20–30 layers of dead, anucleated cells (keratinocytes) on the free surface of the epithelium.

   b. stratum lucidum: seen only in thick skin, this stratum appears clear or white and is superficial to the stratum granulosum.

   c. stratum granulosum: three to five layers of cells which contain numerous dark granules.

   d. stratum spinosum: several layers of cells which, at high magnification, appear to contain numerous spines on their surfaces connecting adjacent cells.

   e. **stratum basale**: the deepest stratum of the epidermis, it consists of a layer of darkly stained cells closest to the dermis.

B. The **dermis** (SKIN MODEL, THICK and THIN SKIN SLIDES) is made up primarily of dense irregular connective tissue and may also be divided into specific layers (Fig. 5.1, 5.6, Table 5.2).

   1. **Papillary layer**: deep to the stratum basale of the epidermis; usually quite thin and light staining; named for the structures which protrude from this layer into the epidermis, the **dermal papillae** (Fig. 5.6; Sobotta, Figs. 472–3).

   2. **Reticular layer**: deep to the papillary layer and much thicker; contains large, coarse bundles of collagen fibers; usually darker staining.

C. The **subcutaneous layer** (hypodermis, superficial fascia) is a layer attaching the skin to underlying structures. It consists of both areolar and adipose connective tissue. Identify it on the MODELS and the THICK SKIN and THIN SKIN SLIDE(S) (Fig. 5.2, Table 5.2).

D. Epidermal derivatives of the integument (*epidermal appendages* of the integument) include hair, nails and glands. Use the MODELS and the THIN SKIN SLIDES to identify the bold terms.

   1. Hair (Fig. 5.1, 5.9; Sobotta, Fig. 483): each hair arises from a **hair follicle**, which is an oblique tube having an epithelial sheath surrounded by connective tissue. Microscope slides usually show only a part of any single follicle because of the orientation of hair in the skin. Identify also the **arrector pili muscle** associated with a follicle.

   2. Nails (Fig. 5.8) are a modification of the stratum corneum of the epidermis. Use your text to review the relation of nails to skin. (Not on slides or models.)

3. Glands (Fig. 5.10): there are several types of glands associated with skin. Use the MODELS and the THIN SKIN SLIDE(S) to identify the following:

   a. **sweat** (sudoriferous) **glands** secrete perspiration through **sweat gland ducts** to cool the body. Identify these also on the THICK SKIN SLIDE.

   b. **sebaceous glands** secrete sebum (oil) to lubricate the skin and hair.

III. Study Tips for this Chapter

A. Identify the layers, specific layers, and structures found in the integument on both the VIRTUAL MICROSCOPE SLIDES and the SKIN MODEL. Don't assume that if you study just one item (e.g., the model only), you will be able to identify the same item on a slide.

B. In lab, have your lab partner "quiz" you on the slides. Your lab partner can display a slide, hide the label, and then you try to identify the tissue or structure that the pointer is on. Reverse roles: YOU set up a slide to quiz your lab partner. Both you and your lab partner will be better able to identify the structures on the slides.

C. At home, make a list of the different *layers* of the skin (epidermis, dermis, subcutaneous layer). Write out characteristics of each.

D. Also at home, make a list of the *specific layers* found in the skin (e.g., stratum corneum, papillary layer). Write out basic characteristics of each. Do the same for the structures found in the skin.

E. Remember to use the VIRTUAL MICROSCOPE to review the tissue types at home!

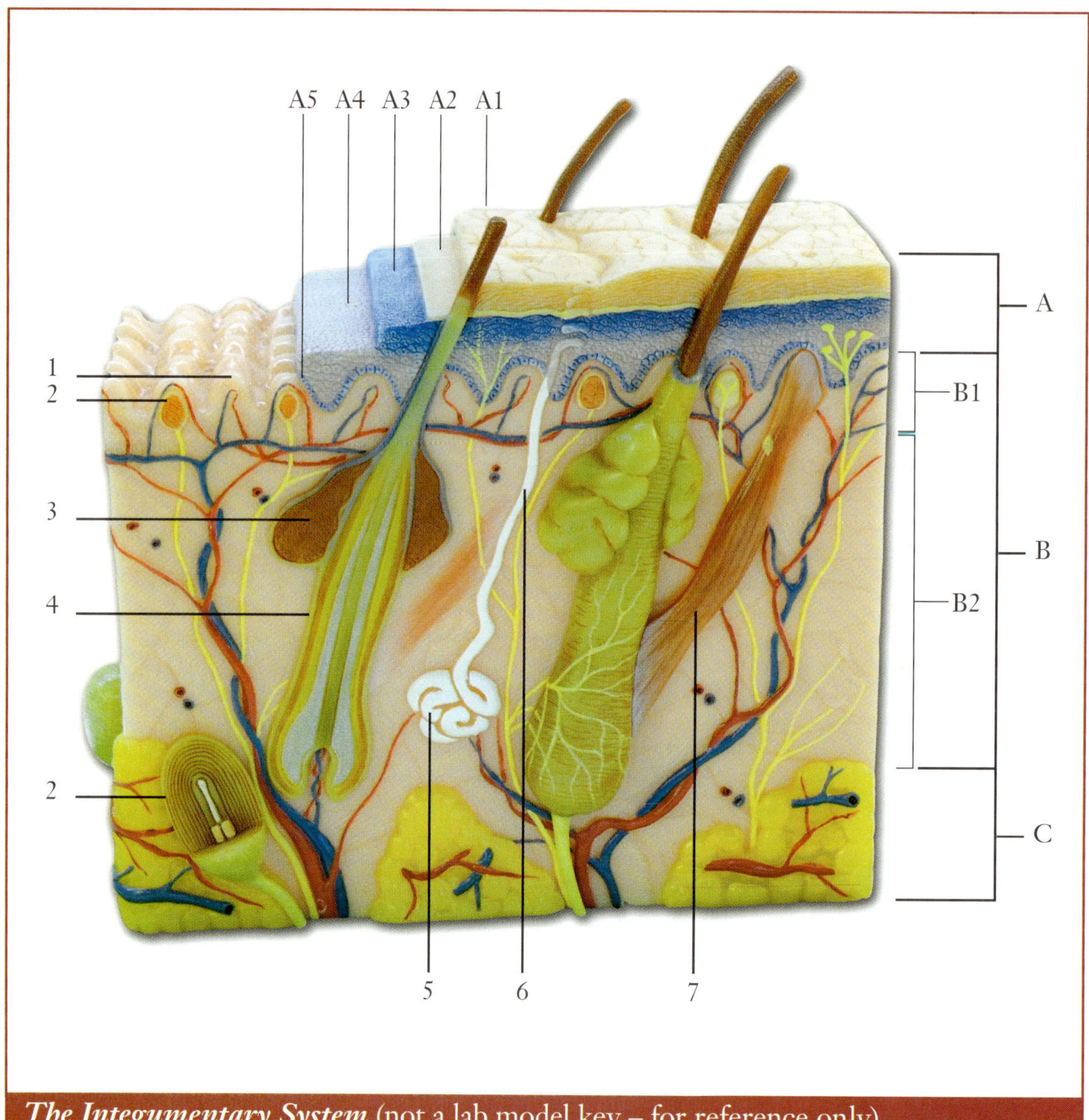

The Integumentary System (not a lab model key – for reference only)

Structures

1. dermal papilla
2. nerve endings
3. sebaceous gland
4. hair follicle
5. (secretory portion of) sweat gland
6. sweat gland duct
7. arrector pili muscle

Layers

A. Epidermis
    A1. stratum corneum
    A2. stratum lucidum
    A3. stratum granulosum
    A4. stratum spinosum
    A5. stratum basale

B. Dermis
    B1. papillary layer
    B2. reticular layer

C. Subcutaneous layer

IV. Integumentary System Model Key

LABEL(S)	TERM

I **epidermis**
   1 **stratum corneum**
   2c **stratum basale**
II **dermis**
   3 **dermal papilla**
   7 **sweat gland** (eccrine)
     sweat gland duct
  d–g, 11, 11a (parts of hair) **hair follicle**
   13 **sebaceous gland**
   14 **arrector pili muscle**
   15a–c (parts of) **sweat gland, sweat gland duct**
III **subcutaneous layer**

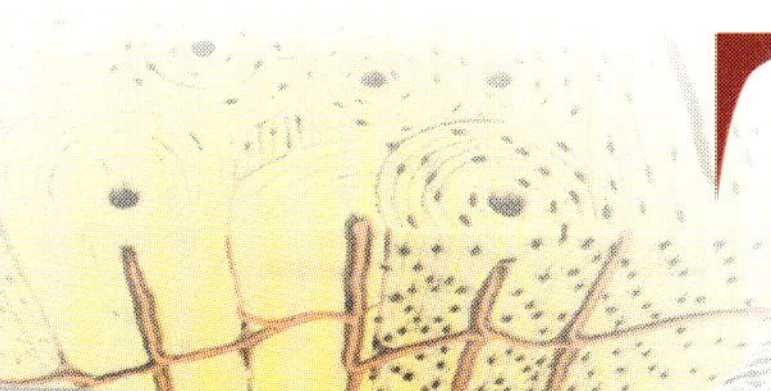

4

CHAPTER

Skeletal System

I. Introduction

II. The Axial Skeleton
    A. The Skull
    B. Named Features of Skull Bones
    C. The Vertebral Column, Ribs, and Sternum

III. The Appendicular Skeleton
    A. Shoulder and Upper Limb
    B. Hip and Lower Limb

IV. Articulations

V. Histology of the Skeletal System
    A. Cartilage
    B. Bone
    C. Osteon Model Key

VI. Study Tips for this Chapter

VII. Skeletal System Model Key

I. Introduction

(pp. 174–175)

A. The skeletal system provides a system of levers for movement and is the body's supportive and protective framework; it is composed of bones and cartilage and the articulations joining these components.

B. Most of your study will be of specific BONES and their features. In examining these in lab, be sure to *use only the soft pointers* provided so that you don't mark or damage them. Some are extremely fragile. Hold the parts of the skull firmly so they do not fall.

C. Familiarity with the descriptive terminology in Chapter 1 of your textbook will be important in learning gross anatomy in the rest of this course. For the skeletal system, review in particular pp. 11–19, Fig. 1.5, Table 1.2, Fig. 1.8, and Table 1.3 on the anatomical position, directional terms, regional terms, and the body planes; several skeletal terms are defined in Fig. 6.17, page 167.

D. You can see or feel many features of the skeleton on yourself (or someone else), and doing so may help you get to know these terms.

E. We will examine cartilage and bone microscopically to understand their structural and functional characteristics.

II. The Axial Skeleton

(pp. 173–214)

The axial skeleton (Fig. 7.1, page 174) is composed of the vertebral column, the ribs, the sternum, and the skull. We will study these using both real bone and molded plastic SKULLS, "EXPLODED" SKULLS, COMPLETE ARTICULATED SKELETONS, and DISARTICULATED SKELETAL ELEMENTS.

A. The skull (pp. 175–203): Identify on the SKULLS the bones and sutures (joints) in bold print below, noting how they are associated with one another. Use the figures in parentheses and the EXPLODED SKULLS to identify and study the structure of each bone. Note which bones are single and which are paired. (*Use pointers!!!!!*) Six bones also have features to identify, as specified in section B.

   1. The skull consists of eight (8) cranial bones and fourteen (14) facial bones (Fig. 7.2). The cranial bones surround the cranial cavity and protect the brain inside it, while the facial bones create the skeletal architecture of the face. These bones have many features and foramina that are for muscle attachments, transmitting vessels and nerves, etc.

   2. The eight (8) cranial bones consist of the following: The **frontal** bone (Fig. 7.4, 7.6, 7.7, 7.9, 7.10, 7.25) forms the forehead, the anterior roof of the skull, and the superior walls of the orbits. Posterior to the frontal bone are the left and right **parietal** bones (Fig. 7.4–7.7, 7.9, 7.11), which form the superior sides of the cranium. The frontal and parietal bones are connected by a fibrous joint called the **coronal suture** (Fig. 7.6, 7.7). The **sagittal suture** (Fig. 7.5) connects the two parietal bones, while the **lambdoid suture** (Fig. 7.5–7.8) connects the parietal bones with the **occipital** bone (Fig. 7.5–7.9, 7.13). The occipital bone is located posteriorly and inferiorly.

   The inferior sides of the cranial vault are formed by the left and right **temporal** bones (Fig. 7.4–7.9, 7.12), which join the parietal bones via a squamosal suture. The **ethmoid** bone (Fig. 7.6, 7.7, 7.9, 7.15, 7.16) and **sphenoid** bone (Fig. 7.4, 7.6, 7.8, 7.9, 7.14, 7.15) also contribute to the formation of the cranium. They are best seen from within the cranial cavity, although they may be seen from the exterior and in the orbit as well.

   3. The 14 facial bones consist of the following: The upper jaw and most of the hard palate are formed by the left and right **maxillae** (Fig. 7.4, 7.6–7.8, 7.21). The posterior third of the hard palate is formed by left and right **palatine** bones (Fig. 7.7, 7.8, 7.15, 7.20).

Connecting with the lateral sides of the maxillae are the left and right **zygomatic** bones (Fig. 7.4–7.6, 7.18, 7.25), which form the prominence of the cheek. The bridge of the nose is formed from left and right **nasal** bones (Fig. 7.4, 7.6, 7.7), while a small portion of the medial wall of the orbits is formed by left and right **lacrimal** bones (Fig. 7.4, 7.6, 7.25).

Within the nasal cavity, the **vomer** (Fig. 7.4, 7.7, 7.8, 7.15, 7.19) forms the inferior part of the nasal septum that divides the nasal cavity into left and right halves. On the lateral sides of the nasal cavity are two small curled bones called the **inferior nasal conchae** (Fig. 7.3, 7.4, 7.15, 7.23; Clemente, Figs. 684–685—see also on the HALF-HEAD MODEL). Finally, the lower jaw is formed by a single bone named the **mandible** (Fig. 7.4–7.7, 7.22).

4. Within each temporal bone are three tiny ear bones or auditory ossicles. (There are a total of 6 auditory ossicles for the entire skull.) These ossicles are the malleus, incus, and stapes, and they help transmit and modify sound impulses through the middle ear. (You will study these bones later in lab with the other parts of the ear.)

5. The **hyoid** bone (Fig. 7.26; Clemente, Fig. 574) is not part of the skull but is associated with it. Single, U-shaped, posterior and inferior to the mandible, it attaches to the bones of the skull via muscles and ligaments and is seen only on the COMPLETE SKELETONS and HALF-HEAD MODEL.

B. Named features of skull bones (Table 7.1): Review the terms defined on page 167 in your text! Descriptions like these or their synonyms will be used to specify what's being asked for on lab exam questions. Then, using the figures in parentheses, find the listed features on both NORMAL and EXPLODED SKULLS. *Note:* the sinuses are *enclosed within* bones (Fig. 7.3, 7.7, 7.23, 7.24), but you should be familiar with their locations, and be able to identify on the materials specified those sinuses that are in bold print.

1. Within the frontal bone is the **frontal sinus** (Fig. 7.3, 7.7, 7.9, 7.23, 7.24). This sinus develops by puberty, and it connects to the nasal cavity via a small duct. See it only on the HALF-HEAD MODEL and BISECTED SKULLS.

2. The occipital bone contains a large hole, appropriately named the **foramen magnum** (Fig. 7.8, 7.9, 7.13). The spinal cord enters the skull through this foramen. On the left and right sides of the foramen magnum are the **occipital condyles** (Fig. 7.8, 7.13a). These condyles articulate with the first cervical vertebra. The **external occipital protuberance** (Fig. 7.5b, 7.8, 7.13a) is a (usually) prominent, pointed projection on the posterior surface of the bone. It is more prominent on male skulls than female skulls.

3. Each temporal bone has a long, slender, anteriorly-projecting **zygomatic process** (Fig. 7.6, 7.8, 7.12), which articulates with the zygomatic bone. Inferior to the proximal end of this process is a rounded depression called the **mandibular fossa** (Fig. 7.8, 7.12a), where the mandible articulates. Posterior to this fossa is the **external acoustic** (or **auditory**) **meatus** (or **canal**) (Fig. 7.6, 7.12a). The **mastoid process** (Fig. 7.5b, 7.6, 7.8, 7.12) is a rounded bump-like elevation posterior to the external acoustic meatus. The **styloid process** (Fig. 7.6–7.8, 7.12) is a thin, pointed projection of bone (broken off several of the lab specimens) , anterior and medial to the mastoid process.

The **petrous part** of the temporal bone (Fig. 7.9, 7.12b) is the dense, bony ridge projecting up into the cranial cavity. It contains the auditory ossicles which will be studied later in connection with the middle ear. Within the cranial cavity the **internal acoustic** (or **auditory**) **meatus** (or **canal**) (Fig. 7.7, 7.9, 7.12b) may be seen on the posterior side of the petrous part. The **jugular foramen** (Fig. 7.8, 7.9) lies in the suture between temporal and occipital bones. Identify the jugular foramen internally and externally. Anterior to this foramen is the **carotid canal** (Fig. 7.8), passing medially and anteriorly as it enters the skull, to end at a posterior corner of the sphenoid bone's sella turcica (see below). Identify the carotid canal internally (Clemente, Fig. 645) and externally (Clemente, Fig. 646).

4. The ethmoid bone contains a horizontal plate of bone called the **cribriform plate** (Fig. 7.9, 7.16). This plate is seen from within the cranial cavity, and is so named because it has numerous tiny holes for the passage of olfactory nerve branches. At right angles to the cribriform plate is the **perpendicular plate** (Fig. 7.3, 7.4, 7.7, 7.16), best seen within the nasal cavity. It forms the superior part of the nasal septum and articulates with the vomer bone. The lateral parts of the ethmoid bone contain 2 **superior nasal conchae** (see Half-Head Model only) and 2 **middle nasal conchae**, on Skulls and the Model (Fig. 7.3, 7.16b, 7.23; Fig. 25.2, p. 745; Clemente, Fig. 684–685).

5. The sphenoid bone is a complex bone that resembles a butterfly. It has a rounded depression called the **sella turcica** (Fig. 7.7, 7.9, 7.14a, 7.23a), in which the pituitary gland rests. Two (2) **optic canals** (or **optic foramina**) (Fig. 7.9, 7.14a) run from within the cranial cavity to each orbit, each carrying an optic nerve. Lateral to the optic canals are the 2 **superior orbital fissures** (Fig. 7.4, 7.14b). The left and right **pterygoid processes** (Fig. 7.7, 7.8, 7.14b; Clemente, Fig. 646), each with 2 vertical plates, may be seen on the inferior side of the skull. Within the body of the sphenoid bone itself is the **sphenoidal sinus** (Fig. 7.7, 7.23a, 7.24) which may have more than one part, and is seen only on the Bisected Skulls and Half-Head Model.

6. Each maxilla contains an **infraorbital foramen** (Fig. 7.4, 7.21a), so named because it is an opening inferior to the orbit. A nerve and vessels are transmitted through this opening. The part of the maxilla that articulates with the horizontal plate of the palatine bone is named the **palatine process** (shown, but not labeled, in Fig. 7.8; labeled in Fig. 7.21b); together they form the hard palate in the roof of the mouth. The **alveolar process** (Fig. 7.21) is the ridge of bone on each maxilla that contains the sockets (alveoli) for the upper teeth.

C. The vertebral column, ribs, and sternum (*pp. 204–214*):

1. The vertebral column (Fig. 7.28) consists of up to 33 vertebrae and is divided into 5 regions on the basis of structural and functional differences among the vertebrae. We will study the vertebral column using Skeletons and Articulated Vertebral Columns. Use the figures in parentheses to help identify the general and regional features of a vertebra.

2. Certain features are common to most vertebrae. Using your text, find the following on the VERTEBRAE in a VERTEBRAL COLUMN (Fig. 7.29, Table 7.5). Each vertebra (except the first) has a rounded **body** (or **centrum**) that connects with a thin arch of bone called the vertebral arch. The body and the vertebral arch surround a space in between, the **vertebral foramen**. (These foramina aligned form the vertebral canal where the spinal cord passes.) On either side of the vertebral arch are **transverse processes**, and located on the posterior part of the arch is a **spinous process**. Also arising from the arch are two **superior articular processes** and two **inferior articular processes**, each one with a surface (facet) for articulation with the adjacent vertebra.

3. Regional characteristics of vertebrae: Use your text (especially Table 7.5) and VERTEBRAL COLUMNS to identify and compare the special features of each region. Study the vertebrae individually so you can recognize by its features which region each is from. Exam questions *could* show an isolated vertebra to identify!

   a. **cervical vertebra** (Table 7.5a, Fig. 7.30): 7 vertebrae, each vertebra having a left and a right **transverse foramen**, passing through a corresponding transverse process.. The first two cervical vertebrae (Fig. 7.30) have specific names. The **atlas** is the first cervical vertebra and lacks a vertebral body. The **axis** is the second cervical vertebra, and has an extension of its vertebral body called the **dens** (or **odontoid process**).

   b. **thoracic vertebra** (Table 7.5b, Fig. 7.29a): 12 vertebrae; each vertebra articulates with ribs at small, smooth areas called **costal facets** on its body and (except for the two most inferior thoracic vertebrae) on its transverse processes. Where a costal facet overlaps two adjacent vertebral bodies, its two parts are called demifacets (see text, p. 209).

   c. **lumbar vertebra** (Table 7.5c, Fig. 7.29b, c): 5 vertebrae, distinguished by their large bodies and broad spinous processes.

   d. **sacral** region (Fig. 7.31): develops as 5 separate vertebrae which fuse to form a single bone, the **sacrum**.

   e. **coccygeal** region (Fig. 7.31): normally 4 small vertebrae which usually fuse to form one bone, the **coccyx**. See also SKELETONS.

4. The ribs and sternum, the costal cartilages connecting them, and the thoracic vertebrae form the skeleton of the thorax (thoracic cage). Identify the parts listed using COMPLETE SKELETONS, INDIVIDUAL RIBS, and a STERNUM (Fig. 7.32):

   a. **Ribs**: There are 12 pairs of ribs. You will *not* be asked the specific level in the thorax a particular rib is from, but you should examine several different ribs to be aware of variations in their appearance among levels. All ribs have a rounded **head** for articulation with 1 or 2 vertebral bodies; ribs 1 through 10 also have a **tubercle** for articulation with a transverse process. The main long portion of the rib is called the **shaft** (or body). Identify these features on COMPLETE SKELETONS and INDIVIDUAL RIBS (Fig.7.33).

b. The **sternum** consists of three parts: the superior **manubrium**, the middle **body**, and the inferior **xiphoid process** (missing on some lab specimens). On the sides of the sternum are **costal notches**, for articulation with the **costal cartilages** from the ribs. Use the COMPLETE SKELETONS and a STERNUM (Fig. 7.32; Clemente Figs. 141–142) to identify this bone and its features.

III. The Appendicular Skeleton

You will *not* be required to tell from which side of the body, right or left, a bone is taken:

A. Shoulder and upper limb *(pp. 221–231)*:

These are grouped as the pectoral girdle, arm, forearm, wrist, hand and fingers. On SKELETONS, INDIVIDUAL BONES, and ARTICULATED PARTS, identify these bones and their features (in **bold** print) using both the Clemente Atlas and your text.

1. The pectoral girdle has two bones per limb, the clavicle and the scapula.

   a. The **clavicle** (Fig. 8.1, 8.2; Clemente, Figs. 138–139) is the S-shaped bone commonly referred to as the collarbone. It has a **sternal end**, which is rounded in cross section and articulates with the manubrium of the sternum, and an **acromial end**, which is flattened in cross section and articulates with the acromion of the scapula.

   b. The **scapula** (Fig. 8.1–8.3; Clemente, Figs. 26–27) is commonly referred to as the shoulder blade. It contains a **medial (or vertebral) border**, and a **lateral (or axillary) border**. On the posterior surface is a projection called the **spine**, which broadens laterally and its end becomes the **acromion** (process). Anterior to this is the knob-like **coracoid process**. The spine separates the posterior surface of the scapula into two fossae: the **infraspinous fossa** (located inferior to the spine) and the **supraspinous fossa** (located superior to the spine). The curved anterior surface of the scapula is named the **subscapular fossa**. On its lateral side is an oval depression named the **glenoid cavity** (or glenoid fossa), where the head of the humerus articulates.

2. Each arm has only one bone, the **humerus** (Fig. 8.4; Clemente, Fig. 83, 84). The rounded proximal portion is the **head**. Lateral to the head are two projections named the **greater tubercle** and **lesser tubercle**. Between these tubercles is the **intertubercular** (or **bicipital**) **sulcus** (or **groove**). On the lateral side of the shaft of the humerus is a roughening, the **deltoid tuberosity**, where the deltoid muscle attaches. On the distal portion of the humerus are two projections named the **lateral epicondyle** and the **medial epicondyle**. Between the epicondyles is the more laterally-placed knob-like **capitulum** (a condyle) and the more medially-placed concave **trochlea** (a condyle). On the posterior distal surface of the shaft is a depression named the **olecranon fossa**.

28

3. The forearm has two bones per limb (Fig. 8.5; Clemente, Figs. 87–90), the medially placed ulna and the laterally placed radius.

    a. The **ulna** has two proximally-located projections: the **olecranon** (process), which fits in the olecranon fossa of the humerus, and the coronoid process. Between these two processes is a depression named the **trochlear** (or semilunar) **notch**. Lateral and inferior to this notch is the **radial notch** (Clemente, Figs. 87–88). On the distal end of the bone is a pointed projection called the **styloid process**.

    b. The **radius** has a proximally-located, rounded **head** which articulates with the capitulum of the humerus and the radial notch of the ulna. On the anteromedial side of the shaft of the radius is the **radial tuberosity**, where the biceps brachii muscle attaches. Like the ulna, the distal end of the radius also has a **styloid process**.

4. Each wrist is composed of eight **carpal** bones (Fig. 8.6; Clemente, Fig. 118). Be able to identify these as a group on a SKELETON or ARTICULATED WRIST AND HAND.

5. The bones of each hand and its fingers will be considered as groups. Use an ARTICULATED WRIST AND HAND to identify the following (Fig. 8.6):

    a. The five **metacarpals** are the bones in the palm of the hand and the base of the thumb.

    b. The **phalanges** (singular: phalanx) are the bones of the fingers. The first digit (thumb) has two phalanges; the other digits have three phalanges each, totaling 14 phalanges per hand.

B. Hip and lower limb *(pp. 230–245)*:

These are grouped as the pelvic girdle, thigh, leg, ankle, foot, and toes. On SKELETONS, INDIVIDUAL BONES, and ARTICULATED PARTS, identify these bones and their listed features using the atlas and your text:

1. The pelvic girdle consists of two ossa coxae (singular = **os coxae**, meaning "bone of the hip"; alternative names: coxal bone, innominate bone). Each os coxae is formed during development (Clemente, Figs. 391–392) by the fusion of three bones which then constitute its three *named regions*. Identify the os coxae, its three regions, and the listed features. Note that all three regions contribute to the acetabulum (Fig. 8.7, 8.9):

    a. The **ilium** is the first of the three named regions. (It is not the "ileum" which is part of the small intestine; see Chapter 9.) Its superior ridge is called the **iliac crest** which terminates at an anterior projection named the **anterior superior iliac spine**. Located inferiorly is the U-shaped **greater sciatic notch** (Fig. 8.9). Part of the ilium forms the rounded socket called the **acetabulum** (Fig. 8.7, 8.9a).

    b. The **ischium** is the second of the three named regions. Part of the ischium forms the **acetabulum**. The **ischial tuberosity** (Fig. 8.9) is a bony projection that is located inferiorly. The ischium articulates with the pubis to form an oval opening named the **obturator foramen**.

c. The **pubis** is the third of the three named regions. It articulates with the ischium to form the **obturator foramen**. Along with the ilium and ischium, it helps form the **acetabulum**. The **pubic tubercle** (Fig. 8.9) is a tiny bump located on the anterior superior surface of the pubis.

2. Each thigh has only one bone, the **femur** (Fig. 8.11; Clemente, Figs. 432–433). The proximal rounded **head** of the femur connects to its shaft via a constricted region named the **neck**. On the lateral side of the proximal part of the shaft is a large prominence named the **greater trochanter**. The **lesser trochanter** is located on the posteromedial surface of the proximal part of the shaft. The distal end of the femur contains two oval knobs, the **medial condyle** and the **lateral condyle**. These condyles articulate with the tibia and help form the knee joint. On either side of these condyles are smaller projections named the **medial epicondyle** and **lateral epicondyle**.

3. Each leg has three bones you should identify along with the following features (Fig. 8.13).

   a. The **patella** (see Complete Skeletons) (Fig. 8.1, 8.12; 8.13d, g) is commonly referred to as the kneecap. This triangular shaped bone helps protect the knee joint, and is held in place by the patellar ligament.

   b. The **tibia** (Fig. 8.13) is the robust, medial bone of the leg. It contains a **medial condyle** and **lateral condyle** (Fig. 8.13a, b, d, e, f). The condyles are located on the proximal end of the bone and, in part, contain concave surfaces which articulate with the medial and lateral condyles of the femur. On the anterior proximal surface of the shaft of the tibia is a large projection named the **tibial tuberosity** (Fig. 8.13a, b). The distal portion of the bone contains the prominent **medial malleolus** (Fig. 8.13a, d) on its medial side; this forms the bump on the medial side of your ankle. On the distal lateral side is the **fibular notch** (Fig. 8.13d; Clemente Fig. 481), where the distal fibula articulates.

   c. The **fibula** (Fig. 8.13) is the long, slender, lateral bone of the leg. The **head** (Fig. 8.13a, d) is the knob-like proximal portion of this bone. On the distal end is the more pointed **lateral malleolus** (Fig. 8.13a, d).

4. Each ankle is composed of seven **tarsals**. Be able to identify these as a group in the articulated ankle. Also recognize the **talus** with its rounded upper surface for articulation with the tibia. The larger **calcaneus** forms the heel. You should be able to identify the talus and calcaneus *both individually and in position*. Use both types of Articulated Ankle and Foot; some are closely wired together while others are loosely strung together permitting examination of individual bones (Fig. 8.14, 8.15).

5. The bones of the foot and toes will be considered as groups. Identify these on the Articulated Ankle and Foot (Fig. 8.14, 8.15; Clemente, Fig. 501, 503):

   a. In each foot are the five **metatarsals**.

   b. The **phalanges** are the bones of the toes. The first digit (large toe) has two phalanges; the other digits have three phalanges each, totaling 14 phalanges per foot.

IV. Articulations: Components of the Knee Joints

(pp. 275–279)

A. On the PLASTIC and PLASTER KNEE MODELS, identify the bones associated with the knee: the **femur**, **patella**, **tibia**, and **fibula**. You should already have identified these bones in lab on other materials.

B. Using Fig. 9.19, identify on the KNEE MODELS the terms in bold print:

The **articular** (or **joint**) **capsule** (PLASTER MODEL only) is cut on the models to expose the joint cavity it encloses (Clemente, Fig. 446). On either side of this capsule are the **tibial** (or **medial**) **collateral ligament** and the **fibular** (or **lateral**) **collateral ligament**. Within the joint cavity are two thin ligaments that form a cross: the **anterior cruciate ligament** and the posterior cruciate ligament (not shown clearly on the MODELS) Between the tibia and femur are two fibrocartilaginous discs: the **medial meniscus** and the **lateral meniscus**. The **patellar ligament** connects the patella to the tibial tuberosity.

C. These structures may also be demonstrated on prosected preserved specimens in lab.

V. Histology of the Skeletal System

We will use projected slides, VIRTUAL MICROSCOPE SLIDES, a MODEL, the Sobotta Atlas, and your textbook to study the microscopic anatomy of the skeletal system.

A. Cartilage *(pp. 102–107, 147–148)*:

Cartilage (Table 4.9, Fig. 6.1) is a specialized connective tissue. Its cells, called **chondrocytes**, reside in spaces called **lacunae** (singular: **lacuna**). Most surfaces of cartilage are covered by a thin dense connective tissue layer called the **perichondrium** (Fig. 6.2, top of page). There are three types of cartilage, each with a unique appearance:

1. **Hyaline cartilage** (Table 4.9a; Fig. 6.1a, b; Sobotta, Fig. 144). The term hyaline refers to the glassy appearance of this type, whether seen grossly or, between the lacunae, on the microscopic level. To see this type of cartilage, view the TRACHEA slide. Identify it and the features of cartilage in bold print above.

2. Elastic cartilage (Table 4.9c; Fig. 6.1a, d; Sobotta, Fig. 142 and 146) has many darkly stained elastic fibers and distinct lacunae. (No microscope slide.)

3. Fibrocartilage (Table 4.9b; Fig. 6.1a, c; Sobotta, Fig. 147) has bundles of fibers and may resemble dense regular connective tissue. (No slide.)

B. **Bone** (*pp. 105–107, 152–156*):

Bone (or osseous connective tissue) is a specialized connective tissue with a great deal of rigidity and strength. Each of its cells, called an **osteocyte**, resides in a space, again called a **lacuna** (Table 4.10; Fig. 6.9a, b). Bone is found generally in two forms, spongy or compact. These can be distinguished grossly in the cut bone(s) on display (Fig. 6.4c). Compact bone is made up of cylindrical **osteons** (also called **Haversian systems**). You should be able to identify these systems, and their parts listed below, on VIRTUAL MICROSCOPE SLIDES of DECALCIFIED BONE and GROUND BONE and on the OSTEON ("Bone Structure") MODEL. Both slides include osteons in cross section. (Fig. 6.8; Fig. 6.9a, b; Sobotta, Fig. 161–2, 164.)

1. **Central** (or **Haversian**) **canal**, runs longitudinally in the center of each cylindrical osteon.

2. **Lacunae**, containing **osteocytes**, between concentric layers of bone.

3. **Canaliculi**, connecting lacunae (seen clearly on GROUND BONE SLIDE and OSTEON MODEL only).

4. **Perforating** (or **Volkmann's**) **canals**, transversely connecting central canals (identify on DECALCIFIED BONE and GROUND BONE SLIDES).

5. **Lamellae** (singular: **lamella**), the concentric layers of bone between lacunae.

Key to Mueller-Ward Model of Bone Structure

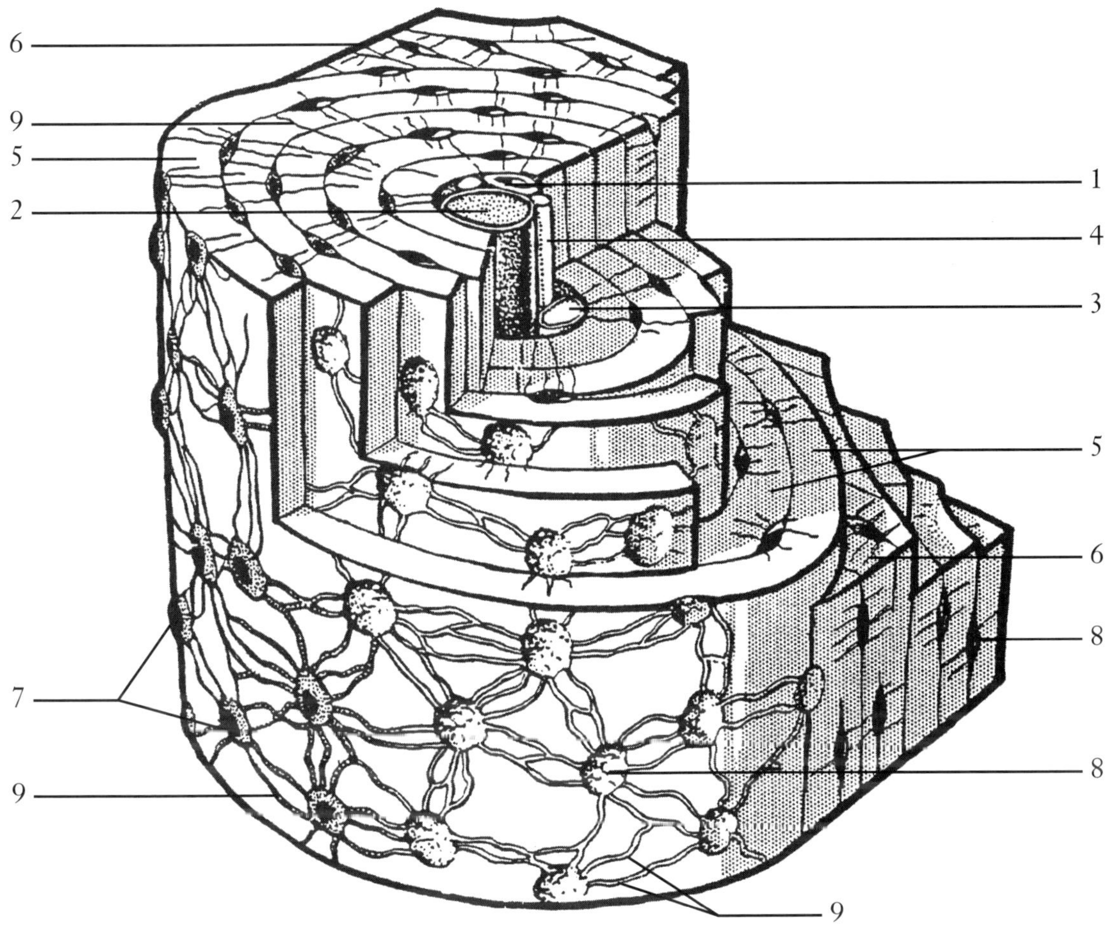

C. Osteon Model Key

Within the **central canal** (or **Haversian canal**):
1. artery
2. vein
3. lymph vessel
4. nerve

5. concentric **lamellae**, within an **osteon**
6. **lamellae** between osteons
7. **osteocytes**
8. **lacunae**
9. **canaliculi**

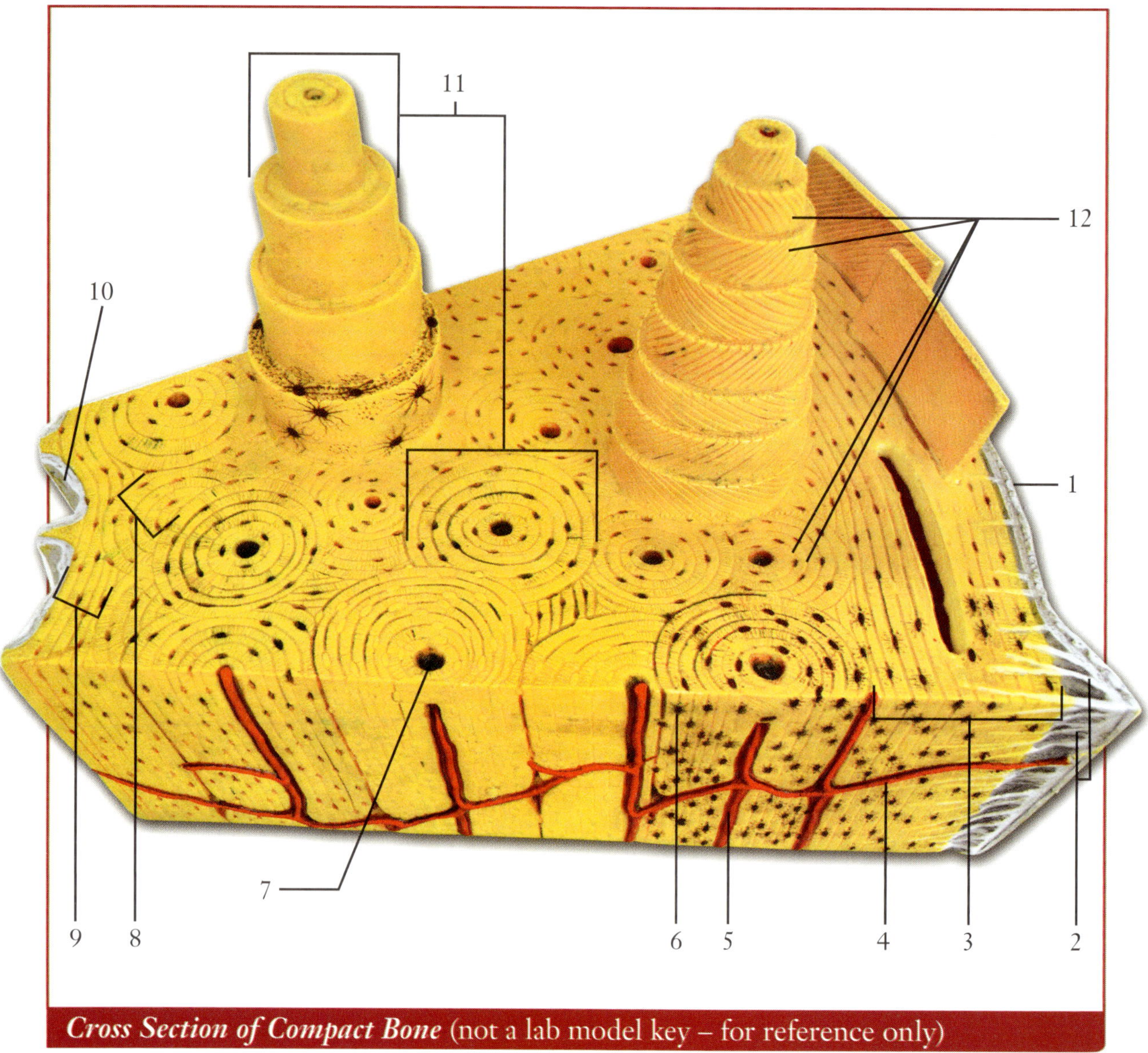

Cross Section of Compact Bone (not a lab model key – for reference only)

1. periosteum
2. perforating fibers
3. external circumferential lamellae
4. artery in perforating (Volkmann's) canal
5. artery in central (Haversian) canal
6. lacuna with osteocyte
7. central (Haversian) canal
8. interstitial lamellae
9. internal circumferential lamellae
10. endosteum
11. osteon (Haversian system)
12. concentric lamellae

VI. Study Tips for this Chapter

A. Use the pictures in your text to help you identify individual BONES and features on the BONES. You can use these text pictures at home to review the bone terminology.

B. Make sure you learn the bones and their features on the COMPLETE SKELETONS, INDIVIDUAL BONES, MODELS, and the EXPLODED SKULLS.

C. At home, make a list of the BONES you learned in lab. Writing the names of the bones over and over again will help you remember their names. Do the same for all of the features of the bones.

D. Are you having trouble remembering particular bones or features? Ask your instructors if they have a tip that helps them remember. In addition, have your lab partner quiz you, and then reverse roles.

E. At home, try to pronounce each of the bone terms. It is very difficult to remember the names if you don't know how to pronounce them.

F. Be careful not to make up "hybrid" bone names! There is no such bone as a "tibula," nor is there a "fibia." If you create one of these hybrid bone names, you will not receive credit on the exam—which is one reason why learning to spell the bone names is very important.

G. Compare and contrast cartilage versus bone tissue. How can you differentiate each when viewing the tissue microscopically?

H. In lab, have your lab partner "quiz" you on the VIRTUAL MICROSCOPE SLIDES. Your lab partner can display a slide, hide the label, and then you try to identify the tissue or structure that the pointer is on. Reverse roles: YOU set up a microscope slide to quiz your lab partner. Both you and your lab partner will be better able to identify the structures on the slides.

I. At home, make a list of the microscopic features and structures you need to identify for cartilage and bone tissue.

J. Remember to use the VIRTUAL MICROSCOPE to review bone and cartilage tissue at home!

VII. Skeletal System Model Key

HALF-HEAD MODELS

- *A.* parietal bone
- *B.* frontal bone
  - *a.* frontal sinus
- *C.* nasal bone
- *D.* ethmoid bone
  - *a.* superior nasal concha
  - *b.* middle nasal concha
- *c.* inferior nasal concha
- *E.* sphenoid bone
  - *b.* sphenoidal sinus
- *F.* occipital bone
- *G.* maxilla
- *H.* palatine bone
- *J.* mandible
- *K.* hyoid bone
- *L.* atlas vertebra
- *M.* axis vertebra

CHAPTER 5

Muscular System

I. Introduction

II. Muscles Associated with the Axial Skeleton
    A. Head
    B. Neck
    C. Trunk

III. Muscles of the Appendages
    A. Shoulder and Upper Limb
    B. Hip and Lower Limb

IV. Histology of Muscle
    A. Smooth
    B. Cardiac
    C. Skeletal

V. Study Tips for this Chapter

VI. Muscular System Model Keys

I. Introduction

A. Your study of the muscular system in the lab will emphasize learning names of individual skeletal muscles, of groups having a similar function or location, or of representative muscles from such groups.

B. Muscles will be demonstrated on MODELS which must be handled and reassembled carefully. In particular, the parts of the ARM and LEG MODELS are not interchangeable among the several examples of each. Parts of each are labeled; be sure to keep them together.

C. Muscles will also be demonstrated on the DONORS; only A.I.s will handle. donors In this and all labs where the donors will be used, *we recommend not wearing wool clothing to lab* because its fibers tend to retain the odor of preserving chemicals.

D. Refer to figures in Chapter 13 of McKinley/O'Loughlin/Pennefather-O'Brien as a guide to the appearance of some muscles on the body surface.

E. You will not be responsible in lab for knowing the origin, insertion, or action of the muscles. That information is provided to facilitate your locating and understanding of the muscles, and to reinforce lecture material.

II. Muscles Associated with the Axial Skeleton

A. Muscles of the Head *(pp. 321–332, Fig. 11.2)*:

We will consider these muscles in 3 groups. Identify them on the DONORS and the HEAD and TORSO MODELS.

1. Muscles of facial expression (Fig. 11.2, 11.3):

   a. The **buccinator** which is located deep on the lateral aspect of the face is responsible for compressing the cheek against the teeth.

   b. The epicranius consists of the two bellies of the **occipitofrontalis** muscle connected by a flat sheet of dense regular connective tissue (galea aponeurotica). The **occipital belly** of the occipitofrontalis (or **occipitalis**) overlies the occipital bone and is responsible for retracting the scalp. The **frontal belly** of the occipitofrontalis (or **frontalis**) overlies the frontal bone; it inserts into the skin of the eyebrows and is responsible for elevating them as well as wrinkling the forehead.

   c. The **orbicularis oculi** which encircles the orbit is responsible for closing the eye (e.g., winking, squinting).

   d. Another circular muscle, the **orbicularis oris** encircles the opening of the oral cavity. It closes and purses (puckers) the mouth.

   e. The most superficial neck muscle is the **platysma**. This broad muscle extends from the sternum and the clavicle and inserts on the mandible. It is primarily responsible for depressing the lower lip.

2. Muscles of mastication (Fig. 11.5):

   a. The large fan-shaped **temporalis** originates on the parietal bone and overlies the temporal bone. It inserts onto the coronoid process of the mandible and it functions to elevate the mandible (i.e., close the mouth) and retract the mandible.

   b. The **masseter** extends from the zygomatic arch to the mandible and assists the temporalis in elevating the mandible. It also protracts the mandible.

3. Extrinsic tongue muscles (Fig. 11.6), seen only on the HEAD and TORSO MODELS:

   a. The **genioglossus** (see only on models showing sagittal plane) comes from the mandible and inserts into the undersurface of the tongue. The position of this muscle allows it to depress (pull downward) the tongue and to protract (stick out) the tongue.

   b. The **hyoglossus** (MUSCULAR HEAD MODEL only) comes from the hyoid bone and inserts into the sides of the tongue. It depresses the sides of the tongue.

B. Muscles of the Anterior and Lateral Neck (*pp. 332–336*):

Considered below in two groups, these muscles can be identified on DONORS and HEAD and TORSO MODELS using text figures.

1. Superficial muscles:

   a. Identify the **platysma** (see II.A.1.e., above).

   b. When the platysma is removed, the **sternocleidomastoid** (Fig. 11.8–9) can be viewed on the lateral aspect of the neck. When both sternocleidomastoid muscles contract, they will flex the neck. However, when only one contracts, it turns the head to the opposite side.

2. Deep muscles, composed of two sets by their relation to the hyoid bone:

   a. Suprahyoid muscles, superior to the hyoid:

      i. The **digastric** (Fig. 11.8, 11.9) has two bellies. The posterior belly originates from near the mastoid process and inserts on the hyoid while the anterior belly extends from the mandible to the hyoid. Thus, it can elevate the hyoid or depress (lower) the mandible.

      ii. The **stylohyoid** (Fig. 11.6, 11.8, 11.9) extends from the styloid process to the hyoid. It can directly elevate the hyoid.

      iii. The **mylohyoid** (Fig. 11.8, 11.9) which is deep to the anterior belly of the digastric, extends from the inferior borders of the mandible to the hyoid. It can elevate the floor of the mouth as well as elevate the hyoid.

      iv. The **geniohyoid** (Fig. 11.6, 11.8) is deep to the mylohyoid and extends from the medial surface of the mandible at the chin to the hyoid. It elevates the hyoid. Identify on HALF-HEAD, MUSCULAR HEAD, and TORSO MODELS only.

   b. Infrahyoid muscles, inferior to the hyoid (Fig. 11.8, 11.9):

      i. The **sternohyoid** is the most medial and it extends from the sternum to the hyoid. Its action is to depress the hyoid.

ii. The **sternothyroid**, which is lateral to the sternohyoid, also originates from the sternum, but it extends just to the thyroid cartilage of the larynx. It depresses the thyroid cartilage (i.e., larynx or voice box). DONORS and HEAD/NECK/SHOULDER MODELS only.

iii. The **thyrohyoid** which is superior to the sternothyroid extends from the thyroid cartilage to the hyoid bone. Because of its intermediate position between the hyoid and the thyroid cartilage, it can either depress the hyoid or elevate the thyroid cartilage.

iv. The long, thin **omohyoid** originates from the scapula and lies deep to the sternocleidomastoid. It inserts onto the clavicle and then continues to the hyoid. It depresses the hyoid.

C. Muscles of the Trunk *(pp. 337–348, 352–357)*:

These muscles will be considered in five groups and can be identified on the DONORS and TORSO MODELS using the text figures noted.

1. Superficial muscles of the back. These act on either the axial skeleton or the limbs; identify the following on TORSO MODELS and DONORS using Fig. 11.1b, 12.2, 12.4b, except as noted:

   a. The large, four-sided **trapezius** extends from the occipital bone, and the spinous processes of the cervical and thoracic vertebrae to the clavicle and the spine of the scapula. Because of its multiple origins and insertions, it has many actions. It elevates, depresses, rotates and adducts (retracts) the scapula, and it can extend the head (see also HEAD and HEAD/NECK/SHOULDER MODELS).

   b. Inferior to the trapezius in the lower half of the back is the large triangular **latissimus dorsi**. It has a very large origin from the lower back and it inserts on the front of the upper humerus. It is known as the "swimmer's muscle" because it adducts and extends the humerus, drawing it posteriorly and inferiorly while it rotates it medially.

   c. The straplike **levator scapulae** lies deep to the trapezius. It extends from the first four cervical vertebrae to the vertebral border of the scapula. When it contracts it elevates the scapula (see also HEAD and HEAD/NECK/SHOULDER MODELS).

   d. The paired **rhomboid** muscles (major and minor) also lie deep to the trapezius. They extend from the spinous processes of the upper thoracic vertebrae to the vertebral border of the scapula. They adduct (retract) and elevate the scapula. Seen only on DONORS and HEAD/NECK/ SHOULDER MODEL.

2. Muscles of the vertebral column (Fig. 11.1b, 11.11, except as noted): include muscles on the posterior (dorsal) side of the vertebral column; on the DONORS, identify:

a. The **erector spinae** is a massive group of deep muscles on the back which extend from the sacrum to the posterior skull. There are 3 groups of muscles: iliocostalis, longissimus, and spinalis. Collectively they act to extend the vertebral column.

b. The broad **splenius** (capitis) muscles are deep to the trapezius muscle. Each splenius extends from the spinous processes of the upper thoracic vertebrae to the back of the head. Each will rotate the head to the same side. When both muscles contract, they extend the neck (Fig. 11.1b, 11.10; Clemente, Fig. 523). See also HEAD and HEAD/NECK/SHOULDER MODELS.

3. Muscles of the thorax: These include two groups and can be identified on DONORS and TORSO MODELS:

   a. Superficial; acting on the upper limb or scapula (Fig. 11.1a, 12.1, 12.4a):

      i. The fan-shaped **pectoralis major** has a broad origin from the clavicle,sternum, and ribs. It inserts onto the humerus, allowing it to flex, adduct, and medially rotate.

      ii. The **pectoralis minor** extends from the 3rd, 4th, and 5th ribs to the coracoid process of the scapula. Along with the serratus anterior (see below), it will protract and depress the scapula. See also HEAD/NECK/SHOULDER MODEL.

      iii. The **serratus anterior** extends from the first 8–9 ribs and inserts on the anteromedial border of the scapula. It is the major protractor and depressor of the scapula.

   b. Deep; assisting breathing (Fig. 11.13; 25.14, p. 762):

      i. The **external intercostals** extend between two ribs and are used during inspiration to increase the diameter of the thoracic cavity by elevating the ribs.

      ii. The deeper **internal intercostals** extend between two ribs and depress the ribs during forced expiration, so as to decrease the lateral dimensions of the thoracic cavity.

      iii. The superiorly located **scalenes** originate from the transverse processes of the cervical vertebrae and insert on the first and second ribs. These muscles assist in elevating the ribs during a forced inspiration. See also HEAD and HEAD/NECK/SHOULDER MODELS.

      iv. The very broad, dome-shaped **diaphragm** (Clemente Fig. 149, 218) flattens out during inspiration in order to increase the vertical dimension of the thoracic cavity.

4. Muscles of the abdomen: These support the abdominal wall and in some circumstances may assist breathing; they are seen most clearly on the DONORS (Fig. 11.1a, 11.14):

a. The long, vertically oriented **rectus abdominis** extends from the inferior margin of the rib cage to the crest of the pubic bone. When this muscle contracts it will flex the vertebral column and compress the abdomen.

b. The medially directed fibers of the **external oblique** extend from the lower eight ribs to the iliac crest. This muscle can compress the abdomen, laterally rotate the trunk, and flex the vertebral column (pull the thorax downward).

c. The deeper **internal oblique** whose fibers are laterally directed extends primarily from the iliac crest to the costal cartilages of the last three to four ribs. It has the same actions as the external oblique.

d. The deepest of these muscles is the **transversus abdominis**. Its horizontally arranged fibers are responsible for compressing the abdomen.

e. The **quadratus lumborum** is located in the posterior abdominal wall (Fig. 11.11; Clemente, Fig. 317, 333). It comes from the iliac crest and the iliolumbar fascia and inserts into the transverse processes of the upper lumbar vertebrae and the lower margin of the 12th rib. When it contracts it will extend the lumbar region and/or laterally flex the vertebral column.

5. Muscles of the pelvis: These form the floor of the abdominopelvic cavity and are known collectively as the "pelvic diaphragm" (Fig. 11.15). Portions can be seen on a Torso Model, but need not be identified.

III. Muscles of the Appendages

A. Shoulder and Upper Limb *(pp. 352–373)*:

These are grouped by their principal action on skeletal elements. Refer to the text and atlas figures to identify these on Donors and on Models of the Arm, Hand, Head/Neck/Shoulder and Torso.

1. Muscles acting on the scapula:

a. Posterior muscles (Fig. 11.1b, 12.2, 12.4b):

i. Identify the **trapezius** (see II.C.1.a., above).

ii. Identify the **rhomboids**, major and minor (see II.C.1.d., above, Donors and Head/Neck/Shoulder Model only).

iii. Identify the **levator scapulae** (see II.C.1.c., above).

b. Anterior muscles (Fig. 11.1a, 11.14a, 12.1, 12.4a):

i. Identify the **pectoralis minor** (II.C.3.a.ii., above).

ii. Identify the **serratus anterior** (II.C.3.a.iii., above).

2. Muscles acting on the arm:

   a. Muscles from the scapula:

      i. The triangularly shaped **deltoid** (Fig. 12.1, 12.2, 12.4) extends from the clavicle and the scapula to the deltoid tuberosity on the humerus. It can extend, flex, and abduct the humerus.

      ii. The **coracobrachialis** (Fig. 12.4a, 12.7) extends from the coracoid process of the scapula to about mid-shaft on the medial aspect of the humerus. Its action is to adduct and flex the humerus.

      iii. The **teres major** (Fig. 12.2, 12.4b, 12.8a; Clemente, Fig. 51) originates from the inferior lateral border of the scapula and inserts on the lesser tubercle of the humerus. It assists the latissimus dorsi in extending, adducting, and medially rotating the humerus.

      iv. The following four muscles make up a group called the "rotator cuff" (Fig. 12.5):

        – The **subscapularis** (Fig. 12.5; Clemente, Fig. 49) extends from the subscapular fossa of the scapula to the lesser tubercle of the humerus. It medially rotates the humerus. Identify only on ARM MODEL.

        – The **supraspinatus** (Fig. 12.2, 12.4b, 12.5; Clemente, Fig. 51) comes from the supraspinous fossa of the scapula to the greater tubercle of the humerus. It abducts the humerus.

        – As its name implies, the **infraspinatus** (Fig. 12.2, 12.4b, 12.5; Clemente, Fig. 51) extends from the infraspinous fossa of the scapula to the greater tubercle of the humerus. It laterally rotates the humerus.

        – The **teres minor** (Fig. 12.2, 12.4b, 12.5; Clemente, Fig. 51) originates from the lateral border of the scapula and inserts on the greater tubercle of the humerus. It laterally rotates the humerus.

   b. Muscles from the axial skeleton:

      i. Identify the **pectoralis major** (anterior) (see II.C.3.a.i., above).

      ii. Identify the **latissimus dorsi** (posterior) (see II.C.1.b., above).

   c. Muscles inserting on the forearm, but also moving the arm:

      i. The powerful, double-headed **biceps brachii** (Fig. 12.1, 12.7) has two origins. The short head comes from the coracoid process and the long head comes from just above the glenoid cavity. They form a common tendon that inserts into the radial tuberosity. It can flex the elbow and supinate the forearm.

      ii. The lateral and medial heads of the three-headed **triceps brachii** (Fig. 12.8) originate from the humerus, whereas the long head comes from just below the glenoid cavity. A common tendon inserts into the olecranon process of the ulna. The muscle is a powerful extensor of the forearm.

3. Muscles acting on the forearm:

    a. Anterior muscles:

       i. Identify the **biceps brachii** (see III.A.2.c.i., above).

      ii. The other major flexor of the forearm at the elbow is the **brachialis** (Fig. 12.7). It extends from the anterior shaft of the humerus to the coronoid process of the ulna.

    b. Posterior muscle: Identify the **triceps brachii** (see III.A.2.c.ii., above).

    c. Muscles primarily or entirely within the forearm:

       i. The laterally positioned **brachioradialis** (Fig. 12.7a, 12.11a, 12.13a) extends from above the lateral epicondyle of the humerus to the styloid process of the radius. It assists the biceps brachii and the brachialis in flexing the forearm.

      ii. The deep, posterior **supinator** (Fig. 12.9, 12.11c, 12.13b) extends from the lateral epicondyle of the humerus and the proximal ulna to the proximal, lateral surface of the radius. It works in conjunction with the biceps brachii to supinate the forearm.

     iii. The **pronator teres** (Fig. 12.9, 12.11a) originates from the medial epicondyle of the humerus and inserts onto the lateral surface of the radius. Along with pronator quadratus (see below), it pronates the forearm.

     iv. The **pronator quadratus** (DONORS only) (Fig. 12.9, 12.11c) extends between the ulna and radius on the distal fourth of the forearm. It pronates the forearm.

4. Muscles acting on the wrist, hand, and fingers are considered in three groups according to location):

    a. Anterior forearm (Fig. 12.10, 12.11; Clemente, Figs. 65–69). In each subgroup, muscles are listed from the lateral to the medial side. Identify the **flexor retinaculum** (Fig. 12.11a) which is a band of dense regular connective tissue connecting the distal ends of the ulna and radius. This retinaculum helps to hold down the tendons on the anterior surface of the wrist.

       i. Superficial muscles: originate from the medial epicondyle of the humerus.

        – The **flexor carpi radialis** (Fig. 12.11a) inserts onto the base of the second and third metacarpal bones. It will flex and abduct the hand at the wrist.

- The **flexor carpi ulnaris** (Fig. 12.11a) attaches to carpal and metacarpal bones. Its action is to flex and adduct the hand at the wrist.

ii. Intermediate muscle: originates from the medial epicondyle of the humerus and the anterior border of the radius.

- The **flexor digitorum superficialis** (Fig. 12.11b) extends to the middle phalanges of digits 2–5. It flexes the wrist and the digits at the MP (metacarpophalangeal) and PIP (proximal interphalangeal) joints. It does *not* move the DIP (distal interphalangeal) joints.

iii. Deep muscle (Clemente, Fig. 69): extends primarily from the upper two-thirds of the ulna.

- The **flexor digitorum profundus** (Fig. 12.11b, c) attaches to the base of the distal phalanges of digits 2–5. It flexes the wrist and the digits at the MP (metacarpophalangeal), PIP (proximal interphalangeal), and DIP (distal interphalangeal) joints.

b. Posterior forearm, from lateral to medial side within each layer (Fig. 12.10, 12.13). Identify these muscles and the **extensor retinaculum** (Fig. 12.13a) which is a mass of dense regular connective tissue running horizontally across the posterior distal ends of the radius and ulna. (Clemente, Figs. 76–78, 103).

i. Superficial muscles: these muscles originate primarily from the lateral epicondyle of the humerus.

- One portion (longus) of the **extensor carpi radialis** (Fig. 12.13a) attaches to the second metacarpal while the other portion (brevis) attaches to the third metacarpal. They work together to extend and abduct the hand at the wrist.

- The centrally located **extensor digitorum** (communis) (Fig. 12.13a) attaches to the base of the distal and middle phalanges of digits 2–5. It will extend the hand at the wrist and the digits at the MP, PIP, and DIP joints.

- The medially positioned **extensor carpi ulnaris** (Fig. 12.13a) extends to the base of the fifth metacarpal. It will extend and adduct the hand at the wrist.

ii. Deep muscles (Clemente, Fig. 77):

- The **abductor pollicis longus** (Fig. 12.13a, b) extends from the distal ends of the ulna and radius to the base of the first metacarpal. When it contracts, it will abduct the thumb and extend (weakly) the wrist.

      – Another muscle whose action affects the thumb is the **extensor pollicis longus** (Fig. 12.13b). It comes from the middle of the ulna and inserts onto the base of the distal phalanx. It can extend the thumb and extend (weakly) the wrist.

  c. Intrinsic muscles of the hand, to be identified as groups. (Fig. 12.14; Clemente, Fig. 108, 114–116.)

    i. Several of the muscles acting on the thumb are grouped together as the **thenar** (Fig. 12.14) muscles. Collectively they abduct, flex, and oppose the thumb to the palm of the hand.

    ii. The muscles which act on the little finger (5th digit) are referred to as the **hypothenar** (Fig. 12.14) muscles. Collectively they abduct, flex, and oppose the little finger to the palm of the hand.

    iii. The intermediate group, or the midpalmar muscles, act on the fingers. There are three groups you should identify:

      – The four worm-shaped **lumbricals** (Fig. 12.14a) are the most superficial on the anterior side. They are responsible for flexing digits 2–5 at the MP joint and extending digits 2–5 at the PIP and DIP joints.

      – The three **palmar interossei** (Fig. 12.14b) are deeper on the anterior side, will adduct digits 2–5 at the MP joints, and may be seen on the Donors.

      – The four **dorsal interossei** (Fig. 12.13b, 12.14c) which are on the posterior side will abduct digits 2–5 at the MP joints.

B. Hip and Lower Limb *(pp. 374–391)*:

These are grouped by their main actions on skeletal elements. Use the text and atlas figures to identify these on Donors and on Torso, Leg, and Foot Models.

  1. Muscles acting on the thigh (femur): Most originate from the pelvis and are grouped below by their primary action:

    a. Flexors of the thigh (Fig. 12.15a, 12.17a): (see also III.B.2.a.ii. below for the rectus femoris).

      i. The long, thick **psoas** (major) extends from the transverse processes of the lumbar vertebrae to the lesser trochanter. It will flex the thigh.

      ii. The **iliacus** originates from the iliac fossa and also inserts onto the lesser trochanter. Its action is the same as the psoas.

    b. Extensors of the thigh:

      i. The large **gluteus maximus** (Fig. 12.15b, c; 12.18a) extends from the ilium, sacrum, and coccyx to the gluteal tuberosity and the iliotibial tract. This is a powerful extensor of the thigh as well as a lateral rotator.

      ii. The hamstring group (see III.B.2.c. below)

    c. The **gluteus medius** (Fig. 12.15b, c; 12.18a) is located deep to the gluteus maximus. It extends from the ilium to the greater trochanter. It is an abductor and medial rotator of the thigh.

    d. There are 3 **adductor** muscles (longus, brevis, and magnus) of the thigh (Fig. 12.15a, 12.17a, 12.18). They extend primarily from the pubis to the linea aspera. Collectively, they adduct, flex, and laterally rotate the thigh.

2. Muscles acting on the leg: These muscles are considered primarily in four compartments based on their location within the thigh (a–d) or behind the knee (e) (Fig. 12.16). Note that a layer of dense connective tissue, the fascia lata, normally covers the thigh superficial to the muscles, but has been removed for the most part on the donors.

    a. The anterior compartment:

        i. The long **sartorius** (Fig. 12.17) goes across two joints. It extends from the ilium to the medial surface of the tibia just below the knee joint. It will flex both the thigh at the hip and the leg at the knee.

        ii. The massive **quadriceps femoris** is composed of four named muscles (Fig. 12.17; Clemente, Fig. 418–20). The muscles have different origins but they all insert onto the patella by a quadriceps (patellar) tendon which continues as the patellar ligament to the tibial tuberosity. They collectively extend the leg.

          – The superficial **rectus femoris** originates from the ilium and thus can also flex the thigh at the hip.

          – The laterally positioned **vastus lateralis** originates from the greater trochanter and the linea aspera of the femur.

          – The medially positioned **vastus medialis** originates from the medial surface and the linea aspera of the femur.

          – The **vastus intermedius** lies deep to the rectus femoris. It originates from the lateral and anterior surfaces of the femur.

    b. The medial compartment contains the 3 **adductor** muscles (see section III.B.1.d., above) and the straplike **gracilis** (Fig. 12.15a, c; 12.17a, 12.18a). The gracilis extends from the pubis to the proximal medial surface of the tibia. It can adduct the thigh and flex both the thigh and leg.

    c. The posterior compartment contains muscles which both extend the thigh and flex the leg. These form the hamstring group (Fig. 12.18; Clemente, Figs. 426–427). They primarily originate from the ischial tuberosity.

        i. The **biceps femoris** lies on the posterolateral thigh and has an additional origin from the linea aspera of the femur.

        ii. On the medial aspect of the posterior thigh is the superficial **semitendinosus.**

      iii. Deep to the semitendinosus on the medial aspect of the posterior thigh is the flatter **semimembranosus**.

d. The lateral compartment contains one muscle, the **tensor fasciae latae** (Fig 12.15b, 12.17a). It originates from the ilium and inserts on a strong band of dense connective tissue, the **iliotibial tract** (or **iliotibial band**) (Fig. 12.15b, 12.17a, 12.18a), part of the fascia lata. When contracted it will abduct the thigh.

e. Behind the knee, deep in the popliteal fossa, locate the **popliteus** (Fig. 12.22b, c) muscle. It extends from the lateral condyle of the femur to the proximal posterior tibia. It is a flexor and medial rotator of the leg.

3. Muscles acting on the ankle, foot, and toes are located either in the leg (considered in three compartments, a–c) or within the foot (d) (Fig. 12.19):

a. The anterior compartment: The muscles here work in "dorsiflexing" the foot (moving the foot upward). Two of them also work in extending (straightening) toes. Tendons pass under the extensor (anterior) retinacula (Fig. 12.20, 12.21a; Clemente, Figs. 464–465):

      i. The centrally located **tibialis anterior** originates from the lateral tibia and inserts medially onto the tarsals and the first metatarsal. It will also invert the foot.

      ii. The superficial, laterally located **extensor digitorum longus** originates from the tibia and fibula and inserts onto the dorsal surface of the distal and middle phalanges of digits 2–5. It extends digits 2–5.

      iii. The deeper **extensor hallucis longus** extends from the fibula to the distal phalanx of the great toe. This muscle extends only the great toe. Identify only on the DONORS.

b. The lateral compartment: The muscles here primarily evert (turn the sole outward) and plantar flex (pull downward) the foot; tendons pass under the fibular retinaculum, by the lateral malleolus (Fig. 12.20, 12.21):

      i. The long, slender, superficial **fibularis** (or peroneus) **longus** comes from the head of the fibula and attaches to the plantar surfaces of one of the tarsals and the first metatarsal.

      ii. The shorter, deeper **fibularis** (or peroneus) **brevis** extends from the lateral aspect of the distal fibula to the proximal end of the fifth metatarsal.

c. The posterior compartment: The muscles here are primarily responsible for plantar flexing the foot and/or flexing the toes; considered in two groups:

      i. The superficial group inserts into the calcaneus via the **calcaneal** (or **Achilles**) **tendon** (or tendo calcaneus) (Fig. 12.21a; 12.22a,b):

        – The superficial **gastrocnemius** (Fig. 12.21a, 12.22a) originates from the lateral and medial condyles of the femur. Thus, it can also flex the leg.

     – The deeper **soleus** extends from the proximal portion of the posterior tibia and fibula to the calcaneus via the calcaneal tendon (Fig. 12.21a, 12.22a).

  ii. The deep group is composed of three muscles whose tendons pass under the flexor retinaculum posterior to the medial malleolus (Fig. 12.22):

     – The medially located **flexor digitorum longus** extends from the posterior tibia to the distal phalanges of digits 2–5. It will flex toes 2–5, and plantar flex the foot.

     – The centrally located **tibialis posterior** originates from the posterolateral tibia and the fibula and inserts onto the plantar surface of tarsal and metatarsal bones. When it contracts it will invert and plantar flex the foot.

     – The laterally located **flexor hallucis longus** extends from the posterior fibula to the distal phalanx of the great toe. It acts to flex the great toe and plantar flex the foot.

  d. The intrinsic muscles of the foot consist of one muscle on the dorsal (superior) side and a group on the plantar (inferior) side (Fig. 12.23). Identify (only on DONORS) the **plantar aponeurosis** (or plantar fascia) (Clemente, Fig. 492) that covers this group.

IV. Histology of Muscle

(pp. 109–111, 288–290, 291–298, 310–313)

Muscle is one of the four basic types of tissue and is specialized for contraction. There are three distinct types of muscle. Be able to identify each type on the appropriate VIRTUAL MICROSCOPE SLIDE along with its distinguishing characteristics.

A. **Smooth muscle** (or **visceral muscle**) (Table 4.12c, Fig. 10.16, Table 10.6; Sobotta, Fig. 170) contains elongated, spindle-shaped cells, each with one centrally located **nucleus**. There are no cross striations. Found in the wall of the SMALL INTESTINE.

B. **Cardiac muscle** (Table 4.12b, Fig. 10.15, Table 10.6; Sobotta, Fig. 177) on the HEART slide has cylindrical cells which may branch. Each has one, or possibly two, **nuclei** along the axis of the cylinder. Cross striations, perpendicular to the axis, are present. Cells meet end-to-end at specialized junctions (gap junctions) called **intercalated discs** which are parallel to, but darker than, the faint striations.

C. **Skeletal Muscle** (Table 4.12a, Fig. 10.1, Table 10.1, 10.6; Sobotta, Fig. 178) contains large diameter cylindrical cells referred to as "muscle fibers." Each has many **nuclei** scattered along its length and located immediately under its cell membrane. Internally, a muscle fiber has lengthwise myofibrils, each composed of a series of segments called sarcomeres. Each sarcomere contains many lengthwise myofilaments. The two types of myofilaments (thick and thin filaments) occur in a regular arrangement which causes the cross **striations** (alternating dark and light bands) to be seen in myofibrils and fibers.

There are two virtual microscope slides of SKELETAL MUSCLE, one of muscle cut in cross section, the other in longitudinal section. Be able to identify this tissue on either section. On the SKELETAL MUSCLE–CROSS SECTION SLIDE, identify also the rounded **skeletal muscle fibers** (or **cells**) and their **nuclei**. On the SKELETAL MUSCLE–LONGITUDINAL SECTION SLIDE, identify also the long **skeletal muscle fibers** (or **cells**), their **nuclei**, and the cross **striations**.

Myofibrils and other small structures of skeletal muscle can be seen only in ELECTRON MICROGRAPHS. Use the two in lab, Plates 26 and 27, to identify the following (Fig. 10.6d, 10.7; Sobotta, Figs. 182 and 195):

1. **Sarcomere**: the functional contractile unit of skeletal muscle. It extends from Z disc to Z disc and narrows during contraction.

2. **Z disc** (or **Z line**): between sarcomeres; within I band.

3. **I band**: thin (actin) filaments; narrows during contraction.

4. **A band**: thick (myosin) and portions of thin (actin) filaments; width unchanged during contraction.

5. **H zone** (or H band): thick (myosin) myofilaments only; within A band, narrows during contraction.

V. Study Tips for this Chapter

A. Use the pictures in your text to help you identify individual MUSCLES. You can use these text pictures at home to review the musculature.

B. Make sure you learn the muscles on the DONORS and selected MODELS. The model keys at the end of this chapter list the muscles that you will be responsible for on a particular model. If a muscle isn't listed on a particular model key, then you do not have to worry about identifying that muscle on that particular model. Ask your instructors for further clarification, if necessary.

C. At home, make a list of the MUSCLES you learned in lab. Writing the names of the muscles over and over again will help you remember their names.

D. In lecture, you learned that muscles can be named according to their shape, their function, or where they are located in the body. For the MUSCLES you have to know in lab, try to figure out how a muscle got its name. That will help you better remember the name in the future, or help you "figure out" the name on an exam.

E. At home, try to pronounce each of the MUSCLE names. It is very difficult to remember the names, if you don't know how to pronounce them.

F. Study lab and lecture material together at home by doing the following: review text pictures and say the names of the muscles aloud. Then, perform the function of that muscle.

G. Compare and contrast the three types of muscle tissue. How can you differentiate each when looking at the tissue microscopically? Remember that you need to identify muscle tissue structures on both VIRTUAL MICROSCOPE SLIDES and ELECTRON MICROGRAPHS.

H. In lab, have your lab partner "quiz" you on the virtual microscope slides. Reverse roles: YOU set up a slide to quiz your lab partner. Both you and your lab partner will be better able to identify the structures on the slides when it comes time for the exam.

I. At home, make a list of the microscopic features and structures you need to identify for each of the muscle tissues.

VI. Muscular System Model Keys

MUSCULAR HEAD MODELS

- *19.* splenius (capitis)
- *20–21.* occipitofrontalis:
    - *20.* frontal belly
    - *21.* occipital belly
- *24–25.* orbicularis oculi
- *28.* orbicularis oris
- *35.* buccinator
- *38.* masseter
- *39.* temporalis
- *41.* sternocleidomastoid
- *42–44.* scalenes (middle, posterior, anterior)
- *45.* levator scapulae
- *45a.* trapezius
- *46–47.* digastric (anterior, posterior bellies)
- *48.* stylohyoid
- *49.* mylohyoid
- *50.* geniohyoid
- *51.* hyoglossus
- *52.* sternohyoid
- *53–54.* omohyoid (superior, inferior bellies)
- (*55.* sternothyroid)
- *56.* thyrohyoid

HALF-HEAD MODELS

- *24–25.* occipitofrontalis:
    - *24.* frontal belly
    - *25.* occipital belly
- *26–27.* orbicularis oculi
- *32.* orbicularis oris
- *35.* buccinator
- *39.* masseter
- *43.* sternocleidomastoid
- *44.* digastric (posterior belly)
- *45.* stylohyoid
- *46.* mylohyoid
- *47.* sternohyoid
- (*48.* sternothyroid)
- (*49.* thyrohyoid)
- *50.* omohyoid (sup. belly)
- *52.* trapezius
- *53.* splenius (capitis)
- *54.* levator scapulae
- *55–57.* scalenes (posterior, middle, anterior)
- *f.* orbicularis oris
- *J–m, k, n.* genioglossus
- *o.* geniohyoid
- *p.* mylohyoid

TORSO MODEL S1 AND S2

(Not all of these structures are labeled)

- *1.* pectoralis major
- *2.* internal intercostals
    - external intercostals
    - scalene (anterior)
    - serratus anterior
- *18.* diaphragm
    - quadratus lumborum
    - psoas (major)
    - iliacus

TORSO MODEL N1

    1. frontal belly
    3. orbicularis oculi
    14. orbicularis oris
    19. masseter
    20. platysma
    23. sternocleidomastoid
52, 54. (right, left) deltoid
    59. pectoralis major
    60. pectoralis minor
    61. serratus anterior
    63. internal oblique
    64. latissimus dorsi
66, 68. rectus abdominis
    80. transversus abdominis
    96. gluteus maximus
    100. gluteus medius

TORSO MODEL N2

100. frontal belly
101. orbicularis oculi
108. orbicularis oris
112. buccinator
114. masseter
119. trapezius
121. sternocleidomastoid
123. omohyoid (superior belly)
129. geniohyoid
134. mylohyoid
135. temporalis
146. omohyoid (inferior belly)
148. supraspinatus
149. deltoid
156. pectoralis minor
158. serratus anterior
159. external intercostals
160. internal intercostals
161. transversus abdominis
162. rectus abdominis
164. external oblique
165. pectoralis major
168. psoas (major)
169. iliacus
179. latissimus dorsi
180. gluteus maximus
184. gluteus medius

HEAD/NECK/SHOULDER MODEL   **Identify** (labels, where present, in parentheses)

on its left – (5 parts may be taken off this side: sternocleidomastoid, trapezius, pectoralis major & deltoid muscles; clavicle)

temporalis (*1*)
trapezius
rhomboids (*33, 34*)
sternocleidomastoid
digastric (*20 [on posterior belly]*)
stylohyoid (*21*)
splenius
levator scapulae (*23*)
pectoralis minor
scalenes (*24, 25, 26*)
thyrohyoid (*27*)
sternothyroid (*29*)
mylohyoid (*30*)
omohyoid
supraspinatus (*31*)
   seen in the midsagittal plane:
   genioglossus
   geniohyoid

on its right –

platysma
occipital belly (*4*)
frontal belly (*5*)
occipitofrontalis
orbicularis oculi (*6, 7*)
buccinator (*11*)
masseter (*13*)
orbicularis oris (*15*)
trapezius (*18*)
sternocleidomastoid (*19*)
splenius (*22*)
   seen in the midsagittal plane:
   genioglossus (*f, g*)
   geniohyoid (*h*)

ARM MODELS A1–A8

1. supraspinatus
2. infraspinatus
3. teres major
4. teres minor
5. latissimus dorsi
6. subscapularis
7. deltoid
8. pectoralis major
9. biceps brachii
9a. coracobrachialis
10. brachialis
11. triceps brachii
12. pronator teres
13. flexor carpi radialis
15. flexor carpi ulnaris
16. extensor carpi ulnaris
17. extensor digitorum
18–19. extensor carpi radialis
20. brachioradialis
(*21.* tendon of extensor pollicis longus)
23. abductor pollicis longus
24. flexor digitorum superficialis
24a. flexor digitorum profundus
25. supinator
27. extensor retinaculum
28–31. thenar muscles
32–34. hypothenar muscles
35. lumbricals
36. dorsal interossei
37. flexor retinaculum
42. tendons of flexor digitorum superficialis
43. tendons of flexor digitorum profundus

WRIST–HAND MODELS

r. flexor retinaculum
l. extensor retinaculum
i, x, v, w. thenar muscles
m, n, o. hypothenar muscles
s. lumbricals
5, k. dorsal interossei

LEG MODELS L1–L10

1. psoas (major)
2. iliacus
3. gluteus maximus
4. gluteus medius
9. tensor fasciae latae
9a. iliotibial tract
10. sartorius
11. quadriceps femoris
   a. rectus femoris
   b. vastus medialis
   c. vastus lateralis
   d. vastus intermedius
13–14. adductors
15. gracilis
16. semitendinosus
17. semimembranosus
18a–b. biceps femoris
19. tibialis anterior
(*20.* extensor hallucis longus)
21. extensor digitorum longus
22. fibularis longus
23. fibularis brevis
24. a–b. gastrocnemius
   c. soleus
   d. calcaneal tendon
26. popliteus
27. flexor digitorum longus
28. tibialis posterior
29. flexor hallucis longus

FOOT MODEL

11. tibialis anterior
(*12.* tendon of extensor hallucis longus)
13. (tendon of) extensor digitorum longus
13a. (body of) extensor digitorum longus
17. fibularis brevis
18. (tendon of) fibularis longus
19. calcaneal tendon
20. flexor hallucis longus
21. flexor digitorum longus
24. (tendon of) tibialis posterior
34–37. retinacula

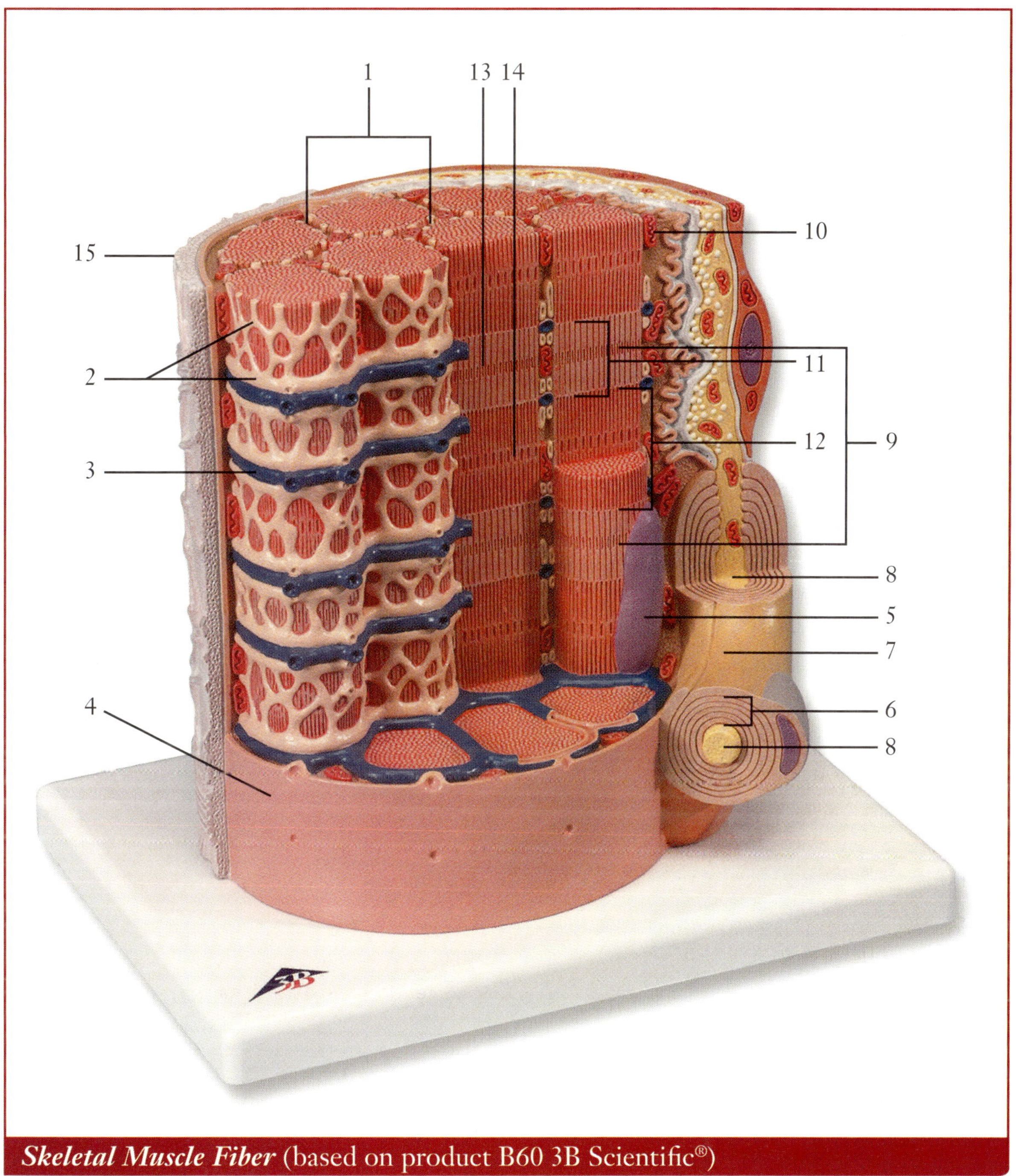

Skeletal Muscle Fiber (based on product B60 3B Scientific®)

1. myofibril (composed of thick and thin filaments)
2. sarcoplasmic reticulum
3. transverse (T-) tubule
4. sarcolemma
5. nucleus of the skeletal muscle fiber
6. myelin sheath
7. neurolemmocyte (Schwann cell)
8. axon of somatic (voluntary) motor neuron
9. sarcomere (for specific details, see the following diagram)
10. mitochondrion in the sarcoplasm
11. I band
12. A band
13. Z disc
14. M line
15. endomysium

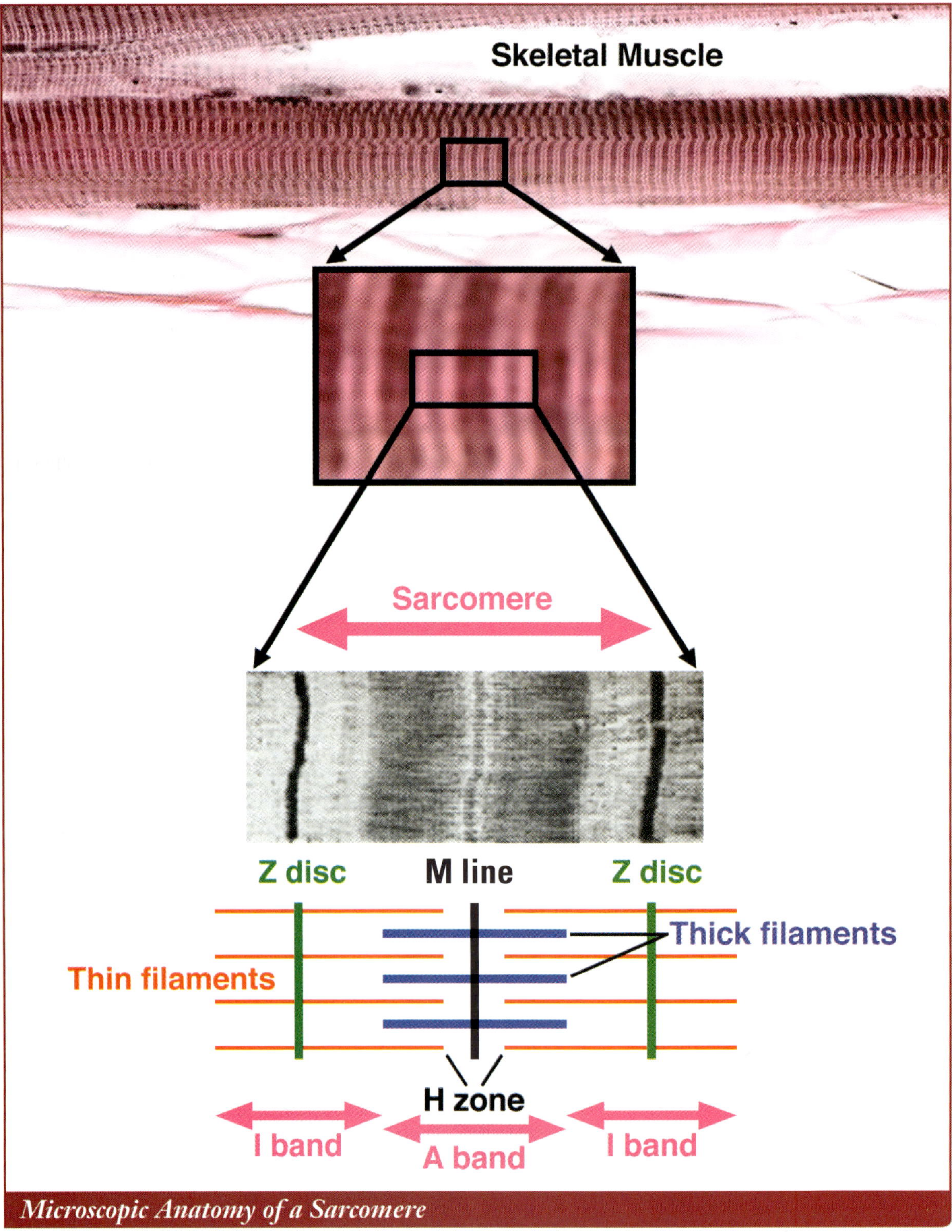

Microscopic Anatomy of a Sarcomere

6

Nervous System

I. Introduction

A. The nervous system can be divided into the central nervous system and the peripheral nervous system. The central nervous system (CNS) includes the brain and spinal cord, while the peripheral nervous system (PNS) includes the cranial nerves, spinal nerves, sensory receptors, and ganglia.

B. We will use the DONORS and MODELS to study the nervous system and two of the organs of the special senses. Most of these materials are quite fragile, so use extreme care in your study.

C. Using introductory and VIRTUAL MICROSCOPE SLIDES, we will examine a few important features of nervous tissues to understand better the nervous system's function and gross organization.

II. Central Nervous System (CNS)
(pp. 433–469, 482–492)

A. General Features

1. The CNS, including its surrounding membranes and fluid, is contained in a protective bony covering.

    a. the brain is almost completely surrounded by the eight skull bones forming the cranial cavity.

    b. the spinal cord is continuous with the brain at the foramen magnum. The spinal cord is centered within the vertebral canal, which is formed from the series of vertebral foramina.

2. Both brain and spinal cord are surrounded by three connective tissue membranes called meninges (singular: meninx) and by cerebrospinal fluid. Two of the meninges can be seen on the DONORS (Fig. 15.4, 16.2).

    a. the innermost pia mater is a delicate vascular membrane which adheres closely to all outer surfaces of the CNS and is difficult to distinguish from the underlying nervous tissue. Know its location.

    b. the **arachnoid mater** (membrane) lies outside the pia mater and is firmly attached to it but does not follow it into all the extensive surface folds of the CNS.

    c. the space between the pia mater and the arachnoid mater, called the subarachnoid space, contains cerebrospinal fluid (CSF). CSF is a clear fluid which protects and supports the CNS. (The subarachnoid space is continuous with the system of ventricles inside the brain [Fig. 15.8] where CSF is produced.)

    d. the outermost membrane is the **dura mater**, composed of dense connective tissue which, in the cranial cavity, adheres closely to surrounding bone and gives rise to septa which divide the cavity into compartments (Fig. 15.5; Clemente, Fig. 637). Identify the dura mater also on the HALF-HEAD and MUSCULAR HEAD MODELS. In the spinal cord, the dura mater is surrounded by the epidural space, which contains areolar and adipose connective tissues (Fig. 16.2).

3. The blood supply to the brain.

    a. the internal carotid and **vertebral arteries** supply blood to the brain. The two vertebral arteries, having passed through the transverse foramina of the cervical vertebrae, enter the cranial cavity through the foramen magnum, and then join to form a single vessel, the **basilar artery**. This vessel sends off various branches to the brain, some of which join with branches from the internal carotid arteries to form the **cerebral arterial circle** (or **circle of Willis**). The cerebral arterial circle provides alternative vascular pathways if one of the major vessels is blocked. Use the BASE-OF-SKULL, TORSO BRAIN, and CERVICAL SPINAL CORD MODELS to identify these vessels (Fig. 23.11a, p. 692).

b. The venous drainage of blood from the brain is through the **dural venous sinuses** located within the dura mater. These sinuses drain into the internal jugular veins. Use the HEAD MODELS to identify these vessels (Fig. 23.11b, p. 692; Clemente, Fig. 637). One of them, the superior sagittal sinus, may be visible on the DONORS.

B. The **spinal cord** is a roughly cylindrical structure occupying the vertebral canal of the vertebral column. The spinal cord is comprised of a central area of **gray matter** (butterfly-shaped in cross-section) containing interneurons, the cell bodies and nerve cell processes of motor neurons, the axons of sensory (afferent) neurons, and glial cells. The gray matter is surrounded by **white matter** consisting largely of bundles (tracts) of myelinated axons running longitudinally along the cord. Some descend to convey information from the brain to the spinal cord (or from upper to lower levels of the cord), others ascend to transmit information in the opposite direction. Axons may cross from one side of the cord to the other.

1. A portion of the spinal cord of the DONORS has been exposed in the lower thoracic and upper lumbar regions. Identify the following bold type structures (Fig. 16.1c, 16.2b; Clemente, Fig. 565, 570):

    a. the **spinal cord** is covered by the same three meninges that cover the brain:

        i. **dura mater**, cut midsagittally and several times transversely

        ii. arachnoid mater (most removed on DONORS)

        iii. pia mater

    b. a series of paired **posterior** (or **dorsal**) **roots** are seen. Each posterior root passes inferiorly from the spinal cord (where it begins as multiple thinner posterior rootlets) to one of the intervertebral foramina where it is enlarged as the **posterior** (or **dorsal**) **root ganglion**.

    c. the **conus medullaris** is the cone-shaped, caudal portion of the spinal cord, usually ending at the level of the first lumbar vertebra.

    d. the **cauda equina** extends from the caudal end of the spinal cord. It is composed of spinal nerve roots and has the appearance of a horse's tail.

2. Cross sections of the **spinal cord** may be studied on the SPINAL CORD CROSS-SECTION MODELS. Identify it and the following regions and structures, and relate them to your microscopic study of the spinal cord (Fig. 16.2–16.5; Clemente, Fig. 571).

    a. On the CERVICAL SPINAL CORD CROSS SECTION MODEL, identify the **dura mater** around the spinal cord.

    b. The **gray matter**, the darker internal portion of the spinal cord, consists of neuron cell bodies, unmyelinated nerve cell processes, supporting cells, and interneurons. It may be subdivided into the following components:

      i. **posterior** (or **dorsal**) **horns**, which contain interneurons and distal portions of axons of sensory (afferent) neurons.

     ii. **anterior** (or **ventral**) **horns**, which contain the cell bodies of somatic (voluntary) motor neurons.

   iii. Lateral horns (present only in the thoracic and lumbar portions of the spinal cord, T1– L2), which contain the cell bodies of autonomic (involuntary; sympathetic) motor neurons.

    iv. A gray commissure connects left horns with the right horns.

     v. The **central canal** is an opening in the center of the gray commissure that contains CSF (cerebrospinal fluid).

  c. The **white matter** is the outer portion of the spinal cord, and consists primarily of myelinated axons.

  d. A **posterior** (or **dorsal**) **root** attaches on each side to the posterior part of the spinal cord, and contains sensory (afferent) axons; MODELS show the narrow rootlets which together form each root. Each posterior root has an enlarged portion, a **posterior** (or **dorsal**) **root ganglion**, which contains the cell bodies of the sensory (afferent) neurons.

  e. An **anterior** (or **ventral**) **root** attaches on each side to the anterior part of the spinal cord, and contains motor (efferent) axons; MODELS again show rootlets.

  f. A **spinal nerve** is formed when a posterior root and an anterior root unite. Thus, a spinal nerve contains both motor (efferent) and sensory (afferent) axons.

C. The brain has six "subdivisions": the cerebrum, diencephalon, midbrain, cerebellum, pons, and medulla oblongata.

Use the various BRAIN and HEAD MODELS and the BRAIN VENTRICLES MODEL, to identify these subdivisions and to locate the bold type structures listed under each. Most are bilaterally paired. (The origins of cranial nerves, part of the PNS, are listed but will be studied separately.)

  1. The **cerebrum** is divided into a **right cerebral hemisphere** and **left cerebral hemisphere** (Fig. 15.10). Each contains the following:

    a. **cortex**, the outer layer composed primarily of unmyelinated nerve cell processes and neuron cell bodies (gray matter), is best seen on the BRAINS of the MUSCULAR HEAD and TORSO N2 MODELS (Fig. 15.3a, 15.4).

    b. white matter, composed of tracts of myelinated axons, is best seen on the BRAINS of the MUSCULAR HEAD and TORSO N2 MODELS (Fig. 15.3a, 15.4, 15.13).

    c. lobes (Fig. 15.1, 15.10, 15.11):

     i. **frontal lobe**, which is responsible for initiating voluntary skeletal muscle movement, the motor movements involved in speech, and also is involved in intellect, personality, and complex decision-making.

     ii. **parietal lobe**, which receives and interprets most somatosensory input.

     iii. **occipital lobe**, primarily involved with interpreting visual stimuli.

     iv. **temporal lobe**, primarily involved with interpreting auditory (sound) stimuli.

     v. insula, of which little is known but may be involved with memory and interpretations of taste.

d. gyri, rounded ridges on the surface of the cerebrum (Fig. 15.1a, 15.10, 15.11). Be aware of the following named gyri:

     i. precentral gyrus (anterior to the central sulcus), which is the primary motor cortex of the brain and initiates skeletal muscle movement.

     ii. postcentral gyrus (posterior to the central sulcus), which is the primary somatosensory cortex of the brain.

e. sulci and fissures, furrows or grooves which separate the gyri and lobes. A fissure is deeper than a sulcus, but the terms are sometimes interchangeable (Fig. 15.1a, c;15.10, 15.11, 15.13b).

     i. **longitudinal fissure**, the deep furrow between right and left hemispheres

     ii. **lateral sulcus** (or fissure), the groove separating the temporal lobe from the frontal and parietal lobes.

     iii. central sulcus (or fissure), the groove that separates the precentral gyrus from the postcentral gyrus,thus separating the frontal lobe from the parietal lobe.

f. **olfactory tract** and, at its distal end, the enlarged **olfactory bulb** (of cranial nerve I) (Fig. 15.1b; 15.24, p. 469; p. 471 of Table 15.8).

g. **corpus callosum**, a broad structure of white matter made up of myelinated axons passing from one hemisphere to the other (Fig. 15.1c, 15.3a, 15.13–15).

h. **lateral ventricles**, one cavity containing CSF (cerebrospinal fluid) in each hemisphere (Fig. 15.6, 15.13b, 15.14).

i. **septum pellucidum**, a membrane in the midline separating right and left lateral ventricles (Fig. 15.14, 15.15 [where "diencephalon" label is to the superior border of that subdivision; it does not include the septum pellucidum]).

j. cerebral nuclei (sometimes called basal nuclei) are structures composed of gray matter. These darker areas may be demonstrated on CORONAL EMBEDDED SECTIONS (Fig. 15.3a, 15.13b, 15.14; 17.8, p. 522), where three (caudate nucleus, putamen, globus pallidus) are labeled. The internal capsule, myelinated axons (white matter) running to and from the cortex, passes between the cerebral nuclei and the thalamus of the diencephalon; it may also be demonstrated on CORONAL EMBEDDED SECTIONS (Fig. 15.14).

2. The **diencephalon** is almost completely surrounded by the cerebral hemispheres. (Fig. 15.15, 15.18).

   a. **pineal gland** (or **pineal body**) (Fig. 15.1c, 15.15).

   b. **pituitary gland** (or hypophysis) (Fig. 15.1b, c; 15.15, 15.17).

   c. **optic chiasm** and **optic tracts** (of cranial nerve II), (midsagittal view in Fig. 15.15, 15.17; inferior view in Fig. 15.1b, 15.18a; 15.24, p. 469; p. 471 of Table 15.8).

   d. **third ventricle**, a flattened midline cavity containing CSF, communicating with each lateral ventricle through an interventricular foramen (Fig. 15.6, 15.13b, 15.14).

   e. **thalamus**, gray matter forming the lateral walls of third ventricle (Fig. 15.1c, 15.13b, 15.14–16, 15.18).

   f. **hypothalamus**, forms the inferior walls and floor of third ventricle (Fig. 15.1c, 15.14, 15.15, 15.17).

3. The **midbrain** (or **mesencephalon**) (Fig. 15.1b, c; 15.18, 15.19) is a constricted region forming part of the brainstem. Locate the following structures.

   a. **cerebral peduncles** (Fig. 15.18, 15.19) large cylindrical bulges on the anterior surface, composed of motor axons connecting the cerebrum with other regions.

   b. two posterior pairs of sensory nuclei, called collectively the tectal plate or corpora quadrigemina (Fig. 15.1c, 15.18b): two **superior colliculi** (singular: colliculus), which contain visual reflex centers; two **inferior colliculi**, which contain auditory reflex centers ("colliculi" is *not* the same word as "canaliculi" of Chapter 4).

   c. cranial nerves (Fig. 15.24, p. 472 of Table 15.8):

      i. oculomotor nerve (III)

      ii. trochlear nerve (IV)

   d. **cerebral aqueduct** (sometimes called the mesencephalic aqueduct), a thin elongated cavity containing CSF in the midline joining the third to the fourth ventricle (Fig. 15.8a, 15.15, 15.19, 15.22).

4. The **cerebellum**, with many slender cortical folds (Fig. 15.1, 15.22). The cerebellum (which is *not* part of the brainstem) coordinates skeletal muscle movement, and helps maintain balance and posture.

5. The **pons** is the second part of the brainstem. It can be divided into an anterior portion containing axonal tracts, and a posterior portion containing a variety of nuclei (groups of neuron cell bodies) and axonal tracts. Identify the following (Fig. 15.1, 15.13b, 15.18, 15.20, 15.24):

    a. **middle cerebellar peduncles** (Fig. 15.18b, 15.20b): One bulge on each side of the pons, containing axonal tracts to the cerebellum.

    b. superior half of the **fourth ventricle**, a tent-shaped cavity containing CSF that lies between the cerebellum posteriorly, and the pons and cranial end of the medulla oblongata anteriorly; continuous with the cerebral aqueduct of the midbrain and the central canal of the spinal cord (Fig. 15.1c, 15.6, 15.18b, 15.20b, 15.21a).

    c. cranial nerves (Fig. 15.24, pp. 473–475 of Table 15.8):

        i. trigeminal nerve (V)

        ii. abducens nerve (VI)

        iii. facial nerve (VII)

        iv. vestibulocochlear nerve (VIII)

6. The **medulla oblongata** (or simply the **medulla**) is the third and final portion of the brainstem. Identify the following (Fig. 15.1, 15.13b, 15.18, 15.21):

    a. **pyramids** (Fig. 15.18a, 15.21), two large columns of motor axonal tracts located on the anterior surface of the medulla, appearing as bulges, one on each side of the midline (Clemente, Fig. 639).

    b. inferior half of the **fourth ventricle** (Fig. 15.1c, 15.6, 15.18b, 15.20b, 15.21a).

    c. cranial nerves (Fig. 15.24, pp. 475–477 of Table 15.8):

        i. glossopharyngeal nerve (IX)

        ii. vagus nerve (X)

        iii. accessory nerve (XI)

        iv. hypoglossal nerve (XII)

III. Peripheral Nervous System (PNS)

(pp. 469–477, 489–504)

A. There are twelve pairs of cranial nerves. They arise from various locations on the brain and/or brainstem noted above (section II.C) with its different regions. Identify the bold-print cranial nerves on the BRAIN MODELS, by *either* the name *or* the identifying *Roman* numeral (Fig. 15.24; Table 15.8, pp. 471–477; Clemente, Fig. 639).

1. **Olfactory nerve** (or **I**), which consists of sensory neurons for smell that pass through the cribriform plate of the ethmoid bone, ending at each olfactory bulb.

2. **Optic nerve** (or **II**), which contains sensory axons for vision that originate from the retina.

3. **Oculomotor nerve** (or **III**), contains motor axons for four extrinsic eye muscles (superior rectus, medial rectus, inferior rectus, and inferior oblique muscles). It also contains some autonomic (parasympathetic) motor axons that help constrict the pupil and contract ciliary muscles to change the shape of the lens.

4. **Trochlear nerve** (or **IV**), contains motor axons for one extrinsic eye muscle (superior oblique muscle).

5. **Trigeminal nerve** (or **V**), contains motor axons for the muscles of mastication. It also contains numerous sensory axons from the face.

6. **Abducens nerve** (or **VI**), contains motor axons for one extrinsic eye muscle (lateral rectus muscle).

7. **Facial nerve** (or **VII**), contains motor axons for the muscles of facial expression. It also contains autonomic (parasympathetic) motor axons to the lacrimal gland and the sublingual and submandibular salivary glands, and it contains sensory axons for taste from the anterior 2/3 of the tongue.

8. **Vestibulocochlear nerve** (or **VIII**), contains sensory axons for hearing (audition) from the cochlear nerve and for equilibrium (balance) from the vestibular nerve.

9. **Glossopharyngeal nerve** (or **IX**), contains sensory axons for taste from the posterior 1/3 of the tongue, motor axons for pharynx muscles, and some autonomic (parasympathetic) motor axons that control the parotid salivary gland.

10. **Vagus nerve** (or **X**), innervates structures in neck, thorax and abdomen. It sends somatic (voluntary) motor axons to some pharynx muscles and many larynx muscles. It also sends autonomic (parasympathetic) motor axons to most of the thoracic and abdominal organs (Fig. 18.5, p. 543). Also identify the left vagus nerve in the thorax on the TORSO MODELS, and on the DONORS in the neck (accompanying the common carotid artery) and thorax (where it innervates the heart and lungs) (Clemente, Fig. 186–7, 581).

11. Accessory nerve (XI), contains motor axons that go to the pharynx, larynx, trapezius muscle, and sternocleidomastoid muscle (not shown clearly on models).

12. **Hypoglossal nerve** (or **XII**), contains motor axons for the intrinsic and most extrinsic tongue muscles.

B. There are 31 pairs of spinal nerves originating from the different regions of the spinal cord, including 8 cervical, 12 thoracic, 5 lumbar, 5 sacral, and l coccygeal (Fig. 16.1a, p. 484). Most are uncomplicated in their paths but in the superior and inferior regions, the anterior rami (branches) of a number of spinal nerves combine on each side and exchange fibers to form various named nerves. These paired areas of interchange are called plexuses (singular: plexus).

1. The cervical plexus (Fig. 16.8), formed from the anterior rami of the first five cervical nerves (C1 to C5), supplies the neck and shoulder, but also forms the **phrenic nerve** (Fig. 16.8; 22.2b, p. 652), which provides motor innervation to the diaphragm. The left phrenic nerve is seen in the neck on the anterior scalene muscle, both on the MUSCULAR HEAD MODEL and on the DONORS. It is also seen on the DONORS in the thoracic cavity on its way to the diaphragm (Clemente, Fig. 581 and 186–7).

2. The **brachial plexus** supplies the upper extremity. Formed primarily from the anterior rami of the last four cervical (C5 to C8) and the first thoracic (T1) nerves, it can be identified on the DONORS and the MUSCULAR HEAD MODEL (Fig. 16.9a; Clemente, Fig. 580). Of the five major nerves (axillary, radial, musculocutaneous, ulnar, and median) which arise from the brachial plexus, be able to identify on the DONORS the left **radial nerve**, **ulnar nerve**, and **median nerve** (Fig. 16.9b, c; Table 16.3; Clemente, Fig. 22).

3. The **lumbosacral plexus**, supplying the lower extremity, can be identified only on the LEG MODELS. It includes both the lumbar plexus (formed from the anterior rami of spinal nerves L1–L4; Fig. 16.10a) and the sacral plexus (formed from the anterior rami of spinal nerves L4–S4; Fig. 16.11a). Each of these plexuses supplies a major nerve to the lower limb. On the DONORS and the LEG and TORSO MODELS, identify the following nerves:

   a. **femoral nerve**, from the lumbar plexus and seen on the anterior thigh (Fig. 16.10, p. 500 of Table 16.4; Clemente, Fig. 418).

   b. **sciatic nerve**, main branch of the sacral plexus and largest nerve in the body, seen on the posterior hip and thigh; in the thigh, splits into its components, the **tibial nerve** and the **common fibular** (or common peroneal) **nerve** (Fig. 16.11b–c, p. 503 of Table 16.5; Clemente, Fig. 428).

IV. Microscopic Anatomy of the Nervous System

(pp. 111–112, 414–417, 418–422)

A. Central Nervous System. Using the following VIRTUAL MICROSCOPE SLIDES, be able to identify:

1. **CEREBRUM**: be able to identify this part of the CNS. Notice its surface layer, the **cortex**, composed of gray matter and containing **cell bodies** and nerve cell processes of neurons as well as smaller glial cells of which only the darker nuclei are seen (Sobotta, Fig. 540–2).

2. **CEREBELLUM**: be able to recognize this part of the CNS. Its surface layer, the **cortex**, composed of gray matter, is highly folded over a thin core of **white matter** (Sobotta, Fig. 536 and 538). Note the larger, distinctive Purkinje cells regularly arranged within the cortex parallel to its surface.

3. **SPINAL CORD**: be able to recognize this part of the CNS:

   Distinguish the **gray matter** and **white matter**. Locate a large **motor neuron** in the anterior horn, and identify the following features of it (Table 4.13, Fig. 14.3):

   a. **Cell body** (or soma) of the motor neuron.

   b. **Nucleus** with a distinct **nucleolus**.

   c. **Chromatophilic substance** (or Nissl bodies), dark granular material within the cytoplasm.

   d. **Nerve cell processes** (or **neuron processes**); there are two types of processes on each neuron, dendrites and an axon. The axon can be distinguished from dendrites because it arises from a lightly staining, cone-shaped area, the **axon hillock** (Sobotta, Fig. 199). You may have to examine many motor neurons before seeing this distinction demonstrated.

B. Peripheral Nervous System. There are two VIRTUAL MICROSCOPE SLIDES of the NERVE, one of the nerve cut in cross section, the other in longitudinal section; be able to recognize each.

1. PERIPHERAL **NERVE**–CROSS SECTION (Fig. 14.12a–b, p. 425; Sobotta, Fig. 205, 209). A peripheral nerve is composed of bundles (fasciculi) of nerve fibers. A nerve fiber consists of an **axon** (a process of a neuron) together with its **myelin sheath** or coverings. Under high magnification the axon appears as a dark spot surrounded by a lighter circular area, the myelin sheath. There are also groups of smaller, poorly-myelinated axons between the large, well-myelinated axons.

2. PERIPHERAL **NERVE**–LONGITUDINAL SECTION (Fig. 14.3, 14.8, 14.12c, p. 425; Sobotta, Fig. 203). **Neurolemmocytes** (or **Schwann cells**) wrap around an **axon** to form a **myelin sheath**, and are arranged sequentially along its length. Where adjacent neurolemmocytes cells meet, a narrow gap (**neurofibril node** or **node of Ranvier**) is seen in the myelin sheath, appearing as an indentation or a thin line perpendicular to the axon.

C. **Pituitary Gland** (or hypophysis). Two parts of this endocrine gland are distinguishable on the PITUITARY GLAND slide when viewed at the low power magnifications. Be able to recognize this gland under the microscope by identifying and comparing the following (Figs. 20.5–20.6, pp. 607–608; Sobotta, Fig. 449):

1. The **posterior pituitary** (or posterior lobe, or neurohypophysis) has a lighter, irregularly fibrous appearance indicating its derivation from the floor of the brain. (A portion of the infundibulum connecting it to the hypothalamus may also be seen.)

2. The larger **anterior pituitary** (or anterior lobe, or adenohypophysis) has darker, more distinct cells of several types and staining properties; more blood vessels are seen.

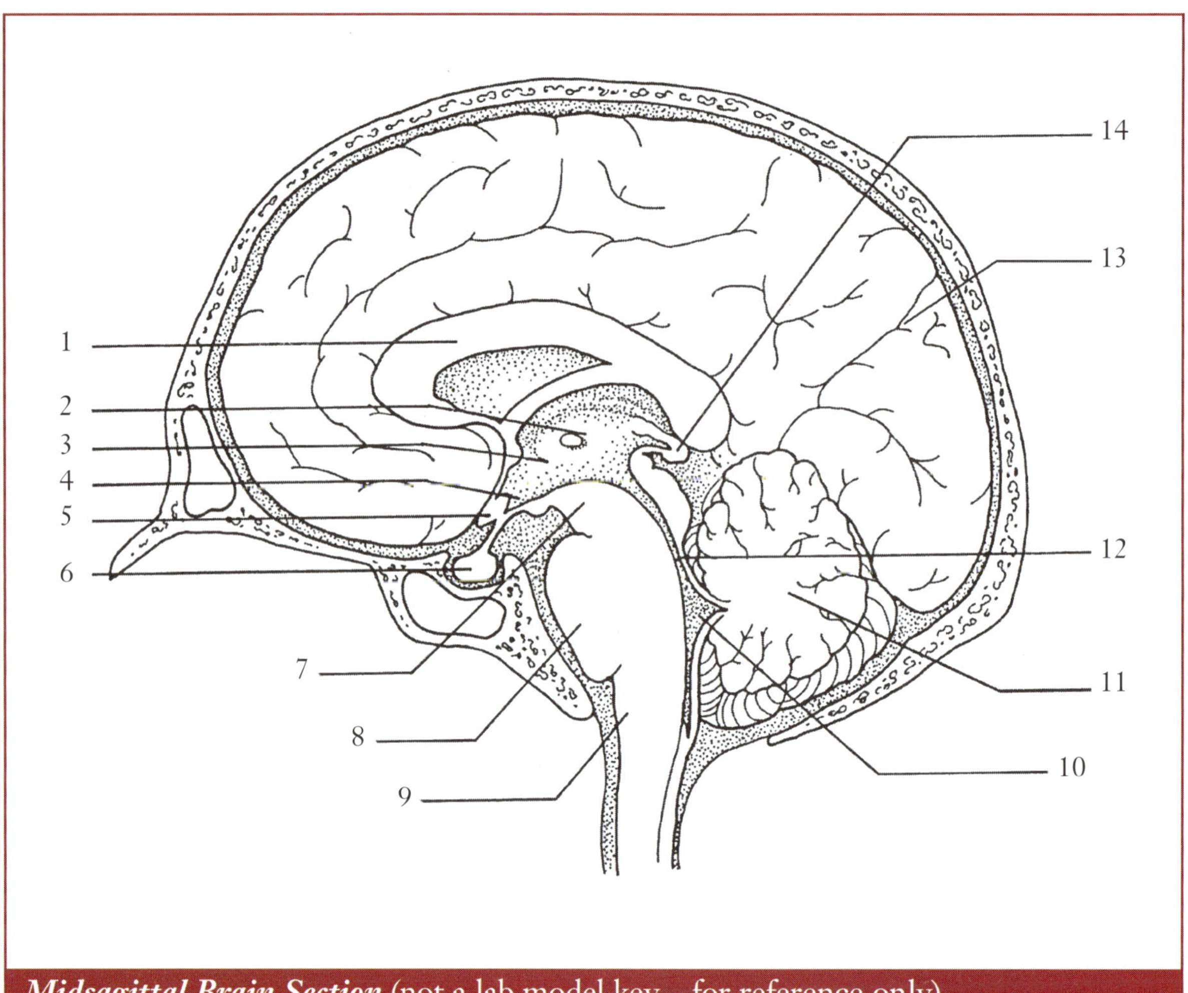

Midsagittal Brain Section (not a lab model key – for reference only)

1. corpus callosum
2. thalamus
3. third ventricle
4. hypothalamus
5. optic chiasm
6. pituitary gland
7. midbrain
8. pons
9. medulla oblongata
10. fourth ventricle
11. cerebellum
12. cerebral (mesencephalic) aqueduct
13. parieto-occipital sulcus
14. pineal gland

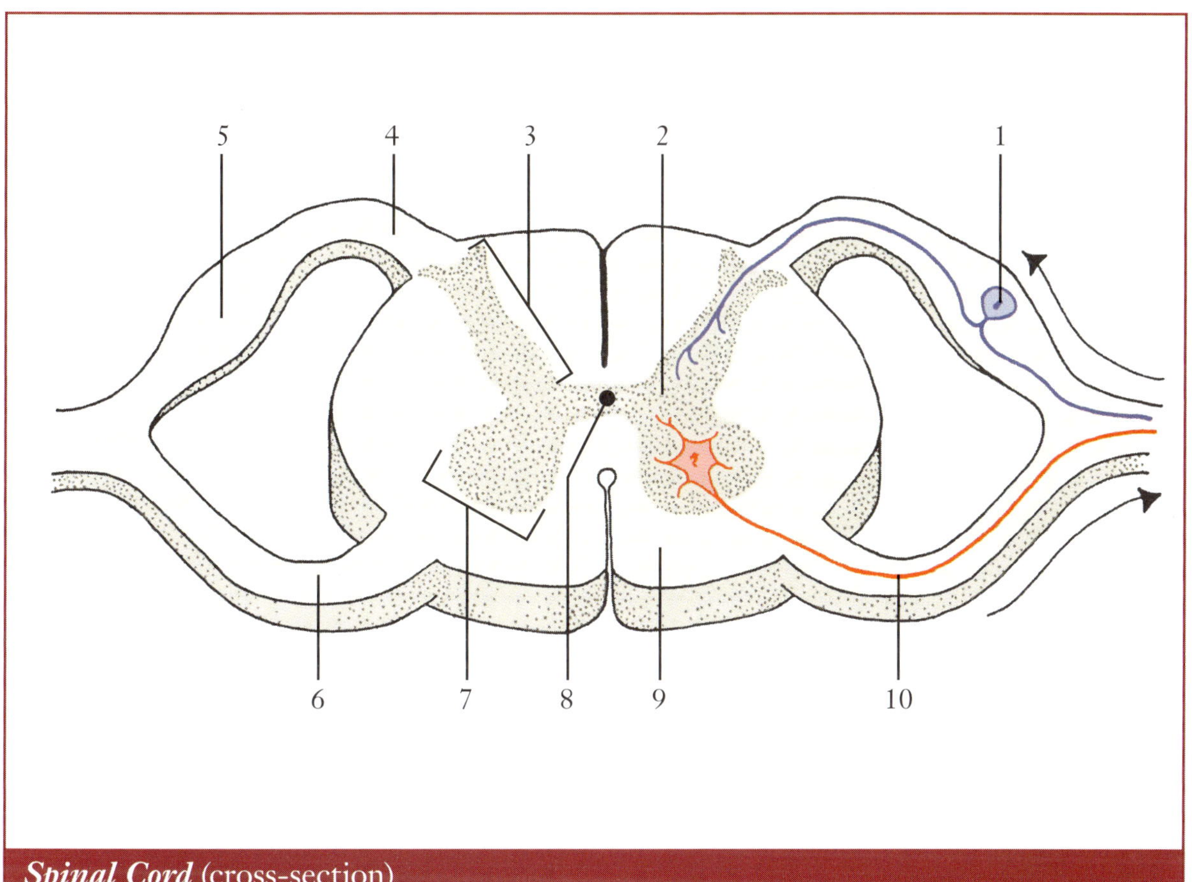

Spinal Cord (cross-section)

1. cell body of sensory (afferent) neuron
2. gray matter
3. posterior (dorsal) horn
4. posterior (dorsal) root
5. posterior (dorsal) root ganglion
6. anterior (ventral) root
7. anterior (ventral) horn
8. central canal
9. white matter
10. axon of motor (efferent) neuron

V. Organs of the Special Senses
(pp. 326–330, 570–596)

A. The special senses of the body are vision, audition (hearing), equilibrium, olfaction, and gustation. In our study of the digestive system, the organs for the sense of gustation (taste) will be identified. These organs are the taste buds, located on the fungiform and vallate papillae. The olfactory epithelium found within the nasal cavity contains the receptors for the sense of olfaction (smell).

B. Eye and Vision. We will use MODELS and a VIRTUAL MICROSCOPE SLIDE to observe various features of the eyeball and associated structures.

   1. Extrinsic eye muscles. There are six muscles originating from the bony orbit to insert on the sclera of the eye. These muscles are responsible for the eye's various movements and (with the two exceptions noted) are innervated by cranial nerve III, the oculomotor nerve. On the MODELS locate the following muscles and note in which direction each one would move the eye (Fig. 11.4, p. 329; Clemente, Fig. 664 through Fig. 668):

      a. rectus (straight) muscles:

         i. **medial rectus muscle**

         ii. **lateral rectus muscle**, (innervated by cranial nerve VI, abducens)

         iii. **superior rectus muscle**

         iv. **inferior rectus muscle**

      b. oblique muscles:

         i. **superior oblique muscle**, (innervated by cranial nerve IV, trochlear)

         ii. **inferior oblique muscle**

   2. Structure of the eyeball. Use the EYE MODELS to identify the bold terms (Fig. 19.11; Clemente, Fig. 680).

      a. the eyeball has 3 basic tunics (layers) (Fig. 19.11a; Table 19.3):

         i. the **fibrous tunic** is the outermost layer. It is divided into a white opaque portion, the **sclera**, which is the posterior five-sixths of the fibrous tunic. The anterior one-sixth is the **cornea**, which is transparent. It is curved more acutely than the sclera and thus it bulges slightly.

         ii. the **vascular tunic** (or uvea) is the middle layer (Fig. 19.11). Most of this tunic is the posterior, darkly pigmented, and highly vascular **choroid**. Near the edge of the cornea, the vascular tunic forms the **ciliary body** (seen best on EYE MODEL E2). The ciliary body includes the ciliary processes and, within the ciliary body, the **ciliary muscles**, made up of smooth muscle cells. The ciliary muscles contribute to changes in the shape of the lens. The most anterior part of the vascular tunic is the **iris**, a thin muscular diaphragm which regulates the amount of light entering the eye through a rounded opening, the **pupil** (Fig. 19.11). The iris is pigmented, giving the eye its color.

   iii. the internal or neural tunic is the innermost layer, and consists of the two-layered **retina**. At the posterior aspect of the neural tunic, two distinct landmarks can be identified. The **blind spot** or **optic disc**, seen internally, is the site where blood vessels and the **optic nerve** (or **cranial nerve II**) enter and leave the eye. Lateral to the optic disc is a slightly yellow area, the **macula lutea**. In the center of the macula is a small depressed area, the **fovea centralis**, which is the area of sharpest vision (Fig. 19.11b, 19.13a, 19.14a).

 b. the **lens** is located behind the pupil. It is clear, elastic, biconvex, and supported around its rim by the fine fibers of the **suspensory ligaments**. The shape of the lens can be changed by the ciliary muscles which are attached to the suspensory ligaments. Contraction of the ciliary muscles reduces the tension that the suspensory ligaments exert on the lens, allowing it to become more convex (thicker) (Fig. 19.11b, 19.15).

 c. cavities and humors. The lens and suspensory ligaments divide the eye into two cavities.

   i. the **anterior cavity** is in front of the lens, and can be subdivided into the **anterior chamber** between the iris and cornea, and the **posterior chamber** between the iris anteriorly and suspensory ligaments and lens posteriorly. The entire anterior cavity is filled with aqueous humor (Fig. 19.11b, 19.16).

   ii. the **posterior cavity** (or **vitreous chamber**) is the four-fifths of the eye behind the lens. It is filled by the **vitreous humor**, a transparent gelatinous mass.

3. Note that the **lacrimal gland** is located outside the eye at the superior lateral aspect of the orbit (Fig. 19.10).

4. Microscopic anatomy of the eyeball. After first examining the slide of the EYE at the lowest magnification, use the higher magnifications to locate the following (Fig. 19.11, 19.13; Sobotta, Fig. 501):

 a. tunics of the eyeball.

   i. fibrous tunic, the outer thick layer composed of the posterior **sclera** (surrounding the posterior cavity) and **cornea** anterior to the iris (Sobotta, Fig. 507).

   ii. vascular tunic, including the dark **choroid**; the **ciliary body** at the edges of the lens; and the **iris** with an opening, the **pupil**, in its center to allow light rays to enter the eye (Sobotta, Fig. 506).

  iii. internal tunic, the **retina**, which lines most of the posterior cavity and includes both the very thin, outer **pigmented layer** (consisting of a simple epithelium and dark pigment granules) and the inner **neural** (or **nervous tissue**) **layer**. The neural layer contains photoreceptors, the rods and cones, and other neurons (Fig. 19.13; Sobotta, Fig. 502). Use high power to distinguish these layers from each other and from the adjacent **choroid** and **sclera**.

 b. the **lens**; a transparent structure that contains cells filled with a protein. The lens is surrounded by a thick elastic capsule to which the suspensory ligaments are attached (Sobotta, Fig. 506).

 c. cavities and chambers (Fig. 19.11b, 19.16).

  i. the anterior cavity is located anterior to the lens and posterior to the cornea. It is divided by the iris into an **anterior chamber** and a **posterior chamber**. Aqueous humor circulates throughout the anterior cavity.

  ii. the **posterior cavity** (or **vitreous chamber**) is located posterior to the lens and contains the vitreous humor, which may not be evident on the slide.

C. Ear: Audition and Equilibrium. The ear has three regions: external, middle, and inner (Fig. 19.19). Use the EAR MODELS to locate these divisions as defined, and the structures in each. (The actual size and orientation of these components may be demonstrated on a cut-open temporal bone.)

 1. The **external ear** consists of *both* the **auricle** (or pinna), which projects from the side of the head, *and* the **external acoustic** (or **auditory**) **meatus** (or **canal**) which leads into the temporal bone. The medial end of the external acoustic meatus is bounded by the **tympanic membrane** (commonly called the eardrum), composed of connective tissue covered by epithelium.

 2. The **middle ear** (containing the air-filled tympanic cavity) is a small six-sided chamber within the temporal bone (Fig. 19.19, 19.20). Crossing the middle ear is a chain of three small bones (the auditory ossicles) which connect the tympanic membrane with the membrane-covered oval window of the inner ear. The three auditory ossicles are, from lateral to medial, the **malleus**, **incus**, and **stapes**. There is a connection, the **auditory** (or **pharyngotympanic** or **Eustachian**) **tube**, permitting the passage of air between the middle ear and nasopharynx.

 3. The **inner ear** lies within the petrous part of the temporal bone and is composed of two complex structures: the outer **bony labyrinth** consisting of spaces in the bone; and the **membranous labyrinth** suspended inside it (Fig. 19.19, 19.21; Clemente, Figs. 802–805). See INNER EAR MODEL.

  a. the components of the **bony labyrinth**:

   i. the central **vestibule**.

72

    ii. three **semicircular canals**, arranged in planes which are 90 degrees apart; enlargements at their bases are the **ampullae**.

    iii. the snail shell-shaped **cochlea**.

    iv. two small membrane-covered openings in its lateral border can be seen from the middle ear: the **oval window**, in contact with the stapes, and the **round window**, situated inferior and posterior to the oval window.

    v. a fluid called perilymph circulates in the bony labyrinth outside the membranous labyrinth.

b. the **membranous labyrinth** follows much the same form as the bony labyrinth since it lies within the bony labyrinth. It contains a fluid called endolymph.

    i. the **utricle** and the **saccule** are enlargements of the membranous labyrinth within the vestibule. The utricle communicates with the five openings of the semicircular ducts. The saccule is connected by small channels to the cochlear duct and the utricle. The receptors that detect changes in the position of the head (linear acceleration and deceleration, and head tilt) are in the utricle and saccule. Note parts of the vestibular branch of CN VIII originating here (Fig. 19.21–22).

    ii. the **semicircular ducts** are located within the semicircular canals. The receptors that detect movement of the head (rotational acceleration and deceleration) are located in enlargements at the ends of the semicircular ducts, called **ampullae** (Fig. 19.21, 19.24, 19.25).

    iii. structures and spaces in and around the membranous labyrinth within the cochlea are examined microscopically below. Nerve cell processes from receptors in its spiral organ form the **cochlear branch of CN VIII** (Fig. 19.21, 19.26) seen on the various EAR MODELS.

c. microscopic anatomy of the cochlea. Identify the following on the slide of the COCHLEA and the COCHLEA CROSS SECTION MODEL (Fig. 19.21, 19.26; Sobotta, Fig. 518):

    i. the **cochlear duct** (or **scala media**), a part of the membranous labyrinth, splits the bony canal of the cochlea into the **scala vestibuli** and **scala tympani** which join only at the apex of the cochlea.

    ii. the thicker **basilar membrane** (Fig. 19.26b–d) is made up of a dense mat of collagen and some elastic fibers; it separates the cochlear duct from the scala tympani. The thinner **vestibular membrane** (Fig. 19.26a, 19.26b) separates the cochlear duct from the scala vestibuli.

iii. the **spiral organ** (or **organ of Corti**) rests on the basilar membrane at the narrow inner curve of the cochlear duct. It consists of **hair cells** with long stereocilia which are normally in contact with the thin, jelly-like **tectorial membrane**. In the preparation of the microscope slide of the cochlea, however, the tectorial membrane may have been separated in places from the stereocilia (Fig. 19.21, 19.26b–d; Sobotta, Fig. 519).

VI. Study Tips for this Chapter

A. Use the pictures in your text to help you identify nervous system structures. You can use these text pictures at home to review these structures.

B. Make sure you learn the nervous system structures on the Donors and selected Models. The model keys at the end of this chapter list many of the structures that you will be responsible for on a particular model.

C. At home, make a list of the 6 subdivisions of the brain you learned in lab. Writing the names over and over again will help you remember their names.

D. At home, list what nervous system structures are found in which subdivision of the brain. Again, writing the names out will help you better remember the material.

E. At home, try to pronounce each of the nervous system names. It is very difficult to remember the names, if you don't know how to pronounce them.

F. Study lab and lecture material together at home by doing the following: review text pictures and say the names of the nervous system structures aloud. Then, look in your lecture notes to determine the function of that nervous system structure.

G. Write out the names of the Cranial Nerves in their numerical order. Note that the first few cranial nerves are toward the front of the brain, whereas the last few cranial nerves are found on the brainstem. By remembering the cranial nerve names in order, you will be able to approximately determine where on the brain the nerve is located.

H. In lab, have your lab partner "quiz" you on the Virtual Microscope Slides. Reverse roles: YOU set up a microscope slide to quiz your lab partner. Both you and your lab partner will be better able to identify the structures on the slides when it comes time for the exam.

I. At home, list the tunics of the eye, and what structures are found in each tunic.

J. At home, list the structures that are found in the external, middle and inner ear.

K. Remember to use the Virtual Microscope to review nervous tissue at home!

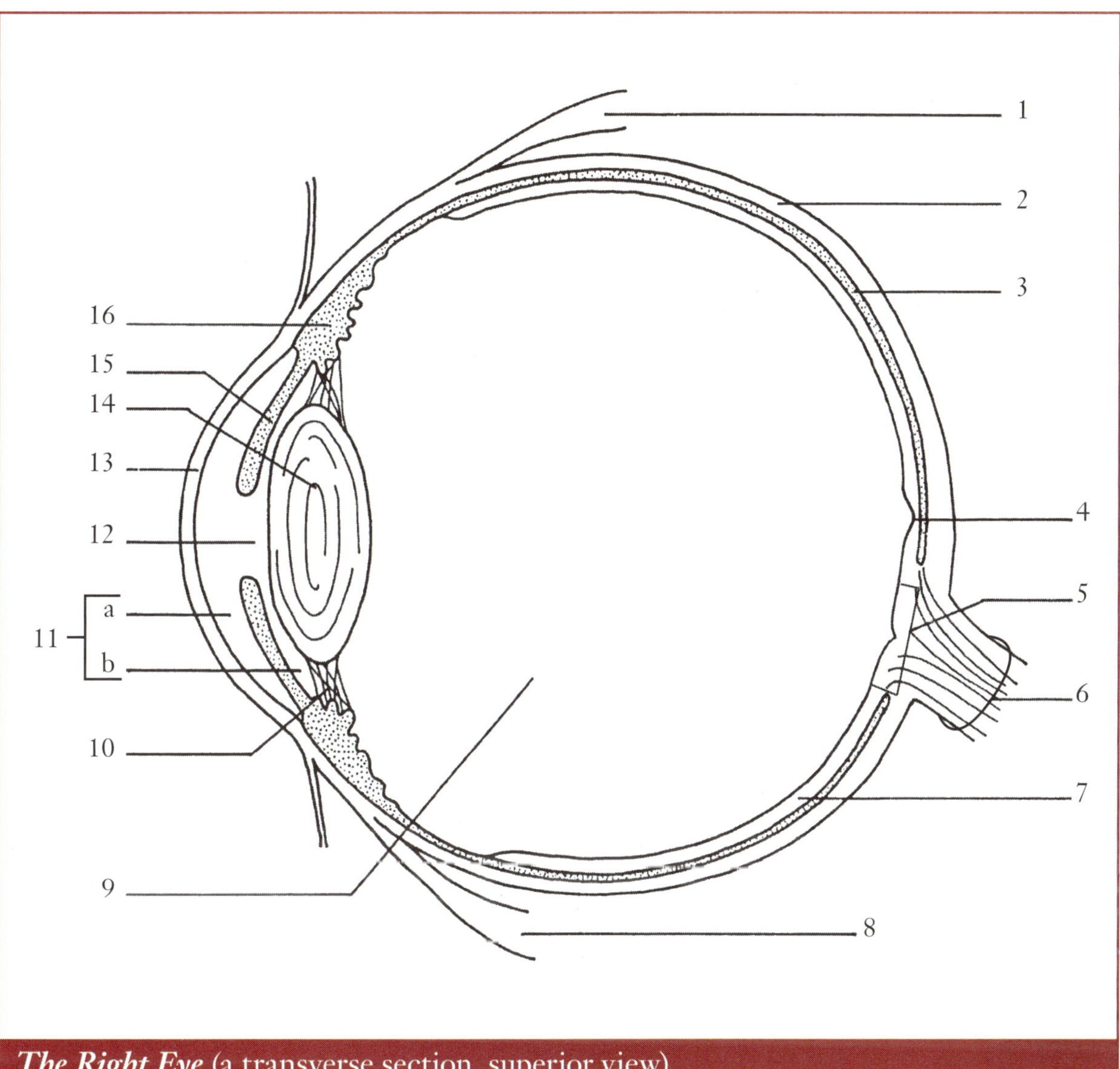

The Right Eye (a transverse section, superior view)

1. lateral rectus muscle
2. sclera
3. choroid
4. fovea centralis
5. blind spot (optic disc)
6. optic nerve (cranial nerve II)
7. retina
8. medial rectus muscle
9. posterior cavity
10. suspensory ligaments
11. anterior cavity
    a. anterior chamber
    b. posterior chamber
12. pupil
13. cornea
14. lens
15. iris
16. ciliary body

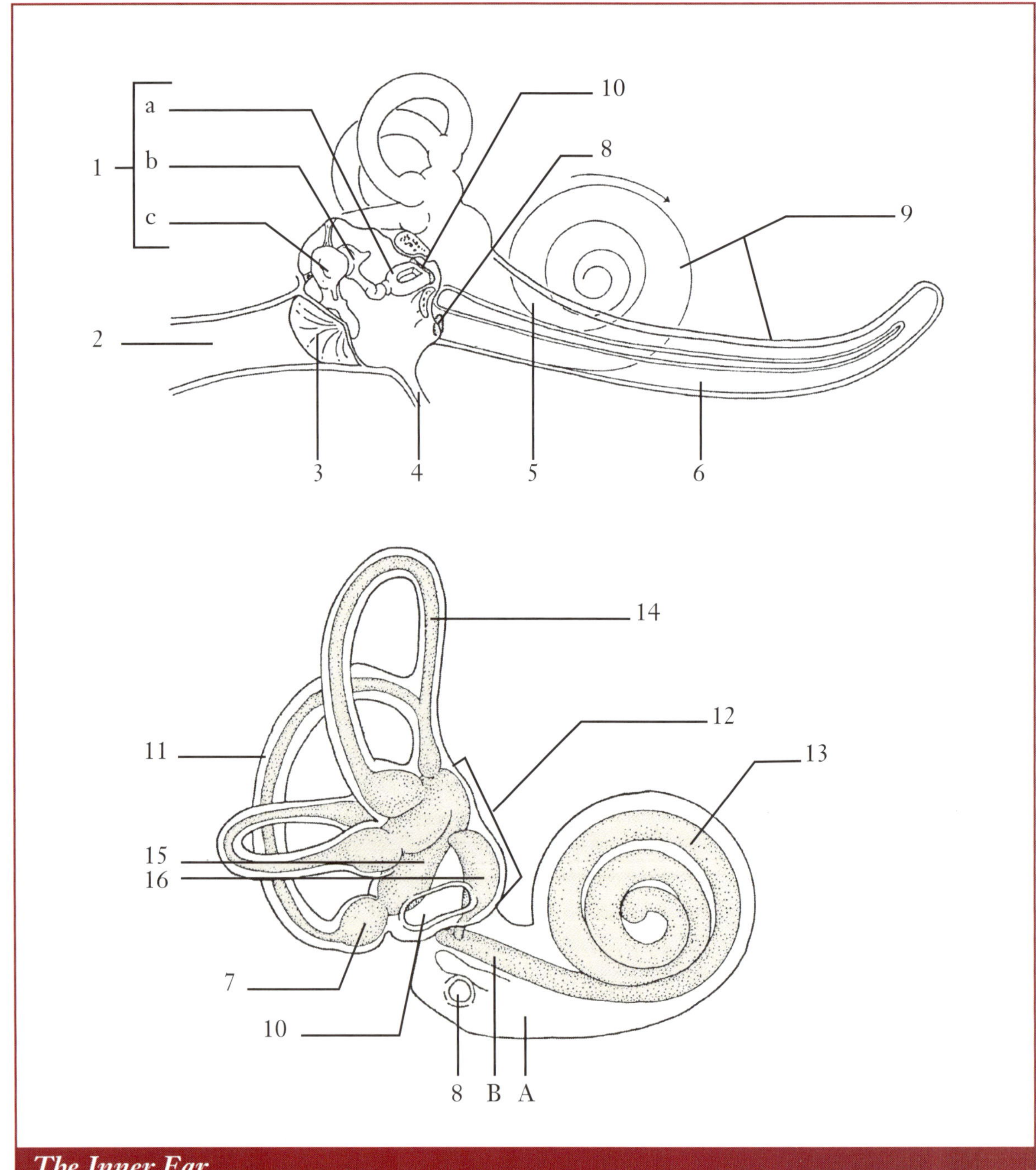

The Inner Ear

1. auditory ossicles
   a. stapes
   b. incus
   c. malleus
2. external acoustic meatus
3. tympanic membrane
4. auditory (pharyngotympanic; Eustachian) tube
5. scala vestibuli
6. scala tympani
7. ampulla

A. bony labyrinth
   8. round window
   9. cochlea
   10. oval window
   11. semicircular canal
   12. vestibule
B. membranous labyrinth
   13. cochlear duct
   14. semicircular duct
   15. utricle
   16. saccule

VII. Nervous System Model Keys

SPINAL CORD CROSS-SECTION MODEL (CERVICAL)

- *7.* vertebral artery
- *9.* dura mater
- *17.* anterior (or ventral) root
- *18.* posterior (or dorsal) root
- *19.* posterior (or dorsal) root ganglion
- *20, 21.* branches from spinal nerve
- *30–32, 33.* white matter
- *34, 36–38.* gray matter
- *35.* central canal
- *36.* anterior (or ventral) horn
- *38.* posterior (or dorsal) horn

BASE-OF-SKULL MODEL

- *1–7.* dural venous sinuses
- *8.* internal carotid artery
- *13.* basilar artery
- *17.* vertebral artery
- *42.* pituitary gland (in sella turcica)
- cerebral arterial circle

MUSCULAR HEAD MODELS (listed by part of the model)

Inside Cranial Cavity

- *102.* dura mater
- *114.* pituitary gland
- *116.* optic nerve (CN II)
- *128–132.* dural venous sinuses

Neck

- *81.* (left) phrenic nerve
- *82.* (left) brachial plexus

Brain

- *140.* frontal lobe
- *141.* parietal lobe
- *142.* occipital lobe
- *143.* temporal lobe
- *144.* lateral sulcus
- *145.* corpus callosum
- *146.* septum pellucidum
- *150.* thalamus
- *152.* hypothalamus
- *154.* pineal gland
- *155.* optic tract
- *156.* midbrain
- *157.* cerebral (mesencephalic) aqueduct
- *158.* third ventricle
- *159.* fourth ventricle
- *161.* pons
- *163–168.* cerebellum
- *169.* olfactory bulb
- *170.* optic chiasm
- *171.* oculomotor nerve (CN III)
- *172.* trochlear nerve (CN IV)
- *173.* trigeminal nerve (CN V)
- *174.* abducens nerve (CN VI)
- *175.* facial nerve (CN VII)
- *176.* vestibulocochlear nerve (CN VIII)
- *177.* glossopharyngeal nerve (CN IX)
- *178.* vagus nerve (CN X)
- *180.* hypoglossal nerve (CN XII)
- *182.* cerebral peduncle
- *183.* pyramid
- *192.* middle cerebellar peduncle

BRAIN MODELS B1–B8 (listed by subdivision of brain and side of labelling)

Labels on Left Half of Model	*Labels on Right Half of Model*

Cerebrum

1. corpus callosum	o, p, q, s. corpus callosum
28. olfactory bulb	28. olfactory bulb (of CN I)
	r. septum pellucidum
	F. frontal lobe
	G. frontal lobe, near posterior border
	H. temporal lobe
	J. occipital lobe
	K. lateral sulcus

Diencephalon

6. interventricular foramen	e, g, n. walls of third ventricle
30. optic nerve (CN II)	
31. optic chiasm	
45. thalamus	
46. pituitary gland (PLEASE DON'T MOVE this part on this model!)	

Cerebellum

B(7, 8, 9, 11)	B(c,f)

Midbrain

inferior colliculus	
14. superior colliculus	
15. cerebral peduncle	
32. oculomotor nerve (CN III)	
33. trochlear nerve (CN IV)	

Pons

D.	a.
18. fourth ventricle	d. fourth ventricle
34. trigeminal nerve (CN V)	
35. abducens nerve (CN VI)	
36. facial nerve (CN VII)	
37. vestibulocochlear nerve (CN VIII)	

Medulla oblongata

E.	
19–20. pyramid	
38. glossopharyngeal nerve (CN IX)	
39. vagus nerve (CN X)	
41. hypoglossal nerve (CN XII)	

HALF-HEAD MODELS (labels on brain and spinal cord)

A. cerebrum
B. diencephalon
C. midbrain
E. medulla oblongata
2. dura mater
3a–c. corpus callosum
8. septum pellucidum
9. thalamus
10. pineal gland

11. pituitary gland
15. cerebellum
16. pons
17. optic chiasm (of CN II)
18. third ventricle
19. fourth ventricle
20. cerebral (mesencephalic) aqueduct
22. spinal cord
dural venous sinuses

TORSO MODEL N1

258. (left) vagus nerve (CN X)
275. femoral nerve

277. sciatic nerve

TORSO MODEL N2

Labeled on Left Side of Brain

250. internal carotid artery at junction with cerebral arterial circle
255. vertebral artery
256. basilar artery
603. temporal lobe
614. third ventricle
621. lateral sulcus
622. precentral gyrus
623. postcentral gyrus
624. contral sulcus
625–627. corpus callosum
636–637. thalamus
639. superior colliculus
640. inferior colliculus
700. pituitary gland

Labeled on Right Side of Brain

601. frontal lobe
602. parietal lobe
604. occipital lobe
605. cerebellum
606. medulla oblongata
608. pons
609–610. cerebral peduncle
611. optic chiasm
612. lateral ventricle
613. corpus callosum
614. third ventricle
615. cerebral (mesencephalic) aqueduct
616. fourth ventricle
644. olfactory bulb (of CN I)
645. optic nerve (CN II)
646. oculomotor nerve (CN III)
647. trochlear nerve (CN IV)
648. trigeminal nerve (CN V)
649. abducens nerve (CN VI)
650. facial nerve (CN VII)
651. vestibulocochlear nerve (CN VIII)
691. middle cerebellar peduncle

Labeled on Torso

685. femoral nerve
690. sciatic nerve
669. (left) vagus nerve (CN X)

LEG MODELS L1–L10

59. femoral nerve
62, 92. lumbosacral plexus

63. sciatic nerve
64. tibial nerve
65. common fibular nerve

EYE MODEL EI

1. superior rectus muscle
(beneath muscle to eyelid)
2. inferior rectus muscle
3. medial rectus muscle
4. lateral rectus muscle
5. superior oblique muscle
6. inferior oblique muscle
7. sclera

On Anterior Part

1–3. lacrimal gland

9. choroid
10. iris
11. retina
12. vitreous humor
13. lens
16. optic nerve (from optic disc)
21. macula lutea (with fovea centralis)

EYE MODEL E2

1. cornea
2. anterior chamber
3, 30–32. iris
4. posterior chamber
5. lens
6. posterior cavity
7, 11. sclera
12. optic nerve (CN II)
14. choroid
16. retina
17. anterior edge of neural layer
of retina (ora serrata)
18. edges of ciliary body
19. ciliary processes

20. suspensory ligaments
21. ciliary muscle, within ciliary body
34. macula lutea
35. fovea centralis
36. optic disc (blind spot)

Detail of Retina

37. axons of optic nerve
38–40. neural layer, including:
41. rod
42. cone
43. pigmented layer

ONE-PIECE EYE MODELS

1. superior rectus muscle
2. inferior rectus muscle
3. medial rectus muscle
5. superior oblique muscle (tendon)
7. sclera
8. cornea
9. choroid

10. iris
11. retina
12. vitreous humor
13. lens
16. optic nerve (CN II)
17. ciliary muscle
21. macula lutea

EYE MODEL E3

External structures (on anterior, removable part of model):
   lacrimal gland (9a,b)

Extrinsic muscles:
   superior rectus (I)
   inferior rectus (II at attachment to sclera)
   medial rectus (III)
   lateral rectus (IV)
   tendon of superior oblique (V)
   inferior oblique (VI)

Components of the eyeball:
   fibrous tunic
      cornea
      sclera (2, A)
   vascular tunic
      iris (3)
      ciliary processes (5, inside)
      choroid (6)

retina (9, C)
   macula lutea
   optic disc (14), origin of optic nerve
lens (15)
vitreous humor (16)

LEFT EAR MODEL 1

A. external ear
   1. auricle
   2. external acoustic meatus
   3. tympanic membrane
B. middle ear
   7. auditory (pharyngotympanic;
      Eustachian) tube
   8. malleus
   9. incus
   11. stapes

C. inner ear
   12. vestibule
   13. oval window
   14. round window
   15–17. semicircular canals
   a, b, c. ampullae of semicircular canals
      18. cochlea
         cochlear branch of CN VIII

INNER EAR MODELS

A. bony labyrinth:
- *1.* vestibule
  - *a.* oval window
  - *b.* round window
- *2–4.* semicircular canals
  - *d.* ampullae of semicircular canals
- *5.* cochlea
- *12.* cochlear branch of CN VIII

B. membranous labyrinth:
(within vestibule)
- *8.* utricle
- *9.* saccule
  - axons to vestibular branch of CN VIII
(within semicircular canals)
- *6–7.* semicircular ducts
(within cochlea)
  - *p.* scala vestibuli
  - *q.* scala tympani
  - *r.* cochlear duct (scala media)

COCHLEA CROSS SECTION MODEL

1, 22, 23. bony substance of cochlea
- *2.* scala vestibuli
- *3.* scala tympani
- *4.* vestibular membrane
- *6, 27.* basilar membrane

8–13, 16. components of spiral organ
- *8–9.* hair cells
- *18.* tectorial membrane
- *19.* cochlear duct (scala media)
- (*24, 25.* parts of sensory neurons)

7

CHAPTER

Circulatory System

I. Introduction

A. We will continue to use DONORS, MODELS, and reference materials as we study the gross anatomy of the circulatory system.

B. Keep in mind that models should be handled carefully and reassembled after use.

C. Try to learn the circuits or sequence of the blood vessels in addition to their names. This will help you to better understand the entire circulatory system.

D. We will again use the VIRTUAL MICROSCOPE SLIDES to examine the histology of the circulatory system.

II. The Heart

(pp. 651–670)

A. Dimensions and Location:

1. The heart is a hollow muscular organ, somewhat conical in shape. An adult's heart is about the size of his or her closed fist.

2. The heart is located in the thorax between the right and left lungs within a region called the mediastinum. Most of the heart lies to the left of the sternum; its **apex** (inferior tip) extends downward and to the left to rest partially on the diaphragm (Fig. 22.2, 22.5a & b). Identify on DONORS, HEARTS and MODELS.

B. External features (Fig. 22.5):

1. The heart is enveloped by a connective tissue sac called the **pericardium**, which is lined by a serous membrane (the serous pericardium), and filled with a very thin layer of serous fluid (Fig. 22.3). On the DONORS, the outer part of the pericardium will have been cut open to expose the surface of the heart.

2. The heart is divided into four "chambers." Locate these chambers on the HEART and TORSO MODELS and (where exposed) on the DONORS.

    a. The **right atrium** receives deoxygenated blood from the venae cavae and the coronary sinus. It pumps blood to the right ventricle.

    b. The **right ventricle** pumps deoxygenated blood through the pulmonary trunk and to the lungs.

    c. The **left atrium** receives the newly oxygenated blood from the lungs, via pulmonary veins. The left atrium pumps blood to the left ventricle.

    d. The **left ventricle** pumps oxygenated blood through the aorta to the rest of the body.

3. On the surface of the heart, locate the following grooves (sulci) which partially separate heart chambers and in which blood vessels lie:

a. anterior side (Fig. 22.5a; Clemente, Fig. 190 and 194):

    i. **coronary sulcus** (or **atrioventricular sulcus**), a groove separating the atria from the ventricles

    ii. **anterior interventricular sulcus**, a groove between the anterior portions of the left and right ventricles

b. posterior side (Fig. 22.5b; Clemente, Fig. 195):

    i. **coronary sulcus** (or **atrioventricular sulcus**), continued from the anterior side

    ii. **posterior interventricular sulcus**, between the posterior parts of the left and right ventricles

C. Internal features:

1. Using the MODELS, observe the interior of the heart. Be aware of the locations and names of the three layers of the heart wall (Fig. 22.3, 22.4):

    a. epicardium (or visceral layer of serous pericardium), the outer surface layer

    b. myocardium, the thickest layer, composed primarily of cardiac muscle. Note difference in thickness among chambers (Clemente, Fig. 201).

    c. endocardium, the inner lining

2. Identify each heart chamber *internally* and its specific *internal* features on the MODELS with the help of Fig. 22.6 and the Clemente figures cited:

    a. **right atrium** (Fig. 22.6; Clemente, Figs. 201–203):

        i. **opening for superior vena cava; opening for inferior vena cava**

        ii. **opening for the coronary sinus** (Clemente, Fig. 202)

        iii. interatrial septum, the internal wall that separates the right and left atria

        iv. **fossa ovalis**, a thin round membrane found in the interatrial septum, (Clemente, Fig. 202). The fossa ovalis covers what was the fetal **foramen ovale** (Fig. 22.15; 23.27). Identify the foramen ovale, a hole in the interatrial septum, on the FETAL HEART MODEL.

        v. **right atrioventricular** opening and **valve**

    b. **right ventricle** (Fig. 22.6; Clemente, Fig. 201, 204):

        i. **right atrioventricular valve** (or **tricuspid valve**)

        ii. associated with the atrioventricular valve:

            – **papillary muscles** are conical muscular projections within the ventricle

      – **chordae tendineae** are string-like bands of connective tissue that attach to the papillary muscles and prevent the valve from everting into the atrium when the ventricle contracts

    iii. **trabeculae carneae** are the ridges of muscle in the wall of the ventricle

    iv. pulmonary trunk opening and **pulmonary semilunar valve**

    v. **interventricular septum**, the internal wall between the ventricles

c. **left atrium** (Fig. 22.6; Clemente, Fig. 201, 206):

    i. **openings for the pulmonary veins**

    ii. **left atrioventricular** opening and **valve**

    iii. **fossa ovalis**

d. **left ventricle** (Fig. 22.6; Clemente, Fig. 201, 206):

    i. **left atrioventricular valve** (or **mitral valve** or **bicuspid valve**)

    ii. associated with the atrioventricular valve:

      – **papillary muscles**

      – **chordae tendineae**

    iii. **trabeculae carneae**

    iv. opening into the aorta and the **aortic semilunar valve** (Clemente, Fig. 207)

    v. **interventricular septum**

D. Vessels associated with the heart:

These vessels can be considered in two distinct groups: the so-called great vessels attached to the base (superior portion) of the heart; and the smaller vessels (vessels of the coronary circulation) which either arise from the aorta to supply blood to the heart itself, or drain blood from the heart, returning it to the right atrium.

1. The great vessels are part of either the pulmonary (lung) circulation or the systemic (general body) circulation. These two circulations or circuits drain into the left atrium and the right atrium, respectively. On the DONORS (where exposed) and on the HEART and TORSO MODELS, locate the following vessels (Fig. 22.5a & b):

a. **superior vena cava**

b. **inferior vena cava**

c. **pulmonary trunk**, branching into the **right pulmonary artery** and **left pulmonary artery**

      d. **pulmonary veins** (usually four)

      e. **ascending aorta**

2. The vessels of the coronary circulation are the blood supply to the heart muscle. (Clemente, Figs. 190–5). Locate the following on the DONORS (where exposed) and on the HEART and TORSO MODELS:

    a. the coronary arteries supply oxygen and nutrients to the heart (Fig. 22.5a, 22.9a). Note the "crown" (Latin: corona) formed in the coronary sulcus in which these vessels lie (Fig. 22.7; Clemente, Fig. 191):

        i. **right coronary artery**

        ii. the less visible **left coronary artery**, having one major branch in the coronary sulcus (or atrioventricular sulcus) and another in the anterior interventricular sulcus

    b. the cardiac veins drain waste products from the heart tissue. Locate two of these, as well as the specialized vein which receives all the venous drainage of the heart (Fig. 22.5a & b, 22.9b):

        i. **great cardiac vein**, in the anterior interventricular sulcus

        ii. **middle cardiac vein**, in the posterior interventricular sulcus

        iii. **coronary sinus**, in the posterior portion of the coronary sulcus (or atrioventricular sulcus).

E. Dissection of the Heart:

You will be provided with a fresh animal heart for dissection and identification of structures you have seen on heart models. Equipment you will need (dissecting pan, scissors, forceps, and a blunt probe) will be provided. Follow the instructions given below, and use your text to help identify structures. PRESERVED HEARTS (whole and dissected) similar to the one you dissect, *if* available in lab later for review, could be used for an exam question.

Note: To observe surface vessels and features clearly, it may be necessary to remove the epicardium and fat. Proceed carefully to avoid damaging the structures you are looking for. Some structures may have been removed or damaged during slaughtering; check with your A.I.s or other lab groups.

1. Anterior side—orientation and surface features:

    a. orientation (Fig. 22.2, 22.5a):

    You can examine the anterior surface by setting the heart on its flat (diaphragmatic) surface in the dissecting pan. The roughly cone-shaped heart has a broad base (superiorly; site of the atria) and a pointed **apex** (inferiorly; formed by the left ventricle).

b. external features (Fig. 22.5, 22.9):

    i. vessels:

- superior vena cava

- **aorta**

- **pulmonary trunk**

- **right coronary artery** and **left coronary artery**

- great cardiac vein

    ii. other structures:

right atrium and **left atrium**

- **right ventricle** and **left ventricle**

- **coronary sulcus** (or atrioventricular sulcus)

- anterior interventricular sulcus

2. Posterior side—orientation and surface features:

a. orientation:

Turn the heart over so its diaphragmatic surface is up. Most of this surface is part of the right ventricle.

b. external features (Fig. 22.5):

    i. vessels:

- inferior vena cava

- pulmonary veins, if present

- **coronary sinus**

- middle cardiac vein

    ii. other structures:

- **right atrium** and **left atrium**

- **right ventricle** and **left ventricle**

- **coronary sulcus** (or atrioventricular sulcus)

- posterior interventricular sulcus

3. Interior of the heart:

When cutting into the heart, proceed with care. Usually, the chambers of the heart will contain clotted blood. Carefully remove the clots, then rinse out the chambers with water.

a. **right atrium** (Fig. 22.6). You will be opening the posterior side of the right atrium. First, find the openings of superior and inferior venae cavae. Start a cut in the posterior wall of the superior vena cava and extend it down the inferior vena cava. Fold the cut edges back to identify the following:

    i. **interatrial septum.**

        – **fossa ovalis** (Remember that this artifact of development is a depression in the interatrial septum.)

        – **opening of the coronary sinus.** Insert the tip of your probe through the opening into the sinus and confirm your identification of the coronary sinus on the surface of the heart.

    ii. pectinate muscles, ridges on part of the interior of the wall of the atrium

    iii. right atrioventricular opening and **right atrioventricular (tricuspid) valve**

b. **right ventricle** (Fig. 22.6; Clemente, Figs. 202–203): Turn the heart over so its anterior surface is up. Begin a cut at the midline of the pulmonary trunk and continue it into the right ventricle alongside the interventricular sulcus to its inferior end. Fold back the cut edges, clean out the chamber as before, and then identify the:

    i. **interventricular septum**

    ii. **trabeculae carneae**

    iii. **right atrioventricular (tricuspid) valve**, with **chordae tendineae** and **papillary muscles**

    iv. pulmonary trunk opening and **pulmonary semilunar valve**

c. **left atrium** (Clemente, Fig. 206): Turn the posterior surface of the heart up. Expose the interior of the left atrium by making a rectangular cut which joins the openings of the pulmonary veins. The atrial lining should appear smooth. Identify the:

    i. **interatrial septum** and **fossa ovalis**

    ii. pectinate muscles (limited)

    iii. left atrioventricular opening and **left atrioventricular (bicuspid, mitral) valve**

d. **left ventricle** (Fig. 22.6; Clemente, Fig. 207): From the anterior surface, begin a cut at the aorta, continue it through the pulmonary trunk into the left ventricle, close to the interventricular septum, toward the apex. Remove any clots and rinse out the chamber to identify the:

    i. **interventricular septum**

    ii. **trabeculae carneae**

      iii. **left atrioventricular (bicuspid, mitral) valve**, with **chordae tendineae** and **papillary muscles**

      iv. aortic opening, **aortic semilunar valve**, and openings into right and left coronary arteries. Follow the course of these arteries by inserting your probe into the openings and confirm their location on the surface of the heart.

4. Review how blood flows through the heart (Fig. 22.13, 22.14) with your partners. Make sure that you can trace the blood flow from the vena cava all the way to the aorta.

5. Dispose of dissection waste as instructed by your A.I.s, clean your station and tools thoroughly and return tools as instructed.

III. Blood Vessels

(pp. 678–708)

Guidelines:

- The number (2) after the name of a blood vessel means there is one on each side of the body.

- Most vessels named in sections A (arteries) and B (veins) have their complete names in bold print (e.g. **axillary artery, subclavian vein**). For these, an exam question will say, "Name the vessel ... " and you must answer with the complete bold-print name for full credit!

- In some cases, though, we do not expect you to distinguish whether a vessel is an artery or a vein. You will see in these cases that the word 'artery' or 'vein' in its name is *not* in bold print (e.g. **radial** artery, **radial** vein). For such cases, an exam question will say, "Name the artery ... " or "Name the vein ... " but you need only answer what was in bold print for full credit!

A. Arteries transport blood away from the heart. This occurs in two separate circuits: the pulmonary circulation and the systemic circulation.

1. The arteries of the pulmonary circulation (Fig. 23.22) carry deoxygenated (oxygen-depleted) blood to the lungs where gas exchange with inspired air occurs. The largest of these arteries (Fig. 22.5) can be identified on the Donors and Torso and Heart Models, and include the:

    a. **pulmonary trunk** (Fig. 22.5a)

    b. **right pulmonary artery** (Fig. 22.5b)

    c. **left pulmonary artery** (Fig. 22.5a & b)

2. The arteries of the systemic circulation (Fig. 23.9a) carry oxygenated (oxygen-rich) blood to tissues and organs of the body. These arteries will be considered in groups according to their origin and the area they supply. Identify the following arteries on Donors and Models:

  a. **ascending aorta** and its branches (Fig. 22.5):

     i. **right coronary artery**, seen on the heart in the coronary sulcus (or atrioventricular sulcus).

     ii. **left coronary artery**, in the coronary sulcus (or atrioventricular sulcus); identify near its origin from the ascending aorta.

  b. **aortic arch** and its branches (Fig. 22.5, 23.12):

     i. **brachiocephalic trunk**, branching into right common carotid and subclavian arteries.

     ii. *left* **common carotid artery**; identify near its origin from the aortic arch.

     iii. *left* **subclavian artery**; identify near its origin from the aortic arch.

  c. arteries to the head and neck (Fig. 23.10, 23.11a; Clemente, Fig. 608, 618, 623):

     i. **common carotid artery** (2): the right is a division of the brachiocephalic trunk, while the left is a branch off the aortic arch; identify in the neck.

     ii. divisions of the common carotid artery just beneath the mandible: **internal carotid artery** (2) carrying blood directly to the internal skull; and **external carotid artery** (2), with branches supplying the neck and the external skull.

     iii. **superficial temporal** artery (2), a continuation in the temporal region from each external carotid artery.

     iv. **vertebral artery** (2), each having ascended through the series of transverse foramina in the cervical vertebrae. These may be found on the BASE-OF-SKULL [superior view] and TORSO BRAIN MODELS.

     v. **basilar artery**, formed where the vertebral arteries join inside the cranial cavity. These may be found on the BASE-OF-SKULL [superior view] and TORSO BRAIN MODELS.

     vi. **cerebral arterial circle** (or **circle of Willis**), a single artery formed by the named arterial sections that connect the basilar and internal carotid arteries beneath the brain (BASE-OF-SKULL [superior view] and TORSO BRAIN MODELS only.)

  d. arteries to the upper limbs, on DONORS and UPPER LIMB and HAND MODELS (Fig. 23.9a, 23.19a, c, & d):

     i. **subclavian artery** (2), the right one being a division of the brachiocephalic trunk, the left one a branch off the aortic arch.

     ii. **axillary artery** (2), each a continuation of that side's subclavian artery after it passes the first rib.

    iii. **brachial artery** (2), each a continuation of that side's axillary artery after it has passed the teres major muscle.

    iv. **radial** artery (2), a branch of each brachial artery passing from the cubital fossa along the anterolateral forearm to the wrist.

    v. **ulnar** artery (2), a branch of each brachial artery passing from the cubital fossa along the anteromedial forearm.

    vi. **superficial palmar arch** (2), an anastomosis (joining) of the radial and ulnar arteries in the palm (Clemente, Fig. 110).

e. arteries of the thorax, seen clearly only on the TORSO MODELS and having two origins (Fig. 23.9a, 23.12; Clemente, Fig. 149, 218):

    i. from each subclavian artery (Fig. 23.12; Clemente, Fig. 149):

      – an **internal thoracic** artery (2) passes down the anterior thorax lateral to the sternum.

      – from each internal thoracic artery, a series of **anterior intercostal** arteries, one beneath each rib on that side.

    ii. branching directly off from the **descending thoracic aorta** is a series of **posterior intercostal arteries** on each side, one beneath each rib (Fig. 23.12; Clemente, Fig. 218); these vessels and their connections are seen in the left thoracic cavity on the TORSO MODELS. The pair of anterior and posterior intercostal arteries beneath each rib anastomose (join) laterally.

f. branches off the **descending abdominal aorta**, that part of the descending aorta beginning at the diaphragm and ending at the common iliac arteries (Fig. 23.9a, 23.12, 23.14). Identify it and its following branches on DONORS and TORSO MODELS.

    i. **celiac trunk**, a large but short artery arising just inferior to the diaphragm and having three branches (left gastric, splenic, and hepatic arteries) which we will identify later with the digestive system (Fig. 23.12, 23.15a).

    ii. **superior mesenteric artery** (Fig. 23.12, 23.15a & b), a large artery arising just inferior to the celiac trunk.

    iii. renal artery (2), to each kidney (to be identified only in Chapter 10.)

    iv. male testicular artery (2) or female ovarian artery (2) to each gonad (to be identified only in Chapter 11.)

    v. **inferior mesenteric artery** (Fig. 23.12, 23.14, 23.15b), a somewhat smaller artery arising much lower in the abdomen.

    vi. **common iliac artery** (2), beginning where the abdominal aorta ends (splits).

g. arteries of the pelvic region, divisions of each **common iliac artery**: Identify on Donors and on Torso and Leg Models (Fig. 23.12, 23.18, 23.20a):

    i. **internal iliac artery** (2), branching posteriorly into the pelvis.

    ii. **external iliac artery** (2), branching anteriorly to pass under the inguinal ligament.

h. arteries to the lower limb, on Donors and on Leg and Foot Models (Fig. 23.20a):

    i. **femoral artery** (2), a continuation of each external iliac artery along the anterior side of the thigh, beginning at the inguinal ligament.

    ii. **popliteal** artery (2), a continuation of each femoral artery along the posterior side of the lower thigh and of the knee.

    iii. **anterior tibial** artery (2), a branch of each popliteal artery that passes laterally to supply the anterior leg.

    iv. **posterior tibial** artery (2), a branch of each popliteal artery that supplies the posterior leg and most of the foot.

    v. **fibular** (or peroneal) artery (2), a branch of each posterior tibial artery supplying the lateral leg and ankle.

B. Veins return blood to the heart. Blood is transported within both the pulmonary circulation and the systemic circulation.

1. In the pulmonary circulation (Fig. 23.22), the **pulmonary veins** transport oxygenated blood from the lungs back to the left atrium of the heart. These veins are best seen on the Torso and Heart Models (Fig. 22.5b, p. 660).

2. The veins of the systemic circulation (Fig. 23.9b) return deoxygenated blood from the tissues and organs of the body back to the right atrium of the heart. They will be classified according to the body region they drain and their location: either deep in the body, usually near an artery; or superficial, near the dermis of the skin and without an accompanying artery. Identify the following veins using the Donors and Models; keep in mind that, for many veins, the paths followed can vary greatly among individuals, and the location in any one person may not be the same as in the textbook:

a. veins from the head and neck (Fig. 23.10b–c):

    i. **internal jugular vein** (2)—deep, running most of its length close to the internal and common carotid arteries, draining to the subclavian vein.

    ii. **external jugular vein** (2)—superficial, from the lateral neck and inferior to the face, over the sternocleidomastoid muscle to the subclavian vein.

iii. **dural venous sinuses** between layers of the dura mater, close to the cranial bones (Fig. 23.11b). See HEAD MODELS only.

b. veins from the upper limb (Fig. 23.19b–d):

  i. deep veins (all bilateral) follow the arteries and have the same names: **radial** vein, **ulnar** vein; **brachial vein** (usually two in each arm, close to the brachial artery), **axillary vein** and **subclavian vein.**

  ii. superficial veins (Clemente, Fig. 13, 40) begin as superficial venous networks which drain into the lateral **cephalic vein** (2) (DONORS and TORSO MODELS) or the medial **basilic vein** (2) (DONORS only). The cephalic vein may be seen in the arm lateral to the biceps brachii and then between the pectoralis major and deltoid. The cephalic and basilic veins are connected by a **median cubital vein** (2) (DONORS only) on the anterior side of the elbow.

c. veins of the thorax (Fig. 23.13, 23.14), seen on TORSO or HEART/ MEDIASTINUM MODELS, in two groups:

  i. anterior (Clemente, Fig. 149, 152):

  – **anterior intercostal** veins (a series on each side)

  – an **internal thoracic** vein (2) on each side of the sternum, draining blood from that side's anterior intercostal veins and into its brachiocephalic vein

  ii. the azygos system including the:

  – **hemiazygos vein,** draining the left lower thoracic cavity (see TORSO and HEART/MEDIASTINUM/DIAPHRAGM MODELS). The accessory hemiazygos vein drains the upper left thoracic cavity.

  – **posterior intercostal veins** (a series on each side, one beneath each rib). In the TORSO MODEL'S left thoracic cavity, one or more of these vessels is seen draining directly into the hemiazygos vein or accessory hemiazygos vein.

  – **azygos vein** (seen only on the HEART/MEDIASTINUM and HEART/MEDIASTINUM/DIAPHRAGM MODELS), draining the right thoracic cavity as well as the hemiazygos and accessory hemiazygos veins, and emptying into the superior vena cava.

d. veins forming the **superior vena cava,** seen on MODELS and DONORS (Fig. 23.10b, 23.13):

  i. **subclavian vein** (2), a continuation of the axillary vein from the first rib to the internal jugular vein.

  ii. **external jugular vein** (2) (see section 2.a).

   iii. **internal jugular vein** (2) (see section 2.a).

   iv. **brachiocephalic vein** (2), each formed by the joining of the subclavian and jugular veins; the left and right brachiocephalic veins join to form the superior vena cava.

e. the **inferior vena cava**, running next to the right side of the descending aorta (Fig. 23.14), receives the venous drainage from the abdomen, pelvis, and lower limbs. Identify the following veins in each of these regions:

   i. veins from the pelvis and abdomen (Fig. 23.13, 23.20b):

- **internal iliac vein** (2), each close to the corresponding artery

- **external iliac vein** (2), each close to the corresponding artery

- **common iliac vein** (2), each close to the corresponding artery

- renal vein (2) (to be identified only in Chapter 10)

- testicular vein (2) or ovarian vein (2) (Clemente, Fig. 321) (to be identified only in Chapter 11)

- hepatic veins (draining and largely obscured by the liver)

Note: Blood returning from the stomach, intestines, spleen, and pancreas does not return directly to the inferior vena cava. Instead, it is transported first to vascular sinuses in the liver by the veins of the "hepatic portal system" (Fig. 23.16). This important system includes the following major veins to be identified later with the digestive system: inferior mesenteric vein; superior mesenteric vein; splenic vein; and the hepatic portal vein, transporting blood to the liver from the mesenteric and splenic veins.

   ii. veins from the lower limb (Fig. 23.20b), emptying into the external iliac vein (all bilateral):

- deep veins follow the arteries of the region and have corresponding names: **femoral vein**; **popliteal** vein, **anterior tibial** vein, **posterior tibial** vein, and **fibular** (or peroneal) vein

- superficial veins begin as networks to form two major veins: the **great saphenous vein**, passing up the medial side of the leg and thigh to drain into the femoral vein in the proximal thigh (Fig. 23.21; Clemente, Fig. 416, 418); and the **small saphenous vein**, seen only on the Donors, beginning at the lateral ankle, passing up the posterior calf to drain posteriorly into the popliteal vein (Clemente, Fig. 472, 475)

IV. Lymphatic System

(pp. 719–735)

A. Definition: The lymphatic system has two components: aggregations of lymphocytes (one of the types of white blood cell) which form lymphatic structures and organs; and a system of small vessels (called lymph vessels) throughout much of the body, connected to lymphatic organs, and draining eventually into the blood circulatory system. Thus the lymphatic system is often studied in relation to the circulatory system.

B. Lymphatic structures: Lymphatic structures are composed of connective tissue and lymphatic cells, and are *not* completely surrounded by a connective tissue capsule. We will consider only lymphatic nodules (Fig. 24.8). They occur in the tonsils, scattered along the wall of the digestive and respiratory tracts, and in lymph nodes, the spleen, and the thymus gland.

   1. The tonsils are groups of lymphatic nodules that are partially surrounded by a connective tissue capsule. The tonsils are embedded deep to, the epithelial lining of the mouth and neighboring pharynx, which "guard" the entrance to the digestive and respiratory systems (Fig. 24.1, 24.8; 25.2). Use the Half-Head and Torso Models to identify three sets of tonsils.

      a. **palatine tonsils** (Clemente, Fig. 726): paired masses of lymphatic tissue on the sides of the oral cavity at its boundary with the oropharynx (below the posterior edge of the soft palate).

      b. **pharyngeal tonsils**, also known as adenoids (Clemente, Fig. 726): paired masses of lymphatic tissue in the posterior wall of the nasopharynx near its boundary with the oropharynx.

      c. **lingual tonsils** (Clemente, Fig. 736): discrete aggregations of lymphatic nodules found beneath the epithelium of the posterior third of the tongue (Half-Head Model only).

C. Lymphatic organs: Lymphatic organs are composed of connective tissue and lymphatic cells, and are *completely* surrounded by a connective tissue capsule. Examples of lymphatic organs include:

   1. **Lymph nodes** are small, round or bean-shaped masses distributed along the course of lymphatic vessels (Fig. 24.1, 24.10). Groups of lymph nodes can be found in the groin, axilla, and neck, and also deep in the body near large arteries (Clemente, Fig. 341). It may be possible to identify these in the groin on the Donors. See also the Heart/Mediastinum/Diaphragm and Torso Models.

   2. The **spleen** is the largest lymphatic organ. It is located against the diaphragm in the upper left quadrant of the abdominal cavity, posterior and lateral to the stomach. Its size and weight vary among individuals as well as with the individual's state of health. Identify the spleen on both Models and Donors. (Fig. 24.1, 24.11; Clemente, Fig. 305 and 316).

3. The thymus gland is a mass of lymphatic tissue deep to the sternum in the superior mediastinum (Fig. 24.1, 24.9). Prominent in early childhood, it decreases in size after puberty and is replaced by adipose tissue. This tissue has been removed during dissection of the donors.

D. Most lymph vessels are extremely small and thin-walled, and will be difficult to locate on the DONORS. Lymph nodes are located along the course of lymph vessels, but the vessels themselves are difficult to distinguish from surrounding connective tissue. There are two major lymph vessels:

1. The **thoracic duct** (Fig. 24.1, 24.4; Clemente, Fig. 221, 223) begins as a sac-like enlargement called the cisterna chyli found anterior to the second lumbar vertebra. The thoracic duct ascends along the anterior side of the vertebral column through the posterior mediastinum (see HEART/ MEDIASTINUM and HEART/MEDIASTINUM/DIAPHRAGM MODELS). As is shown on the TORSO MODELS (and possibly on the DONORS), the thoracic duct drains into the venous circulation at or near the junction of the left subclavian vein with the left internal jugular vein.

2. The right lymphatic duct (Fig. 24.4; Clemente, Fig. 223) is relatively short. It starts at the root of the neck and enters the venous circulation at the junction of the right subclavian vein with the right jugular veins.

V. Histology of the Circulatory System

(pp. 109–111, 634–645; 653–654; 678–685; 729–735)

A. **Blood**: We will use the VIRTUAL MICROSCOPE SLIDE, along with introductory slides, your text, and the Sobotta Atlas to illustrate the microscopic anatomy of the blood so you can recognize its different "formed elements": erythrocytes, specific types of leukocytes, and platelets. Using the BLOOD SMEAR slide, be able to recognize this specific type of tissue microscopically and to identify the following (Fig. 21.2; Table 21.3):

1. **Erythrocytes** (red blood cells) are the most numerous of the formed elements. They do not have a nucleus and, normally, have the shape of a biconcave disc, like a doughnut with a sealed hole. On the slide(s), the center of these cells will appear clear because it is thinner than the surrounding cytoplasm (Fig. 21.3; Sobotta, Figs. 229–235).

2. Leukocytes (white blood cells) are much less numerous than erythrocytes (Fig. 21.2). They are classed as either granulocytes or agranulocytes, depending on whether or not granules are visible within their cytoplasm (Table 21.3).

a. granulocytes: In addition to having granules in its cytoplasm, a granulocyte has a nucleus made of two or more lobes. There are three classes of granulocytes, based on the color of the granules when stained:

i. **neutrophils** make up about 60% of leukocytes. Their granules are very fine and neutral staining. The nucleus may have multiple (3–5) lobes (Sobotta, Fig. 230 and right side of Fig. 229).

  ii. **eosinophils** make up less than 4% of leukocytes. The granules are evident and stained a faint red (eosin is a red dye). The nucleus is usually bilobed (Sobotta, Fig. 232).

  iii. basophils are difficult, if not impossible, to find on a blood smear, making up less than 1% of leukocytes. They have dense aggregations of granules which stain darkly (basic stains). The nucleus is U- or S-shaped (Sobotta, middle of Fig. 229).

 b. agranulocytes have much less prominent granules. The nucleus is usually rounded and takes up much of the cell. There are two types of agranulocyte:

  i. **lymphocytes** make up about 30% of leukocytes. The cytoplasm typically stains a faint blue and the nucleus is round (Sobotta, Fig. 234).

  ii. **monocytes** make up about 6% of leukocytes and are the largest white blood cell. They also typically have pale blue staining cytoplasm and a large indented or C-shaped nucleus and generally takes up nearly all of the cell. (Sobotta, Fig. 235).

 3. **Platelets** (sometimes called thrombocytes) are important for the clotting of blood. They are much smaller than erythrocytes but are fairly numerous (Fig. 21.2, 21.9; Sobotta, left side of Fig. 230).

B. **Heart**: The wall of the heart has three layers (epicardium, myocardium, endocardium), which can be distinguished histologically (Fig. 22.4). On the HEART slide(s), identify bold-print terms in the middle layer (myocardium):

 1. The thin, outer epicardium (visceral layer of serous pericardium) consists of a surface of simple squamous epithelium resting on connective tissue which blends into the myocardium.

 2. The thick myocardium contains an interlacing network of **cardiac muscle** fibers (Sobotta, Fig. 177). Review the characteristics of cardiac muscle in chapter 5, section IV, of the lab guide. Note in particular on the slide(s) the **intercalated discs**, connections between cardiac muscle cells (Table 4.12b, p. 110).

 3. The thin endocardium is the innermost layer of the heart, lining all its chambers and the structures projecting into them. It is composed of connective tissue covered by simple squamous epithelium on its surface.

C. Blood vessels are of three main types: arteries, capillaries, and veins. Each type is described separately below, but both arteries and veins have a 3-layered pattern to their walls, and common terms are defined first.

 1. Use the MESENTERY slide to identify the different layers, or tunics, of a blood vessel's wall as specified in the types of vessels in bold print in section 2 below. The Latin noun "tunica" (covering or coat) is used for this type of layer (Fig. 23.1, 23.3; Sobotta Fig. 272):

    a. the **tunica externa** (or tunica adventitia) is the outermost layer. It consists of connective tissue and, in larger vessels, also contains smaller blood vessels called vasa vasorum (Latin: vessels of vessels).

    b. the **tunica media** contains circularly arranged smooth muscle cells and elastic fibers, but the ratio of these components varies among different types of vessels.

    c. the **tunica intima** (or tunica interna), the innermost layer, consists of connective tissue and simple squamous epithelium (endothelium) forming the lining of the vessel.

2. Arteries carry blood at high pressures, and therefore must have thick walls. In all arteries, the tunica media is the thickest layer, but its composition varies among the three general classes of artery. Find examples on the MESENTERY slide and identify the specified layers in their walls (Fig. 23.4).

    a. elastic arteries (not on MESENTERY slide), large diameter vessels containing many elastic fibers in the tunica media which require special stains to observe (Sobotta, Figs. 266–69).

    b. **muscular** (or distributing) **artery**, (on the MESENTERY slide): smaller in diameter, having many layers of smooth muscle cells in the tunica media (Sobotta, Fig. 272 and Fig. 275). Identify the **tunica externa** (or tunica adventitia), **tunica media**, and **tunica intima** (or tunica interna).

    c. **arteriole**, (smallest type of artery on the MESENTERY slide): has at most a few (6) layers of smooth muscle cells in the **tunica media** (Fig. 23.4c). Identify the **tunica media** and **tunica intima**.

3. Capillaries are functionally the most important vessels in the circulation. Their structure allows exchange of substances between the blood and the body's cells, but makes them difficult to identify microscopically. The following characteristics of capillaries should be remembered:

    a. inner diameter: the same as that of a red blood cell (7.2 microns).

    b. wall: only simple squamous epithelium with its basement membrane.

4. Veins: The blood in veins is at a low pressure as it returns to the heart from capillaries. Therefore, the walls of veins are quite thin in comparison with their diameter and with the walls of companion arteries. Similarly, the three layers of their walls differ in some ways from those of arteries. These differences and the other characteristics are described below (Fig. 23.1, 23.3; Sobotta, Fig. 272). Use the MESENTERY slide to observe various examples of what distinguishes a vein from the artery it accompanies. By comparing the thickness and components of the wall of each, be able to identify a **vein** next to a muscular artery (Fig. 23.2), and a **venule** next to an arteriole. In a larger vein, you may be able to identify the layers in the wall.

    a. the tunica externa is usually thicker than the tunica media, forming the bulk of the wall. It consists primarily of collagenous and elastic fibers. In some veins, particularly of large diameter, it contains longitudinal bundles of smooth muscle as well as vasa vasorum.

      b. the tunica media is quite thin and consists of smooth muscle cells, collagenous fibers, and a few elastic fibers.

      c. the tunica intima. (In veins of the limbs, though not on the slide, the tunica intima is folded in places to form valves similar to the semilunar valves of the pulmonary trunk and aorta. Valves are arranged in such veins so that blood can flow toward the heart but backflow is prevented. [Fig. 23.7])

D. Lymphatic nodules appear in microscopic sections as circular or oval formations of closely packed cells, and sometimes have a lighter central area called a germinal center (Fig. 24.8, 24.10). (The slide of SMALL INTESTINE may show lymphatic nodules; they may be flattened in its wall, or appear as rounded projections into the lumen of the intestine.)

E. Lymphatic organs generally have an outer dense connective tissue capsule and an inner framework of connective tissue which forms trabeculae (Latin for 'small beam'). We will study two lymphatic organs on slides: a single large LYMPH NODE and a section from the SPLEEN.

   1. **Lymph nodes** (Fig. 24.10b) have a capsule and trabeculae. Lymphatic vessels enter the node at various points, penetrating the capsule. They are called afferent lymphatic vessels (Latin: ad=to, ferre=to carry). At its hilum, an indented area, the lymph node is joined to blood vessels and to efferent (Latin: ex=out) lymphatic vessels. Inside the lymph node are two general regions, an outer cortex and an inner medulla. Identify these regions, one component, and the entire organ.

      a. the **cortex** has numerous trabeculae and densely packed lymphocytes, often as **lymphatic nodules** (also called lymphatic follicles), giving it a darker appearance (Sobotta, Fig. 261). (Reminder: the suffix "-ule" is diminutive, so a nodule is smaller than a node!)

      b. the **medulla** is composed of larger interconnected sinuses (spaces) and a meshwork of trabeculae giving this region a lighter staining appearance.

   2. The **spleen** (Fig. 24.11c; Sobotta, Fig. 256) has a capsule and trabeculae, but blood vessels enter and leave the spleen only at its hilum. There are many distinct regions classed as either red pulp or white pulp according to their unstained appearance:

      a. **red pulp** consists of numerous sinuses (spaces) filled with erythrocytes.

      b. **white pulp** is found around the small blood vessels which branch into the red pulp. It typically consists of a light staining central area near each blood vessel, surrounded by a darker staining dense aggregation of lymphocytes.

F. Lymph vessels (Fig. 24.3) collect fluid from tissues for return to the bloodstream. They are all very thin-walled, beginning as lymphatic capillaries where the wall is only a single layer of squamous cells. These capillaries join to form progressively larger lymph vessels which generally travel alongside veins. The fluid within lymph vessels is called lymph, and moves through them at very low pressures. Valves are often found along lymph vessels to ensure that flow is only toward the bloodstream. (No slide.)

VI. Study Tips for this Chapter

A. Use the pictures in your text to help you identify circulatory system structures. You can use these text pictures at home to review these structures.

B. Make sure you learn the circulatory system structures on both the DONORS and selected MODELS. The model keys at the end of this chapter list most of the structures that you will be responsible for on a particular model.

C. At home, make a list of the circulatory system structures you learned in lab. Writing the names of the structures over and over again will help you remember their names.

D. List the 4 heart chambers. Then, list the features that are found in each heart chamber. Try to pronounce each of these terms.

E. Study lab and lecture together by doing the following: review text pictures and say the names of the heart structures aloud. Then, look in your lecture notes to determine the function of those structures. In addition, use your lecture notes to review the pathway of blood through the heart.

F. Do you remember the body region names from the first day of lecture? Blood vessels often are given the same name as the body region in which they travel. Sometimes they are named according to what bone is nearby (ex., radial artery). Remembering these facts will make it easier to remember blood vessel names.

G. Review the lymphatic structures on both the MODELS and DONORS. Use the model keys to determine which lymphatic structures may be found on a particular model.

H. In lab, have your lab partner "quiz" you on the VIRTUAL MICROSCOPE SLIDES. Reverse roles: YOU show a microscope slide with the label not seen to quiz your lab partner. Both you and your lab partner will be better able to identify the structures on the slides when it comes time for the exam.

I. Compare and contrast the different types of formed elements. How can you differentiate each when looking at the *formed elements* microscopically? Drawing pictures of each type of formed element will help.

J. Be able to identify blood vessel layers (e.g., tunica media) on the slides. At home, make a list of the *layers* found in the heart wall and blood vessel walls.

K. Be able to identify specific types of blood vessels on the slides, using the characteristics of each one's wall (tunics) and the type of vessel it is paired with.

L. Be able to identify two lymphatic *organs* (lymph node and spleen) on the slides.

M. Remember to use the VIRTUAL MICROSCOPE to review the circulatory system structures at home!

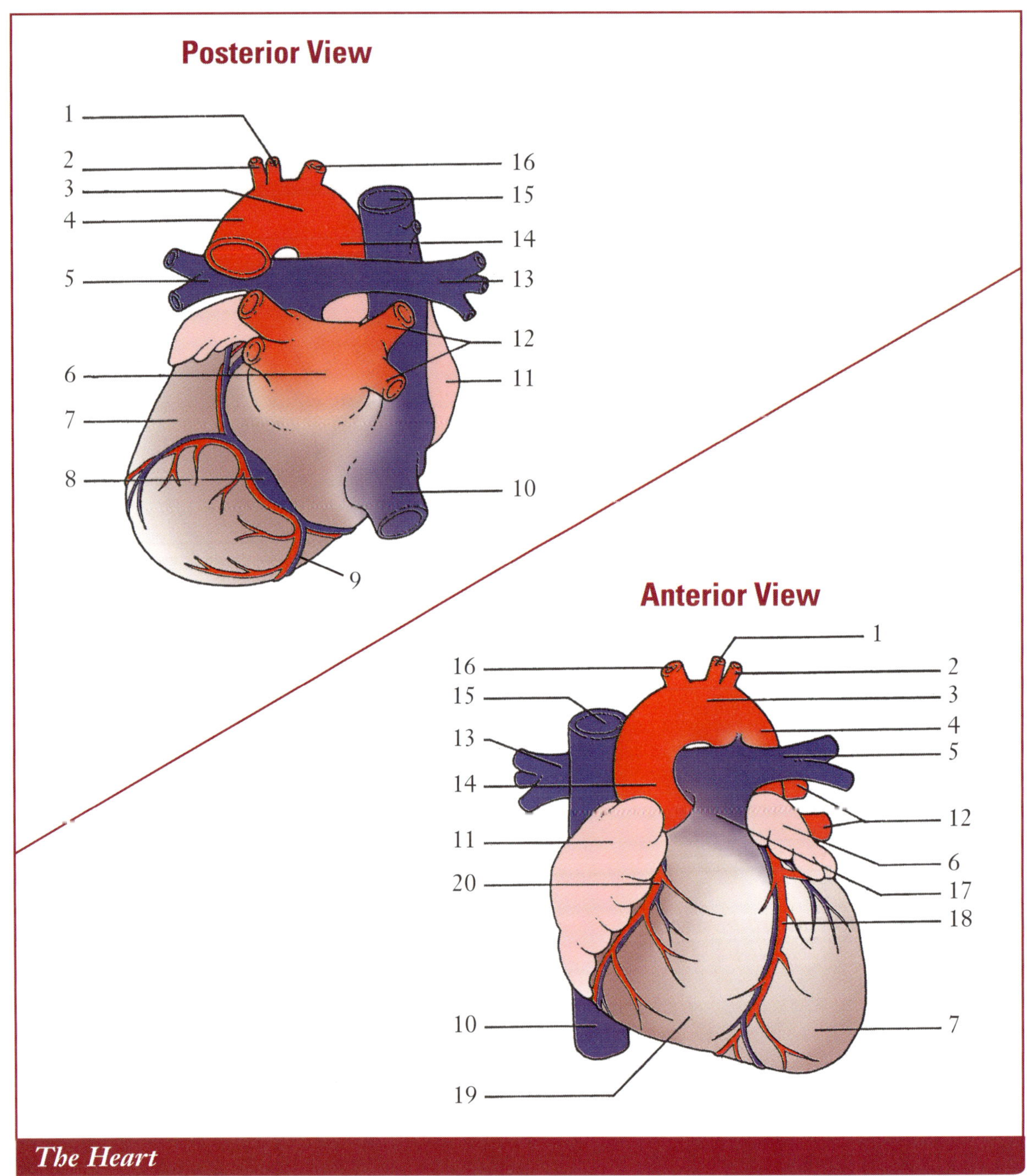

The Heart

1. left common carotid artery
2. left subclavian artery
3. aortic arch
4. descending thoracic aorta
5. left pulmonary artery
6. left atrium
7. left ventricle
8. coronary sinus
9. middle cardiac vein
10. inferior vena cava
11. right atrium
12. pulmonary veins
13. right pulmonary artery
14. ascending aorta
15. superior vena cava
16. brachiocephalic trunk
17. pulmonary trunk
18. anterior interventricular artery
19. right ventricle
20. right coronary artery

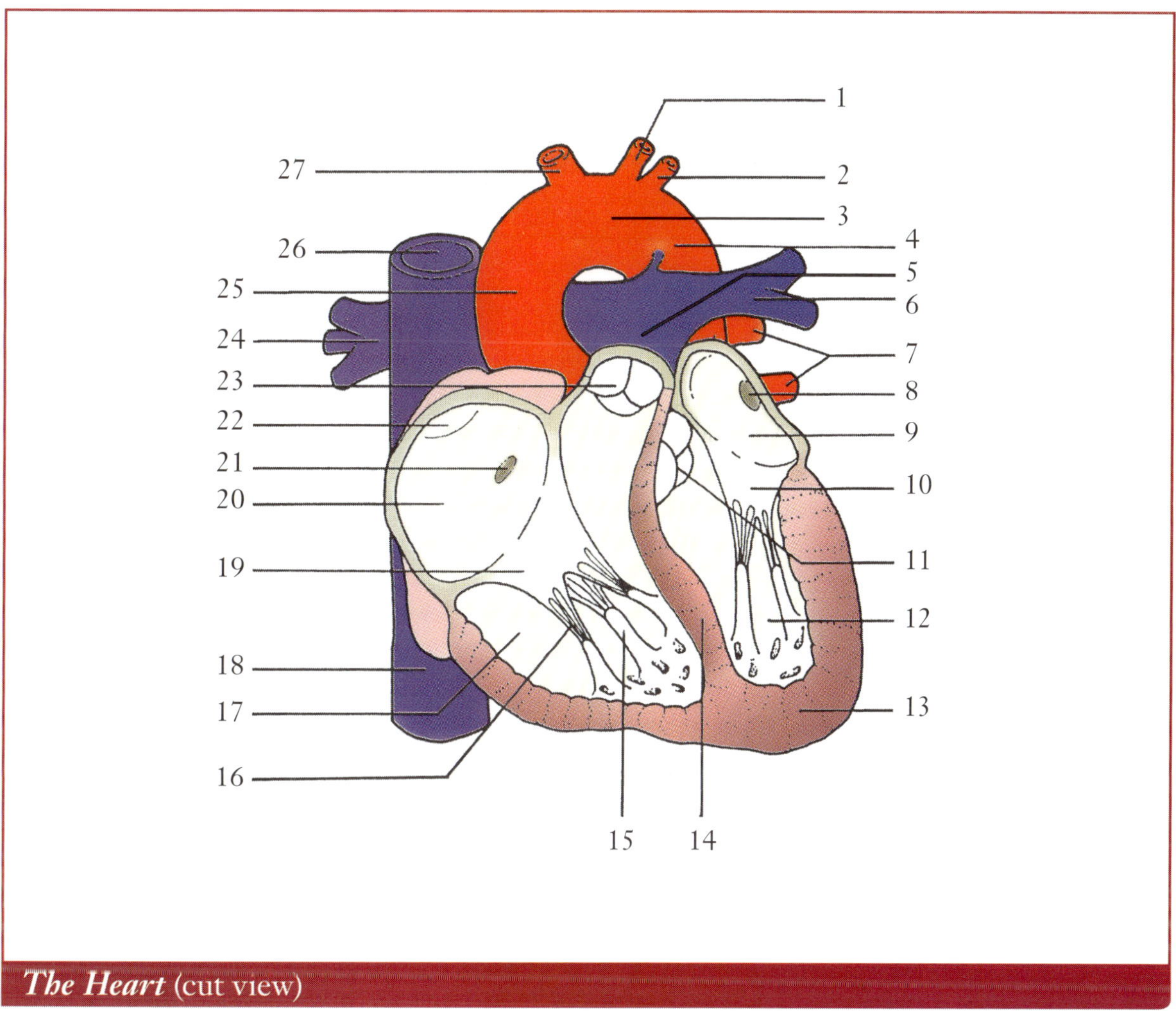

The Heart (cut view)

Anterior View

1. left common carotid artery
2. left subclavian artery
3. aortic arch
4. descending thoracic aorta
5. pulmonary trunk
6. left pulmonary artery
7. left pulmonary veins
8. opening of pulmonary vein
9. left atrium
10. left atrioventricular (bicuspid, mitral) valve
11. aortic semilunar valve
12. left ventricle
13. myocardium
14. interventricular septum
15. papillary muscle
16. chordae tendineae
17. right ventricle
18. inferior vena cava
19. right atrioventricular (tricuspid) valve
20. right atrium
21. opening of coronary sinus
22. opening of superior vena cava
23. pulmonary semilunar valve
24. right pulmonary artery
25. ascending aorta
26. superior vena cava
27. brachiocephalic trunk

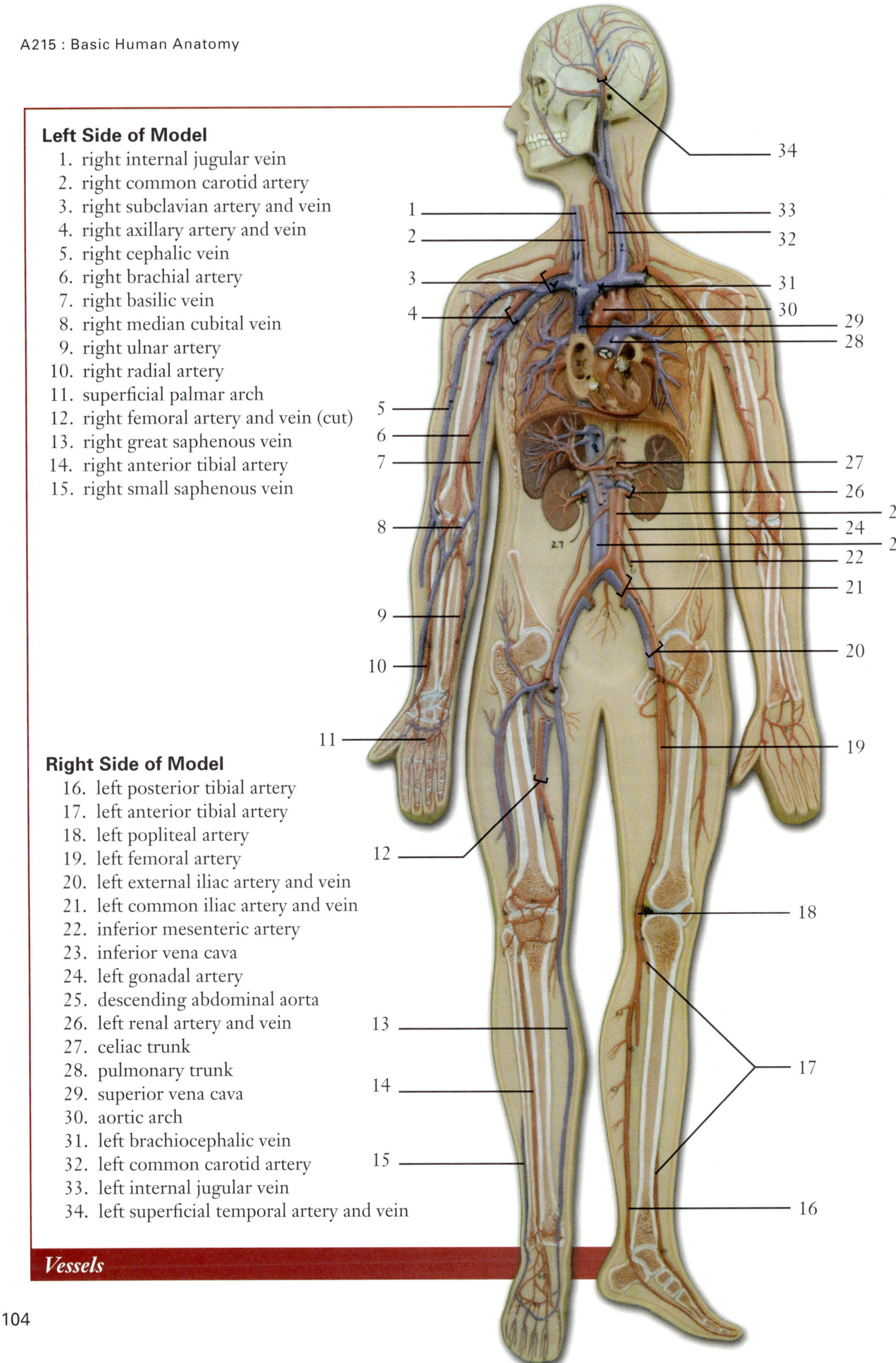

Left Side of Model

1. right internal jugular vein
2. right common carotid artery
3. right subclavian artery and vein
4. right axillary artery and vein
5. right cephalic vein
6. right brachial artery
7. right basilic vein
8. right median cubital vein
9. right ulnar artery
10. right radial artery
11. superficial palmar arch
12. right femoral artery and vein (cut)
13. right great saphenous vein
14. right anterior tibial artery
15. right small saphenous vein

Right Side of Model

16. left posterior tibial artery
17. left anterior tibial artery
18. left popliteal artery
19. left femoral artery
20. left external iliac artery and vein
21. left common iliac artery and vein
22. inferior mesenteric artery
23. inferior vena cava
24. left gonadal artery
25. descending abdominal aorta
26. left renal artery and vein
27. celiac trunk
28. pulmonary trunk
29. superior vena cava
30. aortic arch
31. left brachiocephalic vein
32. left common carotid artery
33. left internal jugular vein
34. left superficial temporal artery and vein

Vessels

VII. Circulatory System Model Keys

NYSTROM HEART MODEL

External

1. right brachiocephalic vein
2. left brachiocephalic vein
3. superior vena cava
4. ascending aorta
5. aortic arch
6. brachiocephalic trunk
7. left common carotid artery
8. left subclavian artery
9. descending thoracic aorta
10. pulmonary trunk
11. right pulmonary artery
12. left pulmonary artery
18. (right) pulmonary veins
19. (left) pulmonary veins
20. inferior vena cava
21. right atrium
(23. right auricle)
24. right ventricle
(25. left auricle)
26. left atrium
27. coronary sulcus
28. left ventricle
32. anterior interventricular sulcus
33. posterior interventricular sulcus
34. apex
36. coronary sinus
37. great cardiac vein
39. middle cardiac vein
45. right coronary artery (beginning at 43 near origin of aorta)
48. left coronary artery (beginning at 44 on aorta)

Internal

51. opening for superior vena cava (3)
52. opening for inferior vena cava (20)
53. opening for coronary sinus (36)
54. fossa ovalis
56. right atrioventricular (or tricuspid) valve
58. papillary muscles
59. chordae tendineae
60. trabeculae carneae
63. pulmonary semilunar valve
64. openings for right pulmonary veins (18)
67. left atrioventricular (or bicuspid or mitral) valve
68. interventricular septum
70. aortic semilunar valve

TWO-PART HEART MODEL

     I. right atrium (a. right auricle)
    II. left atrium (b. left auricle)
   III. right ventricle
   IV. left ventricle
   A. apex
   B. interventricular septum
   1. chordae tendineae (1 and 2 also in right heart)
   2. papillary muscle
3, i. ascending aorta
   4. right coronary artery
   5. left coronary artery
   6. coronary sinus
   7. aortic arch
   c. superior vena cava
   d. inferior vena cava
   e. right atrioventricular (or tricuspid) valve
   f. pulmonary trunk
   g. pulmonary veins
   h. left atrioventricular (or bicuspid or mitral) valve
   k. semilunar valves (right = pulmonary, left = aortic)

FOUR-PART HEART MODEL

Labeled externally

1. superior vena cava
2. inferior vena cava
4. pulmonary trunk
5. pulmonary vein
   (from right lung)
7. ascending aorta
   a. aortic arch
8. right coronary artery
9a. (anterior interventricular
   branch of)
   left coronary artery
9b. (circumflex branch of) left
   coronary artery
10. coronary sinus
10a. great cardiac vein
Ia. (auricle of) right atrium
IIb. (auricle of) left atrium

Labeled internally

I. right atrium
II. left atrium
III. right ventricle
   a. papillary muscle
   b. (cusp of) pulmonary semilunar valve
   3. (cusp of) right atrioventricular valve
IV. left ventricle
   c. papillary muscle
   d. (cusp of) aortic semilunar valve

BOBBITT HEART MODEL – <u>DO NOT MOVE ANY PARTS</u> of these models!

On all models, EXTERNALLY:

1. aortic arch
2. brachiocephalic trunk
3. left common carotid artery
4. left subclavian artery
9. left pulmonary artery
13. posterior intercostal arteries
14. thoracic duct
15. azygos vein
(21. right pulmonary artery)
22. (tracheobronchial) lymph nodes
23. right ventricle
24. left ventricle
25. left atrium
26. right atrium
30. apex
31. pulmonary trunk
32. ascending aorta
33. pericardium
34. superior vena cava
35. right coronary artery
37. left coronary artery
40. great cardiac vein
43. coronary sinus
46. inferior vena cava
47. azygos vein
48. (left) pulmonary veins
49. (right) pulmonary veins
51. coronary sulcus
52. anterior interventricular sulcus

On Heart/Mediastinum/Diaphragm only, EXTERNALLY:

N. descending thoracic aorta
O. azygos vein
P. thoracic duct
U. hemiazygos vein
V. (posterior mediastinal) lymph nodes

On Heart/Mediastinum only, EXTERNALLY:

44. middle cardiac vein

RESPIRATORY ORGAN MODEL

[outside HEART, *Anterior view]*
right ventricle
left ventricle
F. apex (inf. tip of L. ventricle)
10. ascending aorta
18. right atrium (label on auricle)
19. left atrium (label on auricle)

22. superior vena cava
24. pulmonary trunk
30. right coronary artery

[outside HEART, *Posterior view]*
superior vena cava
23. inferior vena cava
right atrium
pulmonary veins (one labeled 27)

left atrium
coronary sinus
right ventricle
left ventricle

[inside HEART, *Anterior view]*
16. right atrium
17. left atrium
20. right ventricle
21. left ventricle
papillary muscles
chordae tendineae

25. right atrioventricular (tricuspid) valve
26. pulmonary semilunar valve
28. left atrioventricular (bicuspid, mitral) valve
29. aortic semilunar valve

TORSO MODEL N1

Lymphatic Structures and Organs

427. pharyngeal tonsils
482. palatine tonsil
514. spleen

Arteries

Base of cranial cavity:

143. internal carotid

Head:

293. superficial temporal

Torso and limbs:

300. internal carotid
302. left common carotid
306. left subclavian
313. brachiocephalic trunk
314. (302)
315. (306)
341. aortic arch
342. descending thoracic aorta
353. posterior intercostal
357. anterior intercostal
363. descending abdominal aorta
364–6. branches of celiac trunk
374. superior mesenteric
398. common iliac
400. external iliac
402. internal iliac
412. femoral

Veins

Torso and limbs:

303. internal jugular
304. external jugular
307. cephalic
310. (right) brachiocephalic
311. (left) brachiocephalic
312. superior vena cava
354. hemiazygos
355. posterior intercostal
395. (right renal)
396. inferior vena cava (segment through
liver not present here)
399. common iliac
401. external iliac
403. internal iliac
417. femoral
420. great saphenous

Lymph Vessels

305. thoracic duct

On or in the Heart

201. right atrium
202. superior vena cava
203. inferior vena cava
205. left atrium
206. left ventricle
207. right ventricle
208. interventricular septum
210. right atrioventricular (or tricuspid) valve
211. chordae tendineae
212. papillary muscle
213. pulmonary semilunar valve
214. pulmonary trunk
215, 216. right, left pulmonary arteries
217, 218. (right, left) pulmonary veins
219. left atrioventricular (or bicuspid or mitral) valve
220. aortic semilunar valve
221. ascending aorta
222. origins of coronary arteries
223. right coronary artery
227. great cardiac vein
228. middle cardiac vein
230. coronary sinus
235. apex
225, 226. branches of left coronary artery

TORSO MODEL N2, CIRCULATORY SYSTEM

Arteries

Base of cranial cavity:

246. (right) internal carotid

Inferior side of brain:

250. (left) internal carotid
255. (left) vertebral
256. basilar, leading to cerebral arterial circle

Anterior thoracic wall:

273. internal thoracic
274. anterior intercostal

Torso and limbs:

214. pulmonary trunk
215. right pulmonary
216. left pulmonary
221. ascending aorta
236. brachiocephalic trunk
237. (right) subclavian
241. (right) common carotid
249. left common carotid
266. (left) superficial temporal
272. left subclavian
282. aortic arch
283. descending thoracic aorta
284. posterior intercostal
287. descending abdominal aorta
291. celiac trunk (branches 292, 293, 296)
304. superior mesenteric
315. inferior mesenteric
321. (right) renal
325. (left) renal
327. (testicular or ovarian)
330. (right) common iliac
331. (right) external iliac
338. (right) internal iliac
348. (left) common iliac
349. (left) external iliac
352. (left) femoral

Veins

Anterior thoracic wall:

275. anterior intercostal
278. internal thoracic

Torso and limbs:

202. superior vena cava
203. inferior vena cava (segment in liver not present here)
217. (right) pulmonary
218. (left) pulmonary
239. axillary
240. (right) subclavian
247. (right) internal jugular
248. (right) brachiocephalic
270. (left) external jugular
271. (left) internal jugular
279. cephalic
280. (left) subclavian
281. (left) brachiocephalic
285. posterior intercostal
286. hemiazygos
322. (right renal)
326. (left renal)
328. (left testicular or ovarian)
329. (right testicular or ovarian)
336. (right) femoral
337. external iliac
346. (right) internal iliac
347. (right) common iliac
353. (left) great saphenous

On or in the Heart

201. right atrium
202. superior vena cava
203. inferior vena cava
205. left atrium
206. left ventricle
207. right ventricle
208. interventricular septum
210. right atrioventricular (or tricuspid) valve
211. chordae tendinae
212. papillary muscle
213. pulmonary semilunar valve
214. pulmonary trunk
215, 216. right, left pulmonary arteries
217, 218. (right, left) pulmonary veins
219. left atrioventricular (or bicuspid or mitral) valve
220. aortic semilunar valve
221. ascending aorta
222. origins of coronary arteries
223. right coronary artery
227. great cardiac vein
228. middle cardiac vein
230. coronary sinus
235. apex
225, 226. (branches of) left coronary artery

Lymphatic Structures, Organs or Lymph Vessels:

381. spleen
382. thoracic duct
411. pharyngeal tonsils
412. (right) palatine tonsil
375. (cervical) lymph node
376. (cervical) lymph vessel
380. (inguinal) lymph node

TORSO MODELS S1 AND S2 (Only some structures are labeled)

HEART and associated vessels

- *(a, I)* right atrium
- *(b, II)* left atrium
- *(17, III)* right ventricle
- *(IV)* left ventricle
- *(j)* ascending aorta
- *(k)* aortic arch
- descending thoracic aorta
- *(h)* pulmonary trunk
- *(c)* superior vena cava
- *(d)* inferior vena cava
- *(e)* pulmonary veins
- coronary sulcus
- coronary sinus
- right coronary artery
- left coronary artery
- great cardiac vein
- middle cardiac vein
- right atrioventricular (or tricuspid) valve
- *(g)* left atrioventricular (or bicuspid or mitral) valve
- chordae tendineae
- papillary muscles
- *(1)* aortic semilunar valve
- *(m)* pulmonary semilunar valve

Arteries

- brachiocephalic trunk
- common carotid, left (and right)
- subclavian, left (and right)
- descending abdominal aorta
- celiac trunk
- superior mesenteric
- common iliac
- internal iliac
- external iliac
- femoral

Veins

- inferior vena cava (segment through liver not present here)
- brachiocephalic
- internal jugular
- subclavian
- common iliac
- internal iliac
- external iliac
- femoral

Lymphatic Organs

- *(24)* spleen
- (inguinal) lymph nodes

BASE-OF-SKULL MODEL

- *1–7.* dural venous sinuses
- *8.* internal carotid artery
- *13.* basilar artery
- *17.* vertebral artery

HALF-HEAD MODELS

- *(58)* common carotid artery
- *(a)* internal carotid artery
- *(b)* external carotid artery
- *(63)* superficial temporal artery
- *(q)* palatine tonsil
- external jugular vein
- dural venous sinuses
- pharyngeal tonsils
- lingual tonsils

MUSCULAR HEAD MODELS (Identify the following)

- *68.* superficial temporal artery
- *70.* external jugular vein
- common carotid artery
- *71.* external carotid artery
- *72.* internal carotid artery
- *83.* subclavian artery
- *84.* subclavian vein
- *85.* internal jugular vein
- *128–132.* dural venous sinuses

ARM MODELS A1–A8

- *45.* axillary artery
- *49.* brachial artery
- *55.* radial artery
- *59.* ulnar artery
- *63.* superficial palmar arch

HAND MODELS

- *1.* radial artery
- *2.* ulnar artery
- *3.* superficial palmar arch

LEG MODELS L1–L10 (Identify the following)

- common iliac artery
- *39.* external iliac artery
- *39a.* external iliac vein
- *40.* internal iliac artery
- *45.* femoral artery
- *45a.* femoral vein
- *51.* popliteal artery
- popliteal vein
- *56.* posterior tibial artery
- *57.* anterior tibial artery
- *58.* fibular artery

FOOT MODEL

- *41.* anterior tibial artery
- *52.* posterior tibial artery
- *61.* fibular artery

8 Respiratory System

I. Introduction

II. Conducting Portion of the Respiratory System
 A. Nasal Cavity
 B. Pharynx
 C. Larynx
 D. Trachea and Bronchial System

III. The Lungs
 A. Orientation and Organization
 B. Blood Supply

IV. Microscopic Anatomy of the Respiratory System
 A. Conducting Portion
 B. Respiratory Portion

V. Study Tips for this Chapter

VI. Respiratory System Model Keys

I. Introduction

(pp. 742–743)

A. The respiratory system includes a conducting portion which allows air passage (during breathing) to and from a respiratory portion where gas exchange with blood occurs. Other functions of the respiratory system include gas conditioning (e.g., warming and humidifying inhaled air), sound production, olfaction (smell) and defense. The anatomy of the respiratory system is intimately related to these functions.

B. Review in Chapter 5 of your lab manual those muscles of the neck, thorax, and abdomen involved in breathing.

C. Various MODELS and the DONORS will be used to study the respiratory system.

D. The histology of the respiratory system will demonstrate important structural and functional differences among its parts. We will examine this histology with the VIRTUAL MICROSCOPE SLIDES.

II. Conducting Portion of the Respiratory System

(pp. 744–755)

A. The **nasal cavity** is a space divided into right and left halves by the nasal septum (Fig. 7.23, p. 199; Fig. 25.1). These two halves open on the face through the external **nares** (commonly called **nostrils**) and posteriorly into the nasopharynx through the internal (posterior) nares (or choanae). The nasal cavity communicates with 4 paired paranasal sinuses (Fig. 25.3). Use the HEAD and TORSO MODELS to identify the following terms in bold print:

    1. The nasal septum (not on MODELS) is made up of the septal cartilage and a bony portion formed by the perpendicular plate of the ethmoid bone and the vomer (Fig. 7.23b, p. 199).

    2. Boundaries of nasal cavity include (Fig. 25.2):

        a. laterally on each side a **superior nasal concha** and a **middle nasal concha** of the ethmoid bone and a separate **inferior nasal concha**.

        b. inferiorly the **hard palate**, formed by the palatine and maxillary bones, and the **soft palate**, which is muscular.

        c. superiorly the cribriform plate of the ethmoid bone.

B. The **pharynx** represents a connection between the respiratory and digestive systems. It is an epithelium-lined muscular region that communicates anteriorly with the oral cavity and nasal cavity, and laterally with the middle ear cavity. Use the HALF-HEAD and TORSO MODELS to identify the three specific regions within the pharynx (Fig. 25.1, 25.2).

    1. The **nasopharynx** is located immediately posterior to the nasal cavity. In each lateral wall is the **opening of the auditory tube** (or **Eustachian tube**, or **pharyngotympanic tube**), the passage to the middle ear cavity. On the posterior wall are the **pharyngeal tonsils** (adenoids) (Fig. 24.8, p. 730).

    2. The **oropharynx** is the part of the pharynx posterior, and open, to the oral cavity. It extends from the soft palate to the laryngopharynx; on its antero-lateral walls are the **palatine tonsils** (Fig. 24.8, p. 730).

    3. The **laryngopharynx** extends from the oropharynx to the esophagus posterior to the larynx.

C. The **larynx** conducts air to and from the trachea (Fig. 25.1, 25.2, 25.4, 25.5). It is formed by nine cartilages, three unpaired and three paired. All but one of these nine (the epiglottis) are composed of hyaline cartilage. Ligaments and muscles hold the cartilages of the larynx together and anchor it to the hyoid bone superiorly and the trachea inferiorly. Be able to identify the larynx as a whole on the LARYNX and RESPIRATORY ORGAN MODELS, and in midsagittal section on HALF-HEAD and TORSO HEAD MODELS.

    1. Laryngeal Cartilages. Use the HEAD, TORSO, RESPIRATORY ORGAN and LARYNX MODELS to identify the following (Fig. 25.4, 25.5):

        a. the **thyroid cartilage** is the largest of the larynx. It is an unpaired cartilage with an anterior median projection, the **laryngeal prominence** (commonly called "Adam's apple"), which is more marked in the male after puberty than in the female. These structures should also be identified on the DONORS (Clemente, Fig. 757 and 759).

    b. the **cricoid cartilage** is smaller, but thicker and stronger, than the thyroid cartilage. It is shaped like a signet or class ring, being narrow anteriorly and broad posteriorly (Clemente, Fig. 757 and 759).

    c. the **epiglottis** is a thin, leaf-shaped cartilage which projects obliquely upwards behind the tongue and the hyoid bone. The epiglottis consists of elastic cartilage (Clemente, Fig. 759).

    d. the **arytenoid cartilages** are paired cartilages located on the superior border of the cricoid cartilage at the back of the larynx. Each arytenoid cartilage is pyramidal in shape. Attached to the arytenoid cartilages anteriorly are the **vocal folds** or (true) **vocal cords** which form the lateral boundaries of the glottis and are important in the production of voice tones (Clemente, Fig. 759 and 761).

    e. the corniculate cartilages are paired, small, conical nodules of hyaline cartilage which articulate with the tops of the arytenoid cartilages (Clemente, Fig. 759 and 761).

    f. the cuneiform cartilages are paired, small, elongated pieces of hyaline cartilage. They lie within the aryepiglottic folds anterosuperior to the corniculate cartilages.

2. The **thyroid gland** is a large endocrine gland located anterolateral to the larynx and upper portion of the trachea. It can be identified on the DONORS, TORSO and HEAD MODELS, one type of LARYNX MODEL, and the RESPIRATORY ORGAN MODEL (Fig. 20.10, p. 613).

D. The trachea and bronchial tree provide the passageway for air to move in and out of the lungs. Use the MODELS and DONORS to identify the various divisions of these structures (Figs. 25.6-7, and Clemente, Figs. 168–9).

1. The **trachea** is a cartilaginous and membranous tube, about 2.5 cm (1 in.) in diameter and 11 cm (4.3 in.) long. It begins at the lower part of the larynx and descends behind the arch of the aorta where it divides into **left** and **right main** (or **primary**) **bronchi** (singular: bronchus; plural: bronchi).

2. The bronchial system begins at the division of the trachea into the two primary bronchi. The bronchi enter the lungs and continue to divide into smaller branches until reaching areas where gas exchange (respiration) can take place. The following portions of the bronchial system can be identified on the MODELS or, in some cases, on the DONORS.

    a. the **right main** (or **primary**) **bronchus** supplies the right lung; it is wider, shorter, and more vertical than the left, and is about 2.5 cm (1 in.) in length.

    b. the **left main** (or **primary**) **bronchus** supplies the left lung and is narrower and more horizontal than the right; it is nearly 5 cm (2 in.) in length.

     c. five **lobar** (or **secondary**) **bronchi** arise from the main bronchi, three from the right main bronchus and two from the left main bronchus; each lobar bronchus supplies one lobe of a lung.

     d. lobar bronchi branch into **segmental** (or **tertiary**) **bronchi**, each segmental bronchus supplying a bronchopulmonary segment of the lung.

III. The Lungs

(pp. 756–759)

A. Orientation and Organization

    1. Orientation: The lungs are the essential organs of respiration; they are situated one on each side within the thorax and separated by the heart and other contents of the mediastinum. Use the DONORS and TORSO MODELS to understand the orientation of the lungs within the thoracic cavity (Figs. 25.10–25.12, and Clemente, Fig. 108).

    2. Organization: Each lung is conical with an apex and base. The lungs are divided into lobes by fissures, and are enclosed by a serous membrane, the pleura. Use the RESPIRATORY ORGAN, LUNG, and TORSO MODELS to identify these organs and features.

     a. lobes: the **right lung** (Clemente, Fig. 161) is divided into a **superior lobe, middle** (*not* medial) **lobe**, and **inferior lobe.** The **left lung** (Clemente, Fig. 160) is exposed on the DONORS; it is divided into a **superior lobe** and **inferior lobe.** Each lobe is divided into two or more **bronchopulmonary segments** (Fig. 25.12; Clemente, Figs. 162–3, 166–7), shown only on the LUNG MODEL SETS.

     b. the pleura is divided into a layer which adheres to the lobes of the lungs, the visceral pleura, and a layer which lines the thoracic cavity, the **parietal pleura** (identify on DONORS) (Fig. 25.10).

B. Blood Supply: The lungs receive blood from both the pulmonary and the systemic circulation. Use the TORSO MODELS and the RESPIRATORY ORGAN MODEL to trace the blood flow of the lungs (Fig. 23.22, 23.23, pp. 707–708).

    1. Pulmonary circulation: The **right pulmonary artery** and **left pulmonary artery** carry deoxygenated blood from the right side of the heart to the areas of their respective lungs where gas exchange can occur. Branches of the pulmonary arteries travel with the branching bronchial system. Oxygenated blood is returned in branches of the pulmonary veins. Four **pulmonary veins** drain into the left atrium (Fig. 22.5, pp. 655–656).

    2. Systemic circulation: Oxygenated blood from the left ventricle of the heart reaches the lungs through the relatively small bronchial arteries. Veins deeper in the lungs drain part of this blood to the pulmonary veins and back to the left atrium; more superficial veins drain into veins of the azygos system (identified in Ch. 7) and to the right atrium.

IV. Microscopic Anatomy of the Respiratory System

(pp. 751–755)

A. The conducting portion, for the most part, is lined by **pseudostratified** (ciliated) **columnar epithelium** with goblet cells (Table 4.2e, p. 88; Sobotta, Fig. 86). Identify some features of the conducting portion on the VIRTUAL MICROSCOPE SLIDES referred to below.

    1. The nasal cavity is lined primarily by pseudostratified ciliated columnar epithelium. Beneath this epithelium is a layer of areolar connective tissue. A small area on the roof and superior walls of each nasal chamber is lined by specialized olfactory epithelium containing nerve endings for the sense of smell. (No slide)

    2. **Trachea**. Use the slide of the TRACHEA to identify this structure and its components (Fig. 25.6; Sobotta Figs. 351–2):

        a. innermost layer, the **mucosa**, with **pseudostratified** (ciliated) **columnar epithelium** supported by areolar connective tissue which contains elastic fibers and blood vessels.

        b. connective tissue submucosa containing seromucous glands.

        c. tracheal **hyaline cartilage**, surrounded by the perichondrium. Each tracheal cartilage is a "C" shaped ring with the open side of the "C" directed posteriorly toward the esophagus. The ends of the tracheal cartilage are bridged by smooth muscle. (This "gap" is seen on the TRACHEA slide. The cartilage ring is not seen in another area as well because of how the tissue was sectioned during slide preparation).

        d. **adventitia**, outermost layer of the trachea consisting of areolar and adipose connective tissue.

    3. Bronchi

        a. main (primary) bronchi are similar to the trachea until they enter the lungs where their cartilage rings are replaced by irregular cartilage plates. (No slide)

        b. with branching into smaller lobar (secondary) and segmental (tertiary) bronchi inside the lung, the cartilage plates become smaller and less numerous, while an inner smooth muscle layer becomes more prevalent. The epithelium is still pseudostratified. A **segmental** (or **tertiary**) **bronchus** can be seen on the slide of the LUNG WITH BRONCHI (Sobotta, Fig. 354a–b).

    4. After the segmental (tertiary) bronchi, the next branchings within the lung that you should identify are the bronchioles. On the slides, they have no cartilage in their walls and fewer goblet cells in the epithelium than do larger air passages. The smallest non-respiratory branches are terminal bronchioles, lined by a simple columnar to cuboidal epithelium with very few goblet cells, and surrounded by a smooth muscle band. Find a small **bronchiole** on the LUNG slides. (Keep in mind that -ole is a diminutive suffix: a bronchiole is smaller than a bronchus.)

B. Respiratory portion. Gas exchange with the blood occurs across the thin walls of alveoli which, collectively, have an extremely large surface area. They are supported by an elaborate network of elastic connective tissue. On slides of the **Lung** (be able to recognize this organ microscopically), identify alveoli and the following structures which connect them to the conducting portion.

   1. **Respiratory bronchioles** branch from the terminal bronchioles. **Alveoli** for gas exchange are scattered or in small groups, but not continuous, along the wall of a respiratory bronchiole. The epithelium of a respiratory bronchiole between alveoli ranges from low cuboidal to almost squamous (Fig. 25.8).

   2. **Alveolar ducts** branch from the respiratory bronchioles. The walls of these ducts contain an almost continuous array of **alveoli**. The lining epithelium between alveoli is squamous. Alveolar ducts end in alveolar sacs, clusters of individual alvcoli (Fig. 25.8; Sobotta, Fig. 356).

   3. Each **alveolus** is a small air space surrounded by an extensive capillary network. The epithelium which lincs the alveoli is an extremely thin simple squamous in close proximity to the capillary walls (Fig. 25.8, 25.9; Sobotta, Figs. 361–2). Alveoli make up the major part of the lung and give it its sponge-like appearance under the microscope.

V. Study Tips for this Chapter

A. Use the pictures in your text to help you identify respiratory system and thyroid gland structures. You can use these text pictures at home to review these structures.

B. Make sure you learn the respiratory system and thyroid gland structures on both the Donors and selected Models. The model keys at the end of this chapter list most structures that you will be responsible for on a particular model.

C. At home, make a list of the respiratory system and thyroid gland structures you learned in lab. Writing the names of the structures over and over again will help you remember their names. Also, practice pronouncing the terms.

D. Be careful with the terms "bronchus" and "bronchiole." Know the difference between the two, and use correct terms on the exam or you will not get credit.

E. Draw out the branching pattern of the bronchial tree. This will help you better remember the terms and the order of branching.

F. In lab, have your lab partner "quiz" you on the Virtual Microscope Slides. Reverse roles: YOU show a microscope slide with the label not seen to quiz your lab partner. Both you and your lab partner will be better able to identify the structures on the slides when it comes time for the exam.

G. At home, make a list of the features you need to identify on the Trachea slide and the Lung slides. Some features (like the epithelium and cartilage) you've seen in earlier lab chapters, so take a few minutes to review your earlier notes.

H. Remember to use the Virtual Microscope to review the respiratory system structures when you get home!

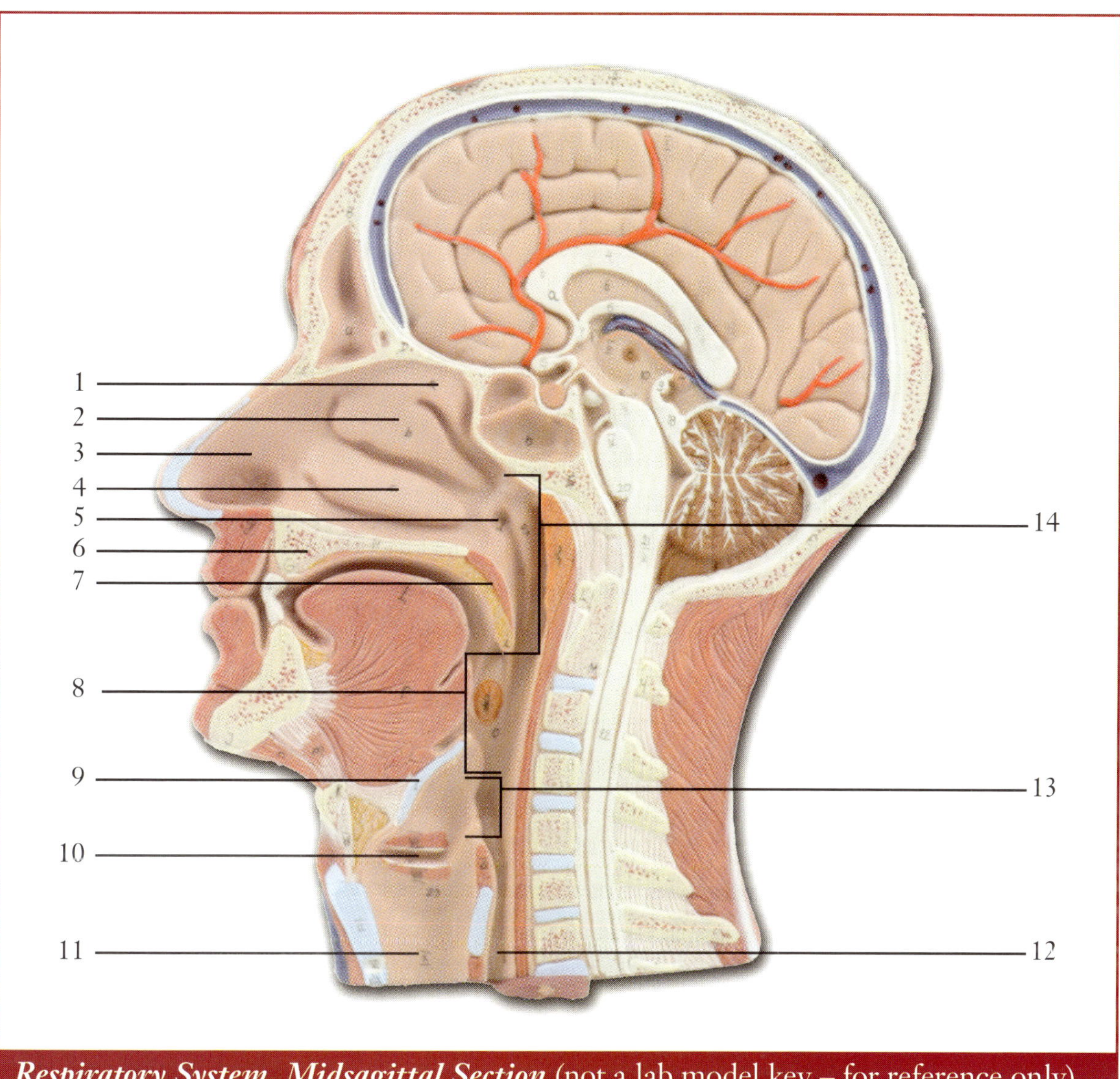

Respiratory System, Midsagittal Section (not a lab model key – for reference only)

1. superior nasal concha
2. middle nasal concha
3. nasal cavity
4. inferior nasal concha
5. opening of auditory (Eustachian, pharyngotympanic) tube
6. hard palate
7. soft palate
8. oropharynx
9. epiglottis
10. vocal cords
11. trachea
12. esophagus
13. laryngopharynx
14. nasopharynx

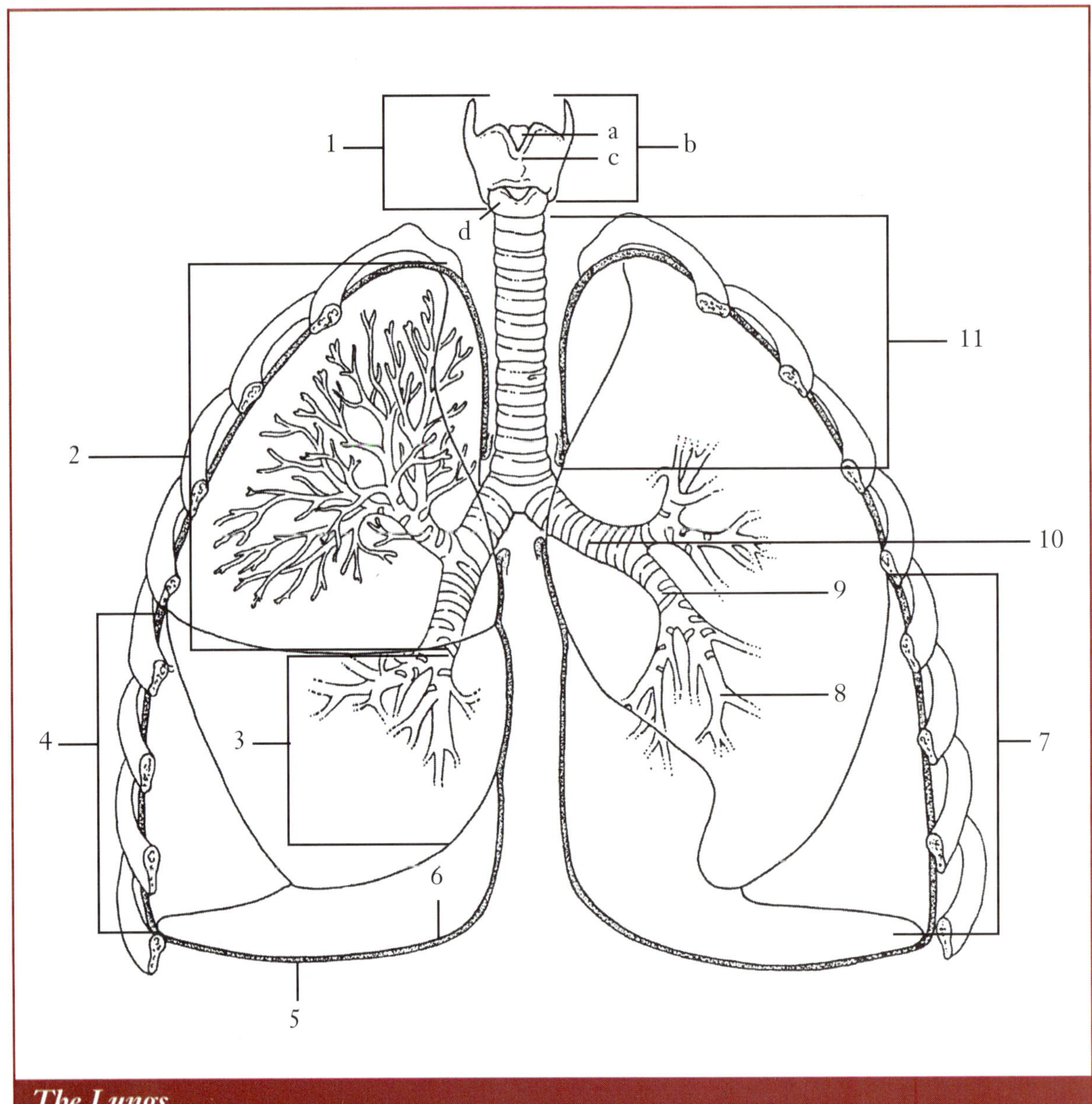

The Lungs

1. larynx
   a. epiglottis
   b. thyroid cartilage
   c. laryngeal prominence
   d. cricoid cartilage
2. right superior lobe
3. right middle lobe
4. right inferior lobe
5. parietal pleura
6. visceral pleura
7. left inferior lobe
8. left segmental (tertiary) bronchus
9. left lobar (secondary) bronchus
10. left main (primary) bronchus
11. trachea

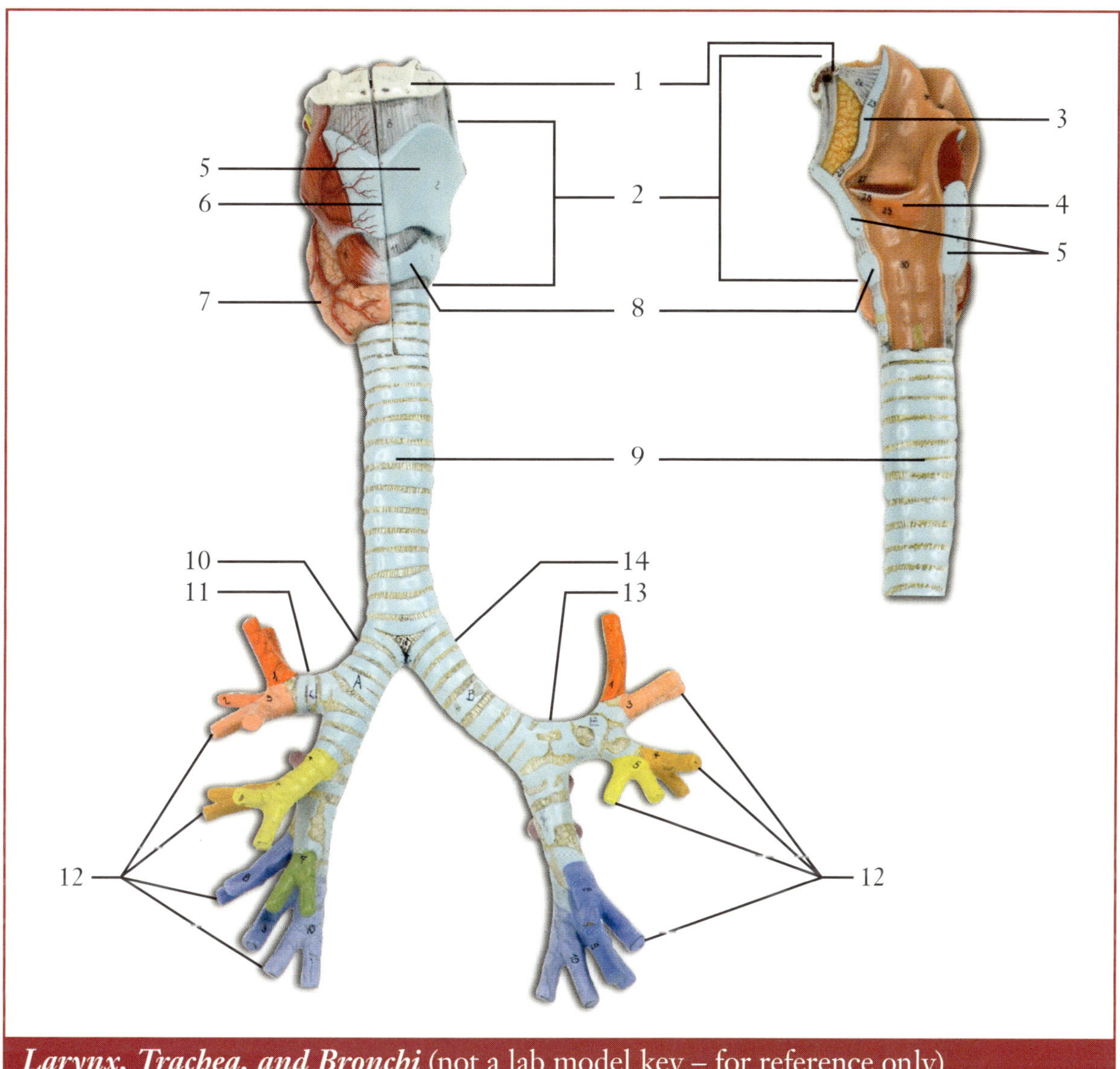

Larynx, Trachea, and Bronchi (not a lab model key – for reference only)

1. hyoid bone
2. larynx
3. epiglottis
4. vocal fold
5. thyroid cartilage
6. laryngeal prominence
7. thyroid gland
8. cricoid cartilage
9. trachea
10. right main (primary) bronchus
11. right lobar (secondary) bronchus
12. segmental (tertiary) bronchi
13. left lobar (secondary) bronchus
14. left main (primary) bronchus

VI. Respiratory System Model Keys

MUSCULAR HEAD MODELS

> external nares (nostrils)
> *90.* thyroid gland
> *91.* thyroid cartilage
> *95.* trachea

HALF-HEAD MODELS

> external naris (nostril)
> nasal cavity
> nasal conchae: superior (a),
>   middle (b), inferior (c)
> hard palate (H, posterior edge)
> soft palate (h)
> opening of auditory or
>   Eustachian or pharyngotympanic tube (d)
> pharynx
>   nasopharynx
>   oropharynx
>   laryngopharynx
>
> pharyngeal tonsils
> palatine tonsil (q)
> larynx
>   epiglottis (I)
>   thyroid cartilage (II)
>   cricoid cartilage,
>   anterior side (III)
>   vocal fold (VII)

LARYNX MODELS L1

> *1.* thyroid cartilage
>   *a.* laryngeal prominence
> *2.* cricoid cartilage
> *3.* epiglottis
>
> *4.* arytenoid cartilage
>   (*g.* corniculate cartilage)
> *5.* trachea (cartilage ring of)

LARYNX MODELS L2

> *2.* thyroid cartilage
> *3.* cricoid cartilage
> *4.* arytenoid cartilage
> *7.* trachea (cartilage ring of)
>   thyroid gland
> *23.* epiglottis
> *28.* vocal fold

> *Note also (not required):*
>   *1.* hyoid bone
>   *5.* corniculate cartilage
>   *6.* cuneiform cartilage
>   *15.* thyrohyoid muscle

RESPIRATORY ORGAN MODEL

larynx
2. thyroid cartilage
3. cricoid cartilage
4. epiglottis
vocal fold
B. thyroid gland
trachea
6. right main (primary) bronchus
7. left main (primary) bronchus
lobar (secondary) bronchi
segmental (tertiary) bronchi

E. lungs
11. (right) superior lobe
12. (right) middle lobe
13. (right) inferior lobe
14. (left) superior lobe
15. (left) inferior lobe
left pulmonary artery (branch of
pulmonary trunk on heart)
pulmonary veins (entering left atrium)
G. diaphragm

TORSO MODELS SI AND S2

1. laryngeal prominence
2. thyroid cartilage
3. thyroid gland
9, 12. trachea
10. right lung
a, b, c. lobes
11. left lung
d, e. lobes

13. right main (primary) bronchus
14. left main (primary) bronchus
15. lobar (secondary) bronchus
segmental (tertiary) bronchi (unlabeled)
h. pulmonary arteries (on heart,
branches of pulmonary trunk)
e. pulmonary veins (where one
enters heart)

TORSO MODEL N1

nasal conchae
422. inferior
424. middle
425. superior
428. nasopharynx
427. pharyngeal tonsils
430. oropharynx
482. palatine tonsil
432. laryngopharynx
436. epiglottis
437–438, 441. thyroid cartilage
442–443. thyroid gland

445–446. trachea
449–451. right lung and lobes
453–454. left lung and lobes
215. (on heart) right pulmonary arteries
216. (on heart) left pulmonary arteries
217. (entering heart) right pulmonary veins
218. (entering heart) left pulmonary veins

TORSO MODEL N2

      16. hard palate
   215. right pulmonary arteries (on heart and lungs)
   216. left pulmonary arteries (on heart and lungs)
   217. (right) pulmonary veins (entering heart)
   218. (left) pulmonary veins (entering heart)
   400. external naris (plural: nares)
   404. superior nasal concha
   405. middle nasal concha
   407. inferior nasal concha
   410. opening of auditory (Eustachian, pharyngotympanic) tube
   411. pharyngeal tonsils
   412. palatine tonsil
   414. epiglottis
   417. vocal fold
   420. thyroid cartilage
   421. cricoid cartilage
   422. trachea
   424. left main (primary) bronchus
   425. right main (primary) bronchus
(427–428. parietal pleura)
429–431. lobes of right lung
432–433. lobes of left lung
  (436. visceral pleura)
   511. soft palate
   701. thyroid gland

9 CHAPTER — *Digestive System*

I. Introduction

(pp. 774–775)

A. In your study of the digestive system keep in mind the relationships of the various components and how they form a functional system.

B. We will use the DONORS and MODELS to study the gross anatomy of the digestive system. As always, use care in handling and reassembling the models.

C. The histology of the digestive system also demonstrates the relationship between its structure and function. Use the VIRTUAL MICROSCOPE SLIDES, MODEL, figures from Sobotta, and your text to help gain an understanding of the microscopic anatomy of the digestive system. Review the "Use of the Virtual Microscope" before observing the slides.

II. Oral Cavity

(pp. 775–779)

A. Boundaries: The **oral cavity**, commonly known as the mouth, is the first part of the gastrointestinal (GI; digestive) tract and extends from the lips to the **oropharynx**. Use the HALF-HEAD and TORSO MODELS, text (Fig. 25.2, p. 745; 26.1, 26.3), and atlas (Clemente, Fig. 726) to locate these and the following structures:

   1. The **vestibule** is the space between the teeth and the lips or cheeks.

   2. The **hard palate** is the anterior portion of the roof of the mouth and is formed by the maxillary and palatine bones.

   3. The **soft palate** extends posteriorly from the hard palate and is formed primarily from skeletal muscle. The soft palate separates the oral cavity from the nasopharynx.

   4. The **palatine tonsils** are paired lateral masses of lymphatic nodules at the border between the oral cavity and the oropharynx (Fig. 26.3).

B. Tongue and Teeth

   1. The **tongue** lies on the floor of the mouth. It is composed of interlacing bundles of skeletal muscle covered by stratified squamous epithelium. The surface of the anterior two-thirds of the tongue contains numerous small projections called papillae. There are four distinct types of papilla which vary in distribution primarily over the dorsal surface of the tongue. While they are visible with the unaided eye, their structures can be seen clearly only with a microscope. For now, note the following characteristics of the papillae and surface of the tongue (Fig. 19.6, p. 565).

      a. filiform papillae: the most numerous, distributed over the entire dorsal surface of the tongue.

      b. fungiform papillae: interspersed among the filiform papillae, but most numerous around the borders of the tongue.

    c. foliate papillae: they extend as ridges on the posterior lateral sides and house only a few taste buds.

    d. **vallate** (or **circumvallate**) **papillae**: usually numbering from eight to twelve, they are macroscopic. The previous three are microscopic. They form an inverted V at the boundary between the anterior two-thirds and posterior one-third of the surface of the tongue. Identify on the HEAD of the TORSO MODEL N1.

    e. the surface of the posterior third of the tongue is free of papillae, but has ridges formed by underlying aggregations of lymphatic nodules, the **lingual tonsils**. Identify on the HALF-HEAD MODELS (Fig. 26.3b).

2. Teeth extend into the oral cavity from sockets (alveoli) within the mandible (inferiorly) and the maxillae (superiorly). Use the TOOTH MODEL and the text (Fig. 26.5) to locate the following:

    a. regions of the tooth:

        i. **crown**, extending into the oral cavity, covered by enamel.

        ii. **neck**, narrow, slightly constricted region below the crown, in contact with the **gingivae** (or **gums**) that cover alveolar processes of the mandible and maxillae.

        iii. **root**, one or more to anchor the tooth into its alveolus.

    b. structural components and their locations:

        i. **dentin** forms the bulk of the tooth; it is a hard, yellowish, calcified substance.

        ii. **enamel** is the hardest substance in the body and is composed largely of inorganic salts. The enamel covers the dentin of the crown.

        iii. **cementum** is a bonelike substance which surrounds the dentin of the root and helps anchor the tooth.

        iv. connective tissue called **pulp**, along with blood vessels and nerves, is found in both the central space called the **pulp cavity** and the narrow core of each root called a **root canal.**

    c. **periodontal ligaments** (sometimes called the periodontal membrane) are composed of dense regular connective tissue and run between the bone of the alveolus and the cementum to anchor the tooth.

C. The salivary glands are exocrine glands and serve as accessory glands for the digestive system. There are three major salivary glands, all of which are paired. Use the HEAD and TORSO MODELS, DONORS and text (Fig. 26.1, 26.4) to locate these:

1. The **parotid glands** are the largest of the salivary glands and are located on each side of the head anterior and inferior to the ear and partially overlying the masseter muscle. The **parotid duct** of each passes over the

masseter muscle, pierces the buccinator muscle, and enters into the vestibule of the oral cavity opposite the second upper molar tooth.

2. The **submandibular glands** are located along the medial aspects of the mandible, each with a superficial portion which is continuous posteriorly around the mylohyoid muscle with a larger deep portion. The duct of each is formed in the deep posterior portion and runs anteriorly to enter the oral cavity at the base of the tongue.

3. The **sublingual glands** are located on the anterior floor of the mouth deep to the oral cavity mucosa. They are the smallest of the salivary glands. Each gland has several small ducts which open separately along the floor of the mouth (HEADS of TORSO MODELS only).

III. The Gastrointestinal (GI) Tract Is a Series of Four Major "Segments"
(pp. 781–797)

A. The **esophagus** is a muscular tube about 25 cm (10 in.) long, connecting the **laryngopharynx** to the stomach. It begins at the level of the cricoid cartilage of the larynx, descends along the posterior aspect of the trachea and anterior to the vertebral column, and pierces the diaphragm to end at the stomach. Use the HEAD and TORSO MODELS to identify the esophagus and trace its course into the abdominal cavity (Fig. 26.1; Clemente, Fig. 216, 217, and 224).

B. The **stomach** joins the esophagus and the small intestine (Fig. 26.1, 26.8, 26.12). It is a J-shaped organ that forms the most expanded segment of the GI tract, lying to the left of the midline of the body just beneath the diaphragm. It is important to note that the shape and position of the stomach are modified by its volume changes and by surrounding structures. Use the DONORS, TORSO MODELS, and text to identify the following:

1. Curvatures. There are two curvatures representing the right and left borders of the stomach. Attached to each of these borders is a membrane composed of a double layer of peritoneum and called an omentum.

   a. the **greater curvature** is the convex, left and inferior border of the stomach. Attached to the greater curvature is the greater omentum, an apron-like fold of peritoneum which covers the anterior surface of the abdominal contents and often contains large amounts of adipose tissue (Clemente, Fig. 259). It probably has been detached from the DONOR'S stomach during dissection, but remains attached to the transverse colon (see below).

   b. the **lesser curvature** is the concave right and superior border of the stomach. Attached to the lesser curvature is the lesser omentum which runs between the stomach and liver. Most of the lesser omentum has probably been cut during dissection of the DONOR.

2. Orifices of the stomach (Clemente, Fig. 268)

   a. **cardiac orifice**, between the abdominal end of the esophagus and the stomach.

b. **pyloric orifice**, opens into the duodenum (first part of the small intestine) toward the right and is surrounded by a thick ring of smooth muscle, the **pyloric sphincter**.

3. Regions of the stomach (Fig. 26.12).

   a. **cardiac**, the area immediately surrounding the cardiac orifice.

   b. **body**, the main, central portion of the stomach.

   c. **fundus**, bulges superior to and to the left of the cardiac orifice.

   d. **pylorus**, tapers toward the pyloric sphincter at the distal end of the stomach.

4. Interior of the stomach. If an empty stomach is opened, its lining shows branching folds, most of which run longitudinally; these are the **gastric folds** (or **rugae**). When the stomach is full, the rugae are stretched and almost flat.

C. The **small intestine** is a long, convoluted tube extending from the pyloric sphincter to the ileocecal valve where it joins the large intestine (Fig. 26.1, 26.8, 26.14). The first and shortest of its specific segments is the **duodenum** which is normally retroperitoneal (behind the parietal peritoneum). The second specific segment is the jejunum which forms about two-fifths of the small intestine. The final three-fifths of the small intestine is the **ileum**. (It is not the "ilium" which is part of the hip bone; see Chapter 4.) Both jejunum and ileum are loosely attached to the posterior abdominal wall by a broad membrane, the **mesentery** (Fig. 26.7, 26.8), which should be identified on the DONORS. Only the duodenum and terminal portion of the ileum will be identified in lab by their locations in the abdomen and their relations to the stomach and large intestine, respectively. Use the DONORS, TORSO MODELS, and text to identify the following specific segments and related components:

   1. The **duodenum** (Fig. 26.1, 26.14, 26.21; and Clemente, Fig. 268, 270, and 285) is the shortest, widest, and most fixed specific segment of the small intestine. It is C-shaped, curving first to the right then back toward the left to end at the jejunum (see also PANCREAS MODEL).

      a. if the duodenum is opened, folds of tissue (Fig. 26.15; Clemente, Fig. 268) characteristic of the small intestine are evident. These are called the **circular folds** (or plicae circulares); unlike the folds of the stomach, they are permanent and are not obliterated when the intestine is full.

      b. on the left border of the curve of the duodenum, ducts from two accessory glands, the liver and pancreas, join to enter its wall. The common entrance of this duct into the duodenum is on the summit of the major **duodenal papilla** (Fig. 26.20, 26.21).

   2. **Ileum**: only the terminal portion of the ileum near the **ileocecal valve** will be identified (Fig. 26.14, 26.16).

D. The **large intestine** extends from the end of the ileum to the anus (Fig. 26.1, 26.8, 26.16). It differs in appearance, structure, size, and arrangement from the small intestine. On the DONORS and TORSO MODELS, notice these differences and use your text to find the following:

1. Differences between the large and small intestine:

   a. generally larger in diameter than the small intestine.

   b. has a more fixed position than most of the small intestine.

   c. the most consistent differences are the following (Fig. 26.16):

      i. the large intestine has longitudinal bundles of smooth muscle fibers forming three distinct bands called the **teniae coli**.

      ii. since the teniae coli tend to be shorter than the rest of the large intestine's wall, the wall tends to form a series of sac-like **haustra** (singular **haustrum**).

      iii. hanging from the haustra are folds of peritoneum filled with adipose tissue and called **omental appendices** (or epiploic appendages) (DONORS only).

2. Specific segments of the large intestine:

   a. the large intestine begins on the lower right side of the abdominal cavity as a short wide pouch, the **cecum**, which lies inferior to the ileocecal junction. Extending inferiorly from the posterior aspect of the cecum is a narrow blind tube, the **vermiform appendix** (Latin *vermis* = worm).

   b. the **ascending colon** ascends along the posterior abdominal wall from the cecum to near the liver.

   c. the **transverse colon** extends from the right border of the abdominal cavity inferior to the liver to its left border near the spleen; the **greater omentum** hangs inferiorly from the transverse colon in front of the small intestine (Clemente, Fig. 259).

   d. the **descending colon** descends along the posterior body wall from near the spleen to the pelvic region.

   e. as the descending colon enters the pelvis, it curves toward the midline of the body as the S-shaped **sigmoid colon**.

   f. the **rectum** begins where the sigmoid colon passes beneath the parietal peritoneum (is retroperitoneal) and runs inferiorly along the sacrum toward the pelvic diaphragm. The rectum lacks haustra and appears to have smooth walls. Identify only on the TORSO and PELVIS MODELS.

   g. the last and shortest specific segment of the large intestine is called the **anal canal** (TORSO and PELVIS MODELS only); it begins at the pelvic diaphragm and ends at the anus, its external opening. The anal canal is surrounded by internal (involuntary) and external (voluntary) **anal sphincter** muscles.

IV. Accessory Organs

(pp. 802–807)

A. The **liver** is the largest internal gland and is situated under the diaphragm in the upper right part of the abdominal cavity. Among its many functions, the liver is an exocrine gland and produces bile (a substance which emulsifies digested lipids). The liver consists of four lobes (Fig. 26.1, 26.8, 26.18). Identify it on the Donors and Torso Models.

B. **Gallbladder** and ducts. Bile produced by the liver is carried by ducts to the gallbladder where it is stored and concentrated until needed. Identify the following on the Donors and Torso Models. (Fig. 26.1, 26.18, 26.20):

    1. the **gallbladder** is located by the inferior surface of the liver at the medial border of the right lobe. It is attached to the liver by connective tissue.

    2. the **common hepatic duct** receives smaller ducts from the lobes of the liver and is joined by a duct from the gallbladder.

    3. the **cystic duct** is the duct from the gallbladder; it carries bile from the common hepatic duct to the gallbladder, or from the gallbladder to the common bile duct.

    4. the **common bile duct** runs from the junction of the common hepatic duct and cystic duct to the duodenal wall; it is joined by the main pancreatic duct to enter the duodenum at the major duodenal papilla. Identify also on the Pancreas Model.

C. The **pancreas** (Fig. 20.15, p. 622; 26.1, 26.21) is located behind the stomach and runs from the inner curve of the duodenum to the vicinity of the spleen. It is lobulated and branched, appearing as a diffuse mass of tissue. On the Donors and Torso and Pancreas Models, locate the pancreas (Clemente, Fig. 277, 285 and 287). On the Models, note the main **pancreatic duct** running the length of the pancreas to join the common bile duct at the duodenum.

V. Blood Supply

(pp. 699–703)

A. Arteries. Major arteries supplying abdominal digestive organs are pictured in Fig. 23.9, 23.12, 23.14, 23.15, pp. 688–696; and in Clemente, Figs. 265–6. Using these figures as a guide, identify the following arteries on the Donors and on the Torso and Pancreas Models:

    1. **Celiac trunk** (or **artery**), with the following branches:

        a. **left gastric artery**

        b. **common hepatic artery** with the following branches:

       i. **gastroduodenal artery** (Clemente, Figs. 265–6)

      ii. **hepatic artery** proper

   c. **splenic artery**

  2. **Superior mesenteric artery**

  3. **Inferior mesenteric artery**

B. Veins. The venous drainage of abdominal digestive organs is summarized in Fig. 23.16 and 23.17, pp. 697–698; and in Clemente, Fig. 266 and 303. Also review the figure and "Learning Strategy!" associated with this system on p. 698. Recall that the hepatic portal system receives blood from these organs and redistributes it to the liver (see section VI below). The hepatic veins then collect blood from the liver and deliver it to the inferior vena cava. Identify the following terms of the hepatic portal system on the DONORS and on the TORSO (where labeled) and PANCREAS MODELS:

  1. **Hepatic portal vein**

  2. **Splenic vein**

  3. **Superior mesenteric vein**

  4. **Inferior mesenteric vein**

VI. Microscopic Anatomy of the Digestive System

(pp. 565, 621–622, 782–803)

A. Oral Cavity—the **tongue** (Fig. 19.6; p. 567). Be able to recognize this organ and distinguish the following papillae on the TONGUE SLIDES:

  1. **filiform papillae** (Sobotta, Fig. 294): the most numerous, slender and tapering to a tip which is usually keratinized (*filum* = thread).

  2. **fungiform papillae** (Sobotta, Fig. 294): less numerous but larger than filiform; having flattened tops (*fungiform* = mushroom-shaped); epithelium may have taste buds.

  3. **vallate** (or **circumvallate**) **papillae** (Sobotta Fig. 292, 295): flattened on top but much larger than fungiform; each surrounded by a circular trench (valley), the epithelium of which contains **taste buds**.

B. Gastrointestinal (GI; digestive) Tract

  1. General scheme. The GI tract is basically a tube with a wall having four different layers or tunics. Each layer has certain components which vary in the different segments along the GI tract. This variation is related to function and aids in the identification of each segment. Keep in mind this scheme as you study slides of three different segments and look for particular components in Section 2. The layers and their components (Fig. 26.9):

a. mucosa, the innermost layer consisting of three parts:

    i. epithelium—lining the lumen of the GI tract.

    ii. lamina propria—areolar connective tissue surrounding vessels, glands, and lymphatics.

    iii. muscularis mucosae—thin layer of smooth muscle cells.

b. submucosa, connective tissue containing larger blood vessels, glands in some segments, and lymphatics.

c. the muscularis is primarily smooth muscle, usually arranged in two layers, the innermost having smooth muscle cells arranged in a circular pattern around the tube, and the outer layer having smooth muscle cells arranged in a longitudinal pattern parallel to the tube.

d. *either* serosa *or* adventitia, the outermost layer:

    i. serosa, connective tissue with a distinct outer covering of simple squamous epithelium, i.e., a serous membrane.

    ii. adventitia, connective tissue only, attaching the segment to adjacent structures.

2. Regional characteristics. Study the VIRTUAL MICROSCOPE SLIDE from each listed segment of the GI tract and identify the bold type features or layers listed with it. Be able to distinguish these segments from each other based on these characteristics.

a. **ESOPHAGUS** (Fig. 26.10):

    i. nonkeratinized **stratified squamous epithelium**

    ii. submucosal glands

    iii. **muscularis.**

b. **STOMACH** (Fig. 26.13):

    i. within the **mucosa**: **simple columnar epithelium**, invaginated into **gastric pits**, into which many long tubular **gastric glands** empty their secretions. On the slide, the parts of gastric glands nearer the pits are composed mainly of round, pink staining (parietal) cells; the deeper parts contain greater numbers of purple staining (chief or zymogenic) cells. The **muscularis mucosae** is the smooth muscle layer forming the deep border of the mucosa.

    ii. **submucosa**—thicker areas of this layer are the bases of rugae (which can also be seen without the microscope).

    iii. **muscularis**—very thick in the stomach; you may be able to distinguish three (not just two) layers.

c. **SMALL INTESTINE** (Fig. 26.15):

Important: In addition to the structures listed here for the SLIDE, identify on the SMALL INTESTINE WALL MODEL those terms in bold print on its key at the end of this chapter.

    i. **simple columnar epithelium** (with goblet cells):

– covers finger-like **villi** (singular: **villus**) projecting into the opening of the intestine, each with a lacteal (lymphatic capillary) in its center.

– **microvillous border**—a thin line indicating the very small microvilli on the apical (free) surface of the epithelial cells

– intestinal glands, invaginations into the intestinal wall between villi

    ii. **muscularis**—note orientation of smooth muscle into an **inner circular layer** and an **outer longitudinal layer** (see 1.c. above).

C. Liver and Pancreas

1. **Liver.** Each lobe of the liver is divided into many lobules, each formed by radially arranged cords or plates of **hepatocytes** (liver cells). Using low magnification, look for lobules on the virtual microscope slide of LIVER. Then use higher magnifications to identify (Fig. 26.19; and Sobotta, Fig. 330, 339):

a. lobule, roughly hexagonal in cross section.

b. **central vein**, in the center of a lobule.

c. a **portal triad** (or **hepatic triad**), at each of a lobule's corners, and its three components (more than one of each may be present in a triad due to branching):

    i. a **branch of the hepatic portal vein**.

    ii. a **branch of the hepatic artery** (often an arteriole).

    iii. a **bile duct branch**, lined by simple cuboidal epithelium.

d. sinusoids, thin-walled vascular spaces draining toward the central vein.

e. **hepatocytes**, the main cell type in the liver, cuboidal in shape, and arranged radially around each central vein to form the walls of the sinusoids.

f. extremely small bile canaliculi or capillaries carry bile between hepatocytes toward the branches of the bile duct, but do not try to find these on the slide.

2. The **pancreas** (Fig. 20.15, p. 622; 26.21; Sobotta, Fig. 343) is composed of two distinct types of glandular tissue. The main mass of tissue is the **acinar**

cells, organized into clusters called pancreatic acini and drained by **exocrine ducts**, of which various sizes form a branching system. This system of exocrine ducts carries digestive enzymes to the pancreatic duct which, in turn, transports them to the duodenum. Embedded within this tissue are clusters of endocrine cells constituting the **pancreatic islets** (islets of Langerhans) which are usually lighter-staining. Use the slide of PANCREAS to identify these structures.

VII. Study Tips for this Chapter

A. Use the pictures in your text to help you identify digestive system structures. You can use these text pictures at home to review these structures.

B. Make sure you learn the digestive system structures on both the DONORS and selected MODELS. The model keys at the end of this chapter list most structures that you will be responsible for on a particular model.

C. At home, make a list of the digestive system structures you learned in lab. Writing the names of the structures over and over again will help you remember their names. Also practice pronouncing the terms.

D. Study lab and lecture material at home by doing the following: review text pictures and say the names of the digestive system structures aloud. Then look in your lecture notes to determine the functions of each digestive system structure. List, in order, the digestive system structures that food goes through before exiting the body.

E. At home, list the 4 *segments* of the GI tract. Then, list any *specific segments* (such as the duodenum).

F. Draw and label a picture of the biliary tree. That will help you better remember the names of the different ducts.

G. Draw and label the branches off of the celiac trunk. Repeat this process many times. Once you can draw this picture without having to look at your text, then you know these branches!

H. In lab, have your lab partner "quiz" you on the VIRTUAL MICROSCOPE SLIDES. Reverse roles: YOU set up slides to quiz your lab partner. Both you and your lab partner will be better able to identify the structures on the slides when it comes time for the exam.

I. Use your lecture notes to help you identify the slides. In lecture we discuss how the layers (tunics) differ in each segment of the GI tract. Use this information to help you identify some digestive organs (like esophagus or stomach) on the slides.

J. At home, make a list of the *organs*, *layers* (or *tunics*), and *structures* you need to identify on the slides.

K. Remember to use the VIRTUAL MICROSCOPE to review the digestive system structures when you get home.

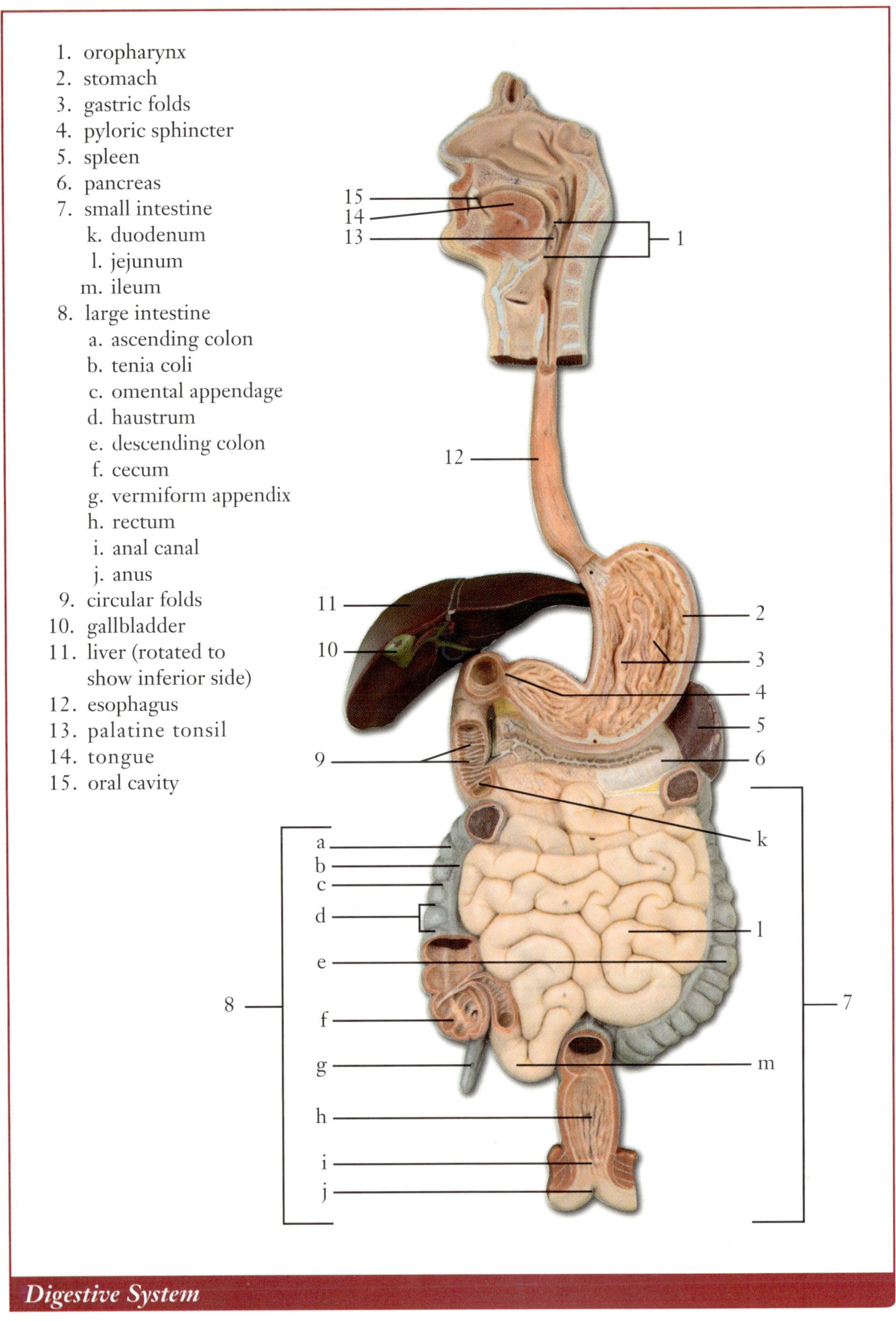

1. oropharynx
2. stomach
3. gastric folds
4. pyloric sphincter
5. spleen
6. pancreas
7. small intestine
k. duodenum
l. jejunum
m. ileum
8. large intestine
a. ascending colon
b. tenia coli
c. omental appendage
d. haustrum
e. descending colon
f. cecum
g. vermiform appendix
h. rectum
i. anal canal
j. anus
9. circular folds
10. gallbladder
11. liver (rotated to
show inferior side)
12. esophagus
13. palatine tonsil
14. tongue
15. oral cavity

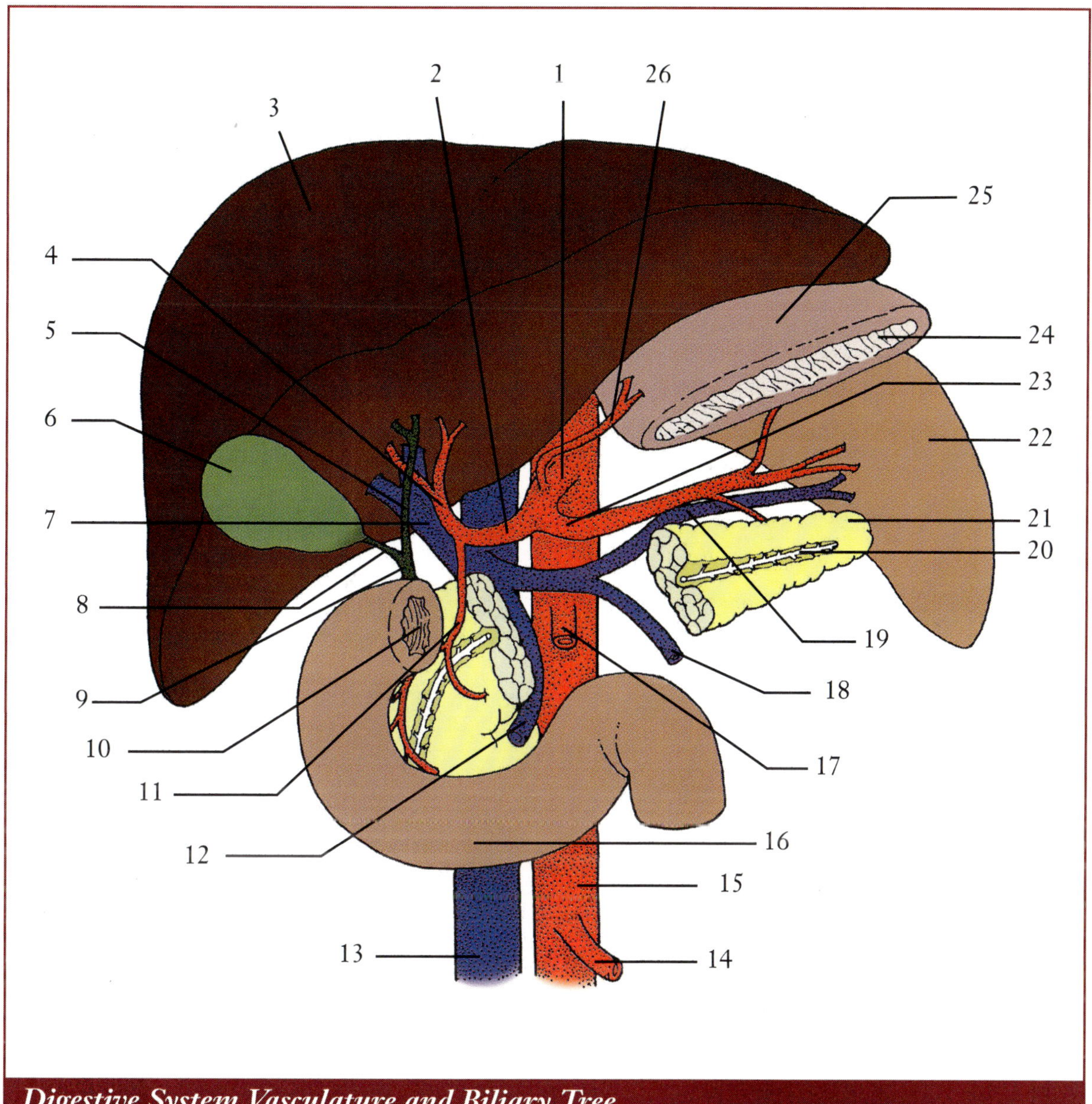

Digestive System Vasculature and Biliary Tree

1. celiac trunk
2. common hepatic artery
3. liver
4. hepatic artery proper
5. common hepatic duct
6. gallbladder
7. hepatic portal vein
8. cystic duct
9. common bile duct
10. circular fold
11. gastroduodenal artery
12. superior mesenteric vein
13. inferior vena cava
14. inferior mesenteric artery
15. descending abdominal aorta
16. duodenum
17. superior mesenteric artery
18. inferior mesenteric vein
19. splenic vein
20. main pancreatic duct
21. pancreas
22. spleen
23. splenic artery
24. gastric fold
25. stomach (cut)
26. left gastric artery

VIII. Digestive System Model Keys

MUSCULAR HEAD MODELS

      parotid gland
66. parotid duct
      submandibular gland
99. esophagus

HALF-HEAD MODELS

79. parotid gland
      parotid duct
      submandibular gland
      oral cavity
      vestibule
H. hard palate
h. soft palate
      lingual tonsils
      oropharynx
      laryngopharynx
      esophagus

TOOTH MODEL

      crown
      neck
      root (two are seen)
2. dentin
1. enamel
10. cementum
3–6. pulp, in the pulp cavity
      root canal (one in each root)
8. periodontal ligament
7. gingiva

TORSO MODEL N1

Head

    oral cavity
    vestibule
    hard palate
    parotid gland
476. vallate papilla
479. sublingual gland
480. submandibular gland
      (deep portion)
481. soft palate
    oropharynx
    laryngopharynx
    esophagus

Torso

483. esophagus

Liver

394. hepatic portal vein
502–505. lobes of liver
506. common bile duct
511. gallbladder
512. cystic duct

Stomach

484. cardiac orifice
485. fundus
486. pyloric region
488. lesser curvature
490. greater curvature

Duodenum, Pancreas, and Large Intestine

373. splenic artery
387. superior mesenteric vein
491. duodenum
493. major duodenal papilla
495, 497, 498. pancreas
496. main pancreatic duct
501. common bile duct
518. cecum
520. ileocecal valve
521. ileum, at junction with cecum
522. ascending colon
524, 527. transverse colon
526. tenia coli (one of three)
    haustra
528. descending colon
529. sigmoid colon
530 from 389. rectum

TORSO MODEL N2

16.	hard palate
291.	celiac trunk
292.	origin of left gastric artery
293.	origin of splenic artery
295.	splenic vein
296.	origin, common hepatic artery
300.	hepatic portal vein
314.	superior mesenteric vein
505–506.	submandibular gland
508.	sublingual gland
509.	parotid gland
510.	parotid duct
511.	soft palate
	oropharynx
	laryngopharynx
515.	esophagus
	stomach
516.	cardiac orifice
517.	fundus
518.	pyloric region
519.	lesser curvature
520.	greater curvature
521–523.	layers of muscularis
525.	rugae
526.	pyloric sphincter
527.	duodenum
529.	major duodenal papilla
530.	common bile duct
531–533.	pancreas
535.	main pancreatic duct
	circular folds (within small intestine)
540.	greater omentum
542.	ileum at junction with cecum
543.	ileocecal valve
544.	cecum
545.	vermiform appendix
546.	ascending colon
548.	transverse colon
549.	tenia coli (one of three)
	haustra
552.	descending colon
553.	sigmoid colon
554 to 319.	rectum
	liver
555, 556, 562, 563.	lobes of liver
564 to 530.	common hepatic duct
565.	cystic duct
566.	gallbladder

TORSO MODELS S1 AND S2

Torso
25. small intestine
16. esophagus

Liver
19. liver (lobes a, b, f, g)
20. gallbladder
21. cystic duct

Stomach
22. stomach
    a. cardiac orifice
    b. pyloric region
    c. lesser curvature
    d. greater curvature
    e. fundus

Pancreas and Intestines
23. pancreas
    main pancreatic duct
    splenic vein
    inferior mesenteric vein
    superior mesenteric vein
    superior mesenteric artery
    celiac trunk
    splenic artery
    common hepatic artery
    gastroduodenal artery
    (origin of) left gastric artery
    common bile duct
25. small intestine
26. duodenum
    major duodenal papilla
    circular folds
28. ileum
30. cecum
    a. vermiform appendix
    b. ileocecal valve
31. colon
    c. ascending
    d. transverse
    e. descending
    haustra
    teniae coli
27. greater omentum
32. sigmoid colon

Pelvic Organs
33. rectum
53, 55. sphincters of anal canal

PELVIS MODELS

Male:
4. anus
61. sphincter muscle of anal canal
62. rectum

Female:
2. anus
30. rectum
43. sphincter muscle of anal canal

HALF-PELVIS MODELS

Male M1–M6:
sigmoid colon
20. rectum
anal sphincter

Female F1–F6:
18. rectum
19. anal sphincter

PANCREAS MODEL

A. Pancreas   (B. Spleen)   C. Duodenum

1. main pancreatic duct
(2. accessory pancreatic duct)
3. common bile duct
4. major duodenal papilla
circular folds
5. hepatic portal vein
6. splenic vein
inferior mesenteric vein
7. superior mesenteric vein
8. celiac trunk
common hepatic artery*
9. hepatic artery proper
10. splenic artery*
11. left gastric artery*
12. gastroduodenal artery
13. superior mesenteric artery

(* = branches of celiac trunk)

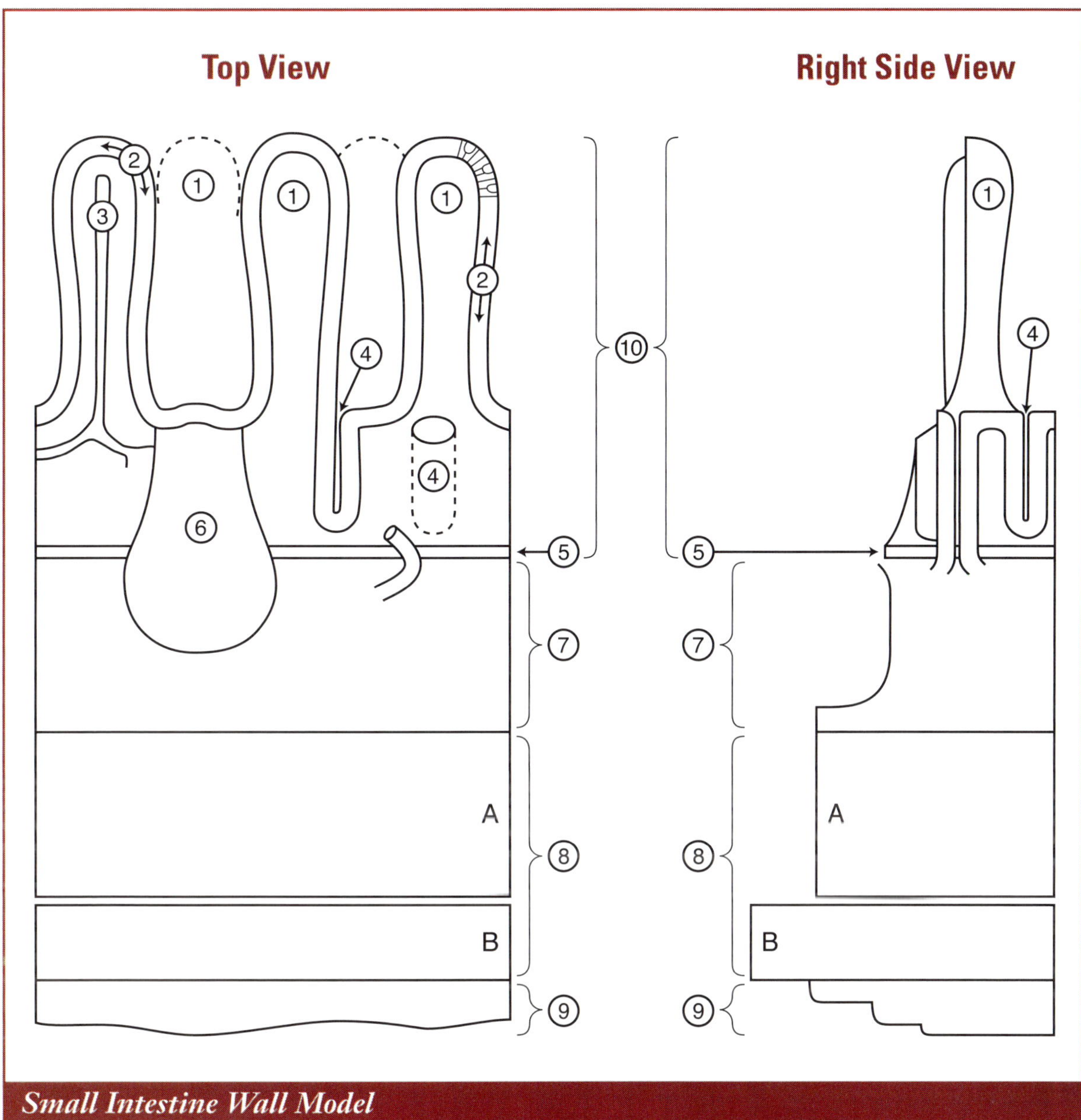

You are responsible for identifying the terms listed in bold print.

1. **villus**
2. **simple columnar epithelium**
3. **lacteal**
4. **intestinal gland**
5. **muscularis mucosae**
6. lymphatic nodule
7. **submucosa**
8. **muscularis**
   A. **inner circular layer**
   B. **outer longitudinal layer**
9. **serosa**
10. **mucosa**

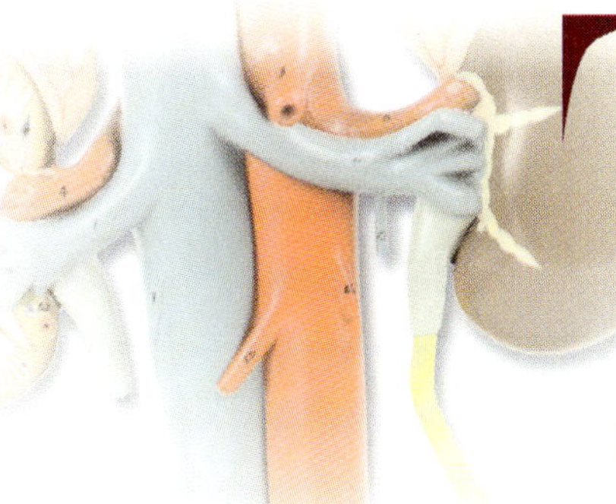

10 Urinary System

CHAPTER

I. Introduction

(pp. 812–813)

A. The urinary system is responsible for removing a variety of metabolic wastes from the body, regulating blood volume, and maintaining ion balance (Fig. 27.1). The **kidneys** are the main excretory organs and their function is critical to maintaining the internal environment. Waste products are taken from the kidneys as urine by the **ureters** and temporarily stored in the **urinary bladder**. The **urethra** leads from the urinary bladder to expel waste products.

B. We will use various MODELS and the DONORS to study the urinary system. The MODELS will be important for the study of the detailed anatomy of the urinary system. The DONORS will be used to demonstrate the location and relationship of the various parts of the urinary system.

C. VIRTUAL MICROSCOPE SLIDES will also be used to study the detail of this system. Familiarity with the microscopic anatomy of the kidney is particularly important in understanding its function and its gross structure.

145

II. The Kidneys

(pp. 814–817)

A. Orientation: Use the DONORS and TORSO MODELS.

1. Location and size (Figs. 27.1–27.3): The **kidneys** are paired organs about 12 cm long, lying against the posterior wall of the abdominal cavity between the peritoneum (retroperitoneal) and the muscles of the back. The right kidney usually lies slightly more inferiorly than the left, due to its relationship to the liver.

2. Surrounding connective tissues (Fig. 27.2; Clemente, Fig. 321): Much of these has been removed on the DONORS and MODELS.

    a. the perinephric fat is located external to the fibrous capsule of the kidney.

    b. renal fascia encloses both the kidney and perinephric fat.

    c. paranephric fat surrounds the renal fascia.

3. The **adrenal** (or **suprarenal**) **glands** are pyramid-shaped endocrine glands located behind the peritoneum (retroperitoneal) close to the superior border of each kidney. With a lobulated appearance, they are difficult to distinguish from surrounding adipose connective tissue in the DONOR and may have been removed during dissection (Fig. 20.14, pp. 617–619). Identify on the MODELS.

B. Gross Anatomy (Clemente, Figs. 326–7, 329):

1. External (Figs. 27.1–27.4), Identify the following on the DONORS and TORSO and KIDNEY MODELS:

    a. each kidney has a convex lateral border and a concave medial border.

    b. the **renal hilum** is an indentation of the medial border where the **renal artery** enters the kidney and the **renal vein** and **ureter** leave.

    c. each kidney is covered by a thin **fibrous** (or **renal**) **capsule**.

2. Internal (Fig. 27.3, 27.4). Identify the following regions and structures on the KIDNEY MODELS:

    a. the **renal cortex**, the outer region, is granular in appearance and forms about the outer third of the kidney except at the hilum. It has inward extensions called the **renal columns**.

    b. a second region, the **renal medulla**, has a lined appearance and consists mainly of the **renal pyramids**. Their bases rest on the cortex and between the renal columns. Their rounded tips, known as **renal papillae**, project inward.

    c. urine from collecting ducts at each renal papilla is collected in a **minor calyx** (*calyx* = cup or chalice). A small number of minor calyces funnel urine into a **major calyx**; major calyces funnel urine into a central cavity or region, called the **renal pelvis**.

    d. the renal pelvis is continuous with the **ureter** at the hilum.

3. Blood Vessels (Fig. 27.4): Identify the following on the KIDNEY and KIDNEY LOBULE MODELS:

    a. arteries:

        i. **renal artery**, one to each kidney from the abdominal aorta. Identify it on the TORSO MODELS also. It may be visible on the DONORS as well.

        ii. each renal artery branches outside the kidney into segmental arteries. These branch into **interlobar arteries** which pass between renal pyramids in the renal columns toward the surface of the kidney.

        iii. interlobar arteries branch into **arcuate arteries** which run along the border of the cortex and medulla near the bases of the renal pyramids.

        iv. **interlobular arteries** branch off into the cortex from the arcuate arteries.

    b. veins: **interlobular veins, arcuate veins, interlobar veins** and larger branches run with corresponding arteries. Each **renal vein** drains into the inferior vena cava; identify it also on DONORS and TORSO MODELS.

III. Ureters, Urinary Bladder, and Urethra
(pp. 822–828; Fig. 27.1, 27.9–27.11)

A. The **ureters** are two tubes, each having two layers of smooth muscle in its wall. Peristaltic contractions in the ureters convey urine from the kidneys to the urinary bladder. Each ureter is from 25 to 30 cm (10 to 12 in.) in length, and is a thick-walled, narrow, tube which begins at the renal pelvis. It runs downward and medially, enters the pelvis, and opens into the base of the **urinary bladder**. Identify the ureters on the DONORS and the TORSO and PELVIS MODELS (Fig. 27.9; Clemente, Fig. 321).

B. The **urinary bladder** is a hollow, muscular reservoir resting on the floor of the pelvic cavity. It varies in its size, shape, position, and relations according to the amount of urine it contains. In males the bladder is anterior to the rectum. In females the bladder is anterior to the uterus and the superior portion of the vagina. Identify the urinary bladder on the DONORS, TORSO MODELS, and PELVIS MODELS (Fig. 27.10; Clemente, Fig. 321, 343, 374, and 377).

C. The **urethra** is a fibromuscular tube leading from the base of the urinary bladder. In the male, the urethra is from 18 to 20 cm (7 to 8 in.) long. It passes through the prostate gland and the urogenital diaphragm to travel within the corpus spongiosum of the penis. In the female, the urethra is about 4 cm (1.5 in.) long. It runs anteroinferiorly behind the pubic symphysis, embedded in the anterior wall of the vagina, to end directly anterior to the opening of the vagina. Use both the MALE and FEMALE PELVIS and the TORSO MODELS to identify the urethra (Fig. 27.11; Clemente, Fig. 343 and 377).

IV. Microscopic Anatomy of the Urinary System

(pp. 817–826; Fig. 27.4–27.10)

A. The **KIDNEY**: The basic unit of structure and function of the kidney is the nephron (Figs. 27.4–27.7). The nephron consists of a filtering unit (the "renal corpuscle") and a tubular portion which modifies the glomerular filtrate. There are over one million nephrons in each kidney, and it is the arrangement of the nephrons which gives the organ a cortex and a medulla. View the VIRTUAL MICROSCOPE SLIDE of KIDNEY at low magnification to distinguish the cortex from the medulla. Then identify the following regions and structures on the SLIDE at higher magnifications, as well as on the KIDNEY LOBULE and RENAL CORPUSCLE MODELS:

1. The outer region or the **renal cortex**, containing many small, round renal corpuscles, much of the tubule system, and blood vessels.

2. The **renal medulla** is the region internal to the cortex that contains parallel tubules and blood vessels. Their shape on the slide depends on how they're sectioned. The absence of renal corpuscles distinguishes the medulla (Sobotta, Fig. 377, 379).

3. Specific parts of the nephron:

   a. the renal corpuscle has two components, the **glomerulus** and the **glomerular** (or Bowman) **capsule** (Fig. 27.5, 27.7, and Sobotta, Fig. 373):

      i. the **glomerulus** is a "knot" or "tuft" of coiled capillaries, and appears on the slide as a solid round structure surrounded by a thin circular clear space.

      ii. the **glomerular capsule** (RENAL CORPUSCLE MODEL only) consists of simple epithelium: a specialized inner (visceral) layer next to the glomerulus; and a squamous outer (parietal) layer which is continuous with the first portion of the tubule system of the nephron. The thin **capsular space** (SLIDE and MODEL) between these layers collects the glomerular filtrate.

   b. the tubule system (Figs. 27.5–27.8):

      i. The **proximal convoluted tubule** (Sobotta, Figs. 373–4) begins at the glomerular capsule. It is lined by thick simple cuboidal epithelium with tall microvilli, which cause the lumen of the tubule to appear "fuzzy" or congested. The proximal convoluted tubule has a very long tortuous course within the cortex, so that in a microscopic section, proximal tubules outnumber others about 7-to-1.

      ii. The **nephron loop** (or **loop of Henle**), the next segment of the nephron after the proximal tubule, projects into the medulla. It is divided into a thick descending limb, lined with simple cuboidal epithelium; a thin segment (first descending, then turning and ascending) lined with simple squamous epithelium; and a thick ascending limb with cuboidal epithelium, which passes back toward the cortex (Sobotta, Fig. 377, 379). On the Kidney Slide, most nephron loops are seen in cross section, but a small number in the outer medulla have been sectioned longitudinally and show clearly the U-shaped turn in the thin segment. Be able to identify these nephron loops.

 iii. The **distal convoluted tubule** is a continuation of the ascending limb of the nephron loop within the cortex, and is lined with a somewhat thinner simple cuboidal epithelium. These cuboidal cells have fewer, short microvilli and are not as darkly staining as the cells of the proximal tubule (Fig. 27.8; Sobotta, Fig. 374). At the renal corpuscle of the same nephron, the distal tubule contacts the blood vessel (afferent arteriole—see below) which formed its glomerulus. The portion of the distal tubule wall which contacts the vessel is the **macula densa**, a plate of closely packed cuboidal cells with prominent nuclei; you should see examples on the slide (Fig. 27.7; Sobotta, Fig. 373).

4. Fluid from the distal convoluted tubules drains into a system of collecting tubules which then drain into **collecting ducts** (Fig. 27.4, 27.5, 27.8). These ducts pass through the medulla, merging with each other until 10–25 end at each renal papilla. Collecting tubules and ducts are lined by cuboidal to tall columnar cells which are very lightly staining (Sobotta, Fig. 377, 379); you may be able to distinguish collecting tubules in the cortex and collecting ducts in the medulla on the Kidney Slide. However, you need to identify only collecting ducts, and only on the Kidney Lobule Models.

5. Blood vessels (Models only; Fig. 27.4, 27.6):

 a. **afferent arterioles** are branches off the interlobular arteries. An afferent arteriole branches into capillaries inside a glomerular capsule to form a **glomerulus**. Identify a glomerulus *also* on the Kidney Slide.

 b. an **efferent arteriole** leaves a glomerulus and has a smaller diameter than the corresponding afferent arteriole. Efferent arterioles then branch again to form both **peritubular capillaries** supplying tubules within the cortex, and **vasa recta** which are capillaries that run into the medulla largely *parallel* to the nephron loops.

B. Ureters, urinary bladder and urethra:

1. The **ureters** have walls with three principal layers. Use the slide of Ureter to identify the ureter and the following components (Fig. 27.9; Sobotta, Fig. 387).

 a. the inner mucosa, including a surface of **transitional epithelium** and underlying areolar connective tissue.

 b. **muscularis**, containing smooth muscle, with inner layers arranged more longitudinally and outer layers more circularly.

 c. the outer layer (adventitia), formed by areolar connective tissue.

2. The **urinary bladder** has a four-layered wall similar to the ureters but with several differences. Use the slide of Urinary Bladder to identify the bladder and the following components (Fig. 27.10; Sobotta, Fig. 388):

    a. mucosa, including a surface of **transitional epithelium** and the immediately underlying areolar connective tissue.

    b. a submucosa of dense irregular connective tissue.

    c. **muscularis**, containing three thick layers of smooth muscle, known collectively as the detrusor muscle.

    d. either serosa (where the bladder has a peritoneal covering over areolar connective tissue) or adventitia, the areolar connective tissue joining the bladder to adjacent structures.

3. The urethra is composed of a mucous membrane supported by submucosal connective tissue. The epithelial lining varies from transitional near the bladder, to stratified columnar, to stratified squamous near its termination. (No microscope slide.)

C. The **adrenal** (or **suprarenal**) **gland** (Fig. 20.14, pp. 617–619) has an outer cortex and an inner medulla which can be distinguished at low magnification on the slide of Adrenal Gland (Sobotta, Fig. 465). Viewed microscopically, a thin connective tissue capsule covers the gland. Beneath it, the adrenal **cortex** has layers of cells in three groups (each a "zona") with distinct arrangements and staining. The cells of the adrenal **medulla** are primarily of one type and are more darkly stained on the slide (may be seen in only part of the section on the slide, so examine the entire section). Because of its endocrine functions, the adrenal has numerous blood vessels.

V. Study Tips for this Chapter

A. Use the pictures in your text to help you identify urinary system and adrenal gland structures. You can use these text pictures at home to review these structures.

B. Make sure you learn the urinary system and adrenal gland structures on both the Donors and selected Models. The model keys at the end of this chapter list most structures that you will be responsible for on a particular model.

C. At home, make a list of the urinary system and adrenal gland structures you learned in lab. Writing the names of the structures over and over again will help you remember their names. Also practice pronouncing the terms.

D. Study lecture and lab material together by doing the following:

    1. Identify and name the urinary organs in lab (and at home, using the pictures in your text). Then use your lecture notes to determine the function of each of these organs.

    2. Identify the urinary organs in lab, and then use your lecture notes to determine the urine pathway through these organs.

3. Identify the urinary organs in lab, and then use your lecture notes to determine the urine pathway through these organs.

E. The microscopic anatomy of the kidney is quite complicated. Remember that you will have to identify microscopic structures both on the VIRTUAL MICROSCOPE SLIDES and on the KIDNEY LOBULE and RENAL CORPUSCLE MODELS. You can better learn this material if you:

1. Remember which portions of the nephron and collecting ducts are located in the cortex of the kidney and which are found in the medulla of the kidney.

2. Remember which blood vessels are associated primarily with the proximal and distal convoluted tubules, and which blood vessels are associated with the nephron loops.

3. Review your lecture notes concerning the production of urine in the kidney. Once you learn this pathway, you will have an easier time learning the microscopic kidney structures in lab.

F. In lab, have your lab partner "quiz" you on the VIRTUAL MICROSCOPE SLIDES. Reverse roles: YOU set up a slide to quiz your lab partner. Both you and your lab partner will be better able to identify the structures on the slides when it comes time for the exam.

G. Use your lecture notes to help you identify the other VIRTUAL MICROSCOPE SLIDES. In lecture, we discuss the differences between the layers (or tunics) of the ureter and urinary bladder. Use this information to help you differentiate these two structures on the slides.

H. At home, make a list of the *organs*, *layers* (or *tunics*), and *structures* you need to identify on the slides.

I. Remember to use the VIRTUAL MICROSCOPE to review the urinary system structures and adrenal gland when you get home.

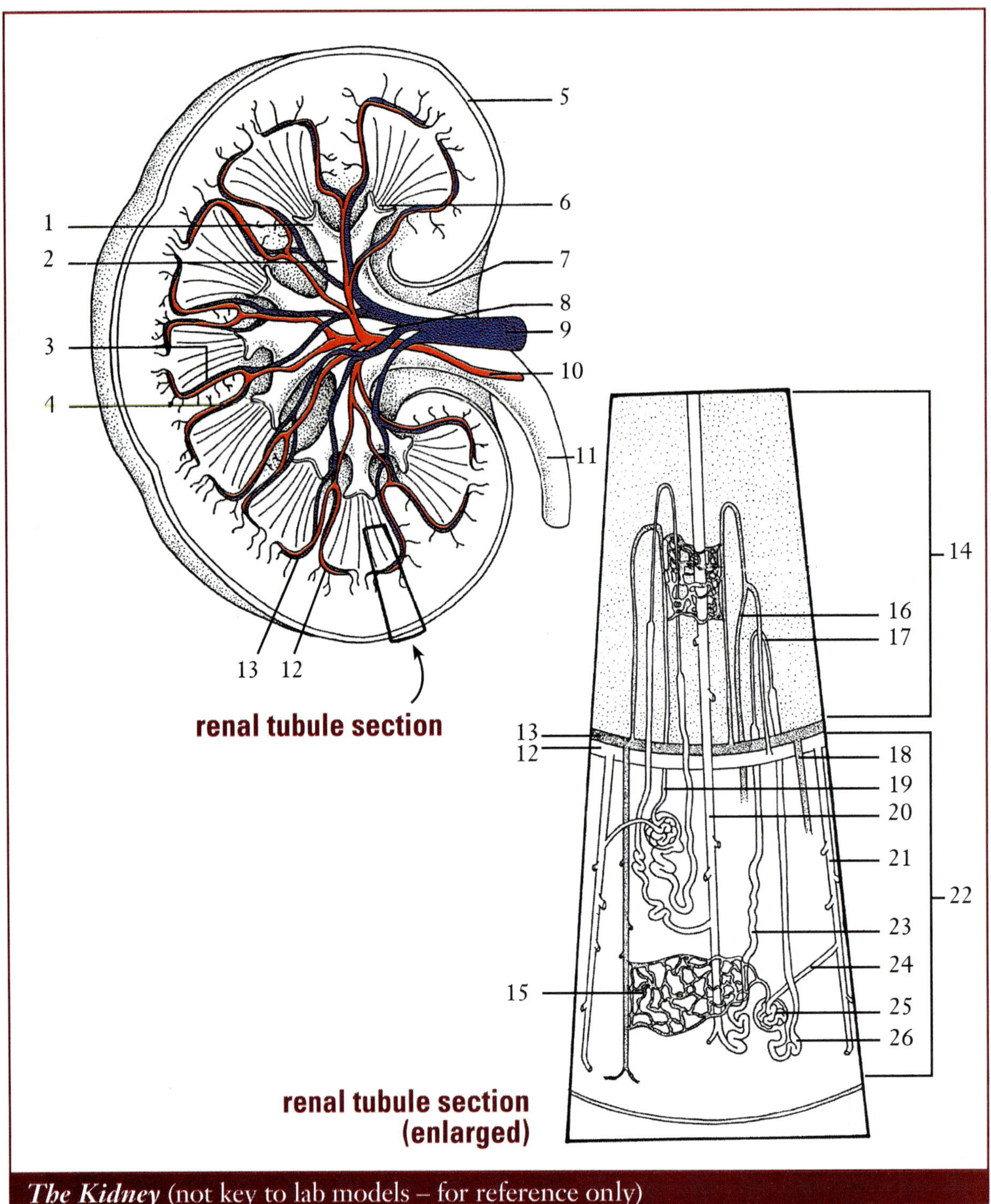

The Kidney (not key to lab models – for reference only)

1. minor calyx
2. major calyx
3. interlobar vein
4. interlobar artery
5. fibrous (renal) capsule
6. renal papilla
7. renal hilum
8. renal pelvis
9. renal vein
10. renal artery
11. ureter
12. arcuate artery
13. arcuate vein
14. renal medulla
15. peritubular capillaries
16. vasa recta
17. nephron loop
18. interlobular vein
19. efferent arteriole
20. collecting duct
21. interlobular artery
22. renal cortex
23. distal convoluted tubule
24. afferent arteriole
25. glomerulus
26. proximal convoluted tubule

VI. Urinary System Model Keys

TORSO MODEL N1

392, 531. adrenal gland
532. (right) kidney
537. (left) kidney
538. (right) ureter
539. (left) ureter
540, 571–3. urinary bladder
577, 586. urethra

395. (left) renal vein
(right) renal vein
renal arteries (right and left)

TORSO MODEL N2

703. adrenal glands
750. kidney (right)
756. renal pelvis
751, 757. ureters (right and left)
urinary bladder

321, 325. (right, left) renal artery
322, 326. (right, left) renal vein

TORSO MODELS S1 AND S2

34. kidney (right)
a. renal cortex
b, d. renal medulla
e. renal papilla
renal pelvis
36. kidney (left)
35. adrenal gland
52. ureters
51. urinary bladder
urethra

(right, left) renal artery
(right, left) renal vein

PELVIS MODELS

Male

36. ureter
37. urinary bladder
44, 45. urethra

Female

31. urethra
32. urinary bladder
33. ureter

HALF-PELVIS MODELS

Male M1–M6

4. urinary bladder
6. urethra
9. ureter

Female F1–F6

7. urethra
8. urinary bladder
9. ureter

Keys to Mueller-Ward Kidney Models

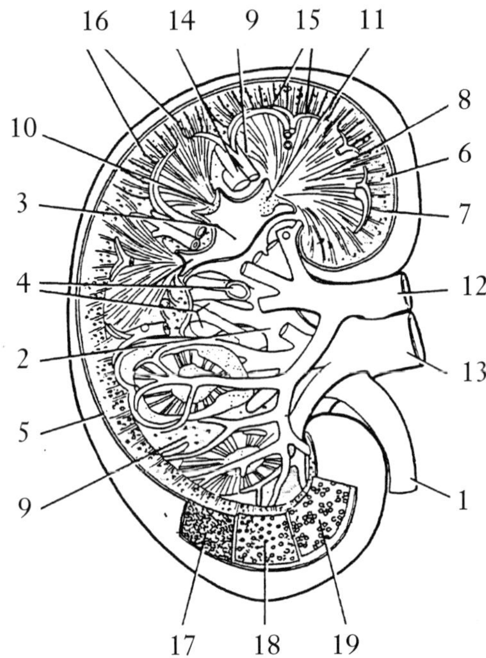

KIDNEY MODEL
(Human – 2.5×)

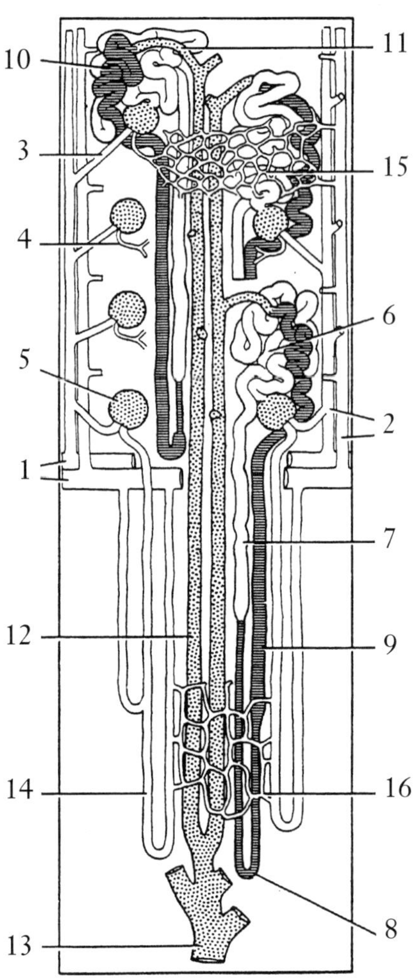

KIDNEY LOBULE MODEL
(diagrammatic)

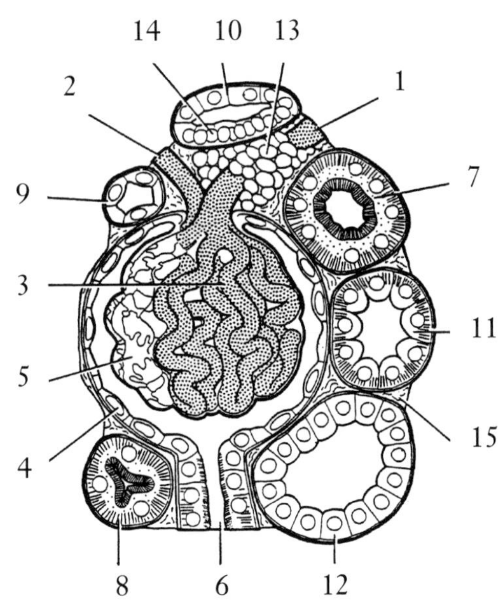

RENAL CORPUSCLE MODEL
(diagrammatic)

MUELLER-WARD KIDNEY MODEL

   1. ureter
   2. renal pelvis
   3. major calyx
   4, 11. minor calyces
   5. fibrous (renal) capsule
   6, 7. renal cortex
   8. renal pyramid
   9. renal column
   10. renal papilla
   12. renal artery
   13. renal vein
   14. interlobar vein and artery
   15. arcuate vein and artery
   16. interlobular veins and arteries
   17–19. layers of cortex

RENAL CORPUSCLE MODEL

   1. afferent arteriole
   2. efferent arteriole
   3. capillaries of glomerulus*
   4–5. glomerular capsule*
   (*4.* parietal layer)
       capsular space
   (*5.* visceral layer)
   6–8. proximal convoluted tubule
   (*9.* thin segment-most are in medulla,
       not in cortex)
   10–11. distal convoluted tubule
   (*12.* collecting duct)
   (*13.* juxtaglomerular cells**)
   14. macula densa**
   (*15.* connective tissue)

   (* components of renal corpuscle)
   (** components of juxtaglomerular
       apparatus)

KIDNEY LOBULE MODEL

   1. arcuate artery and vein
   2. interlobular artery and vein
   3. afferent arteriole
   4. efferent arteriole
   (*5.* renal corpuscle)
   6. proximal convoluted tubule
   7–9. nephron loop (loop of Henle)
       7. descending limb
       8. thin segment
       9. ascending limb
   10. distal convoluted tubule
   11,12. collecting tubule, collecting duct
   13. collecting duct near renal papilla
   14. vasa recta
   15. peritubular capillaries
   (*16.* peritubular capillaries in medulla)

SOMSO KIDNEY MODEL

       renal hilum (undissected side)
       fibrous capsule
   1. renal vein
   2. renal artery
   3. ureter
       renal cortex
       renal medulla
       renal column
   4. renal pelvis
   5. minor calyx (others seen)
       major calyces
   6, 19. renal papillae (others seen)
   7. renal pyramid (others seen)
       interlobar veins
       interlobar arteries
   13. interlobular artery (others seen)
   16. arcuate artery
   17. interlobular vein (others seen)
   18. arcuate vein

11
CHAPTER

Reproductive System

I. Introduction

(pp. 837–838)

A. Although differences between male and female obviously are greater in the reproductive system than in other systems, both reproductive systems are concerned with the production, development, and transport of gametes, and both have endocrine functions. You should relate structures you study to their cooperative performance of these functions and, in the female, to potential pregnancy.

B. The embryonic origin of some male and female structures is the same despite differences in their mature form and function. Keep such "homologous" relationships in mind.

C. Use care in studying and reassembling MODELS. Do not touch models with pen or pencil tip.

D. One organ from the male reproductive system and two from the female will be examined microscopically. Be able to identify these with the VIRTUAL MICROSCOPE SLIDES, and understand the functional relationships of the structures studied.

II. The Male Reproductive System

(pp. 855–864)

A. Scrotum and Testes

1. The **scrotum** (Fig. 28.11, 28.12, 28.17a) (MALE DONOR and MALE TORSO, PELVIS and HALF-PELVIS MODELS) is a thin-walled, divided sac beneath the pelvic arch. It contains and helps support the paired **testes** (Figs. 28.11–13a, 28.15a) in an environment cooler than the body core. The testes contain tubular systems which produce the male gametes, spermatozoa, and separate cells which produce the hormone testosterone.

2. Exterior of testis. Note the following on the MALE DONOR and the MALE TORSO and PELVIS MODELS:

    a. Each **testis** is oval or ellipsoid in shape, compressed laterally, and positioned obliquely in the scrotum (Fig. 28.11, 28.12).

    b. Each testis is covered by a tough, bluish-white, fibrous membrane, the **tunica albuginea** (Fig. 28.13a). A portion on the MALE DONOR is dissected free of the testis.

    c. Outside and adhering to the tunica albuginea, on the front and sides of each testis, is the **tunica vaginalis**, a double-layered serous sac derived from the peritoneum (Fig. 28.13a; Clemente, Fig. 343). A portion of its outer layer is seen only on the MALE DONOR where it is dissected free of the scrotum.

3. Interior of **testis**. Identify the following structures on the WHOLE PELVIS MODEL (Fig. 28.13a).

    a. Septa are thin extensions of the **tunica albuginea** into the testis, separating it into lobules (or compartments). Seminiferous tubules, in which spermatogenesis and spermiogenesis occur, are highly convoluted tubules found within each lobule. At the apex of each lobule, sperm leave the seminiferous tubules through short tubuli recti.

    b. The tubuli recti converge on a network of tubules called the rete testis, located in the posterior part of the testis and supported by connective tissue from the tunica albuginea in a region called the **mediastinum testis**, seen in section on the MODEL (Fig. 28.13a). Efferent ductules leave the rete testis, perforating the tunica albuginea.

4. Blood supply. In both sexes, arteries supplying the gonads branch from the abdominal aorta. Identify **gonadal arteries** on the N2 TORSO MODELS (Fig. 23.9a, p. 688; 23.12, p. 693) as well as **gonadal veins** (Fig. 23.9b, p. 689; 23.13, p. 694), the right one draining into the inferior vena cava, the left into the left renal vein. On the MALE DONOR, you must identify the corresponding vessels as **testicular arteries** and **testicular veins** (Fig. 28.12; Clemente, Fig. 321).

B. The genital ducts and associated structures should be identified on the MALE DONOR and MALE TORSO, PELVIS and HALF-PELVIS MODELS unless otherwise noted (Figs. 28.11–13a, 28.15a, 28.17).

1. The **epididymis** (Figs. 28.11–13a, 28.15a) is a comma-shaped structure found along the posterior surface of the testis. It begins at the superior end of the testis, winds inferiorly and eventually becomes continuous with the ductus deferens. Within the epididymis is a highly coiled structure called the duct of the epididymis. It is within this duct that sperm are stored and mature after they leave the testis.

2. The **ductus** (or **vas**) **deferens** (Figs. 28.11–13a, 28.15a) is the continuation of the duct of the epididymis. It originates at the inferior region of the epididymis and ascends along the posterior border of the testis and the medial side of the epididymis. It travels superiorly with other structures as part of the cylindrical **spermatic cord** (Fig. 28.12, 28.13a), entering the pelvis through the inguinal canal. Within the pelvic cavity, each ductus deferens passes posteriorly and inferiorly to join with the duct of the corresponding seminal vesicle near the region where the urinary bladder and prostate gland meet. Follow the path of the ductus deferens on both MODELS and the MALE DONOR, identifying it within both the spermatic cord and the pelvic cavity.

3. The **spermatic cord** (Fig. 28.12, 28.13a) suspends the testis in the scrotum and extends from the deep inguinal ring down to the posterior border of the testis. It is composed of arteries, veins, lymph vessels, nerves, and the ductus deferens, held together by areolar connective tissue. Bundles of skeletal muscle, extending down from the internal abdominal oblique, loop around the spermatic cord and testis as the cremaster muscle.

4. Each **ejaculatory duct** (Fig. 28.11, 28.15a) is formed by the union of the duct of a seminal vesicle with the terminal part of the corresponding ductus deferens. It originates posterior to prostate gland, and runs anteroinferiorly to join the prostatic urethra (MODELS only).

5. The male **urethra** (Fig. 27.11b, p. 827; 28.11, 28.15a, 28.17b) serves both the urinary and reproductive systems. The urethra may be considered in three segments: prostatic, membranous, and spongy (penile) (MODELS only).

6. (MODELS only) The **penis** (Fig. 28.11, 28.12, 28.17) is the male organ of copulation. It consists of a **body** (or **shaft**) (Fig. 28.17a), covered by thin, loosely attached skin, and an expanded tip, the **glans** (Fig. 28.11, 28.15a, 28.17a). The skin which folds over the glans is the prepuce (foreskin) and is usually surgically removed (circumcision). The penis contains two cylindrical masses, the **corpora cavernosa**, and a single mass, the **corpus spongiosum**, beneath them (Fig. 28.15a, 28.17).

   a. Each **corpus cavernosum** is composed of erectile tissue; the **corpora cavernosa** are covered and separated by strong fibrous capsules.

   b. The **corpus spongiosum** is erectile tissue surrounding the third segment of the urethra. The **glans** of the penis is an expanded conical tip of the corpus spongiosum.

C. Accessory glands of the male reproductive system include the following which can be located on the TORSO and the PELVIS and HALF-PELVIS MODELS (Fig. 28.11, 28.15a, 28.16).

1. Each of the two **seminal vesicles** is a sacculated tube on the posteroinferior aspect of the bladder. As mentioned earlier, the duct of the seminal vesicle merges with the ductus deferens to form the ejaculatory duct. Each seminal vesicle is found lateral to the corresponding ductus deferens.

2. The **prostate gland** is a rounded, encapsulated organ located at the base of the bladder. The prostate gland surrounds the initial portion of the male urethra.

3. The bulbourethral glands are two small, round bodies. Each is located lateral to the membranous urethra, within the urogenital diaphragm (PELVIS MODEL only).

D. Microscopic Anatomy: TESTIS and associated structures

First examine the VIRTUAL MICROSCOPE SLIDE(S) of TESTIS at the lowest magnification and recognize the testis, tunica albuginea, and epididymis; then use higher magnifications to identify the following.

1. The thick **tunica albuginea** is composed of dense connective tissue surrounding the testis. It also forms much thinner connective tissue septa that divide the testis into lobules (Fig. 28.13a; Sobotta, Fig. 398).

2. **Seminiferous tubules** are found within each lobule (Fig. 28.13a). At higher magnification, the cells within these tubules can be seen at the various stages of spermatogenesis. You will be asked to identify only the **spermatogonia**, which are located along the basement membrane of the tubule, and the supporting **sustentacular** (or **nurse** or **Sertoli**) **cells**, also found extending inward from the basement membrane. The sustentacular cells have a pale-staining, often triangular nucleus with a small darker nucleolus (Fig. 28.13b, 28.14a; Sobotta, Figs. 401–2).

3. **Interstitial cells** (of Leydig) are found in groups outside the seminiferous tubules and within the connective tissue between the tubules. The interstitial cells produce the hormone testosterone and thus are the endocrine portion of the testes (Fig. 28.13b, 28.14a; Sobotta, Figs. 401–2).

4. Within the mediastinum testis are the irregular spaces of the rete testis (Sobotta, right side of Fig. 404).

5. Several efferent ductules leave the rete testis and enter the epididymis. Each of these ductules is surrounded by a thin layer of smooth muscle and lined by patches of low cuboidal epithelium interspersed with patches of columnar epithelium (Sobotta, Figs. 405–406).

6. The **duct of the epididymis** is typically lined with pseudostratified columnar epithelium with long microvilli which, because of their superficial resemblance to cilia, are often called stereocilia (Fig. 28.15c; Sobotta, Fig. 407). Sections of this single, long coiled tube are seen on the TESTIS slide(s) outside the tunica albuginea.

7. The **ductus** (or **vas**) **deferens** has a very thick wall of smooth muscle and is also lined with pseudostratified columnar epithelium (Fig. 28.15b; Sobotta, Fig. 410). It may be present on the TESTIS slide(s); one or more cross sections can be seen on the slide of DUCTUS (VAS) DEFERENS.

III. The Female Reproductive System

(pp. 838–855)

A. Internal genital organs, within the pelvic cavity (Fig. 28.2, 28.3, 28.7a, and Clemente, Fig. 374, 377–9). Identify the following on the FEMALE DONOR and FEMALE TORSO, PELVIS, and HALF-PELVIS MODELS:

1. The **ovaries** are homologous to the male testes. Within the ovaries, the female gametes (oocytes) are housed, and the hormones estrogen and progesterone are produced. The ovaries are situated one on each side of the uterus close to the lateral wall of the pelvis. Each ovary is almond-shaped and supported by the broad ligament of the uterus (Fig. 28.2, 28.3, 28.7a). Identify the ovaries on the FEMALE DONOR and MODELS.

2. Blood supply. As above (section II.A.4), identify **gonadal arteries** and **gonadal veins** on the N2 TORSO MODELS (Fig. 23.9a–b, pp. 688–689; 23.12–13, pp. 693–694). On the FEMALE DONOR and the FEMALE HALF-PELVIS MODEL, you must identify the corresponding vessels as **ovarian arteries** and **ovarian veins** (Fig. 28.3a; Clemente, Fig. 318).

3. Genital tract (Fig. 28.2, 28.3, 28.7a):

   a. The **uterine** (or **Fallopian**) **tubes** transmit oocytes from the ovaries to the cavity of the uterus, and are situated in the upper margins of the broad ligaments. Each tube is about 10 cm long, its medial end opening into the superior portion of the uterine cavity, its lateral end into the peritoneal cavity close to the ovary. At the lateral end are located finger-like projections, the **fimbriae**. The fimbriae overlie each ovary and help direct an ovuluated oocyte into the uterine tube.

   b. The **uterus** is a hollow, thick-walled, muscular organ normally located between the urinary bladder anteriorly and the rectum posteriorly. It is pear-shaped with a narrower, more cylindrical area, the **cervix** (Fig. 28.2, 28.3a, 28.7) (see MODELS), projecting into the vagina.

   c. The uterus is supported by several connective tissue ligaments. The broad ligament drapes over the uterus and uterine tubes, and the ovaries attach to its posterior aspect. The **round ligaments** (Fig. 28.7a) are two narrow, flat bands that provide lateral support for the uterus. From the lateral angle of the uterus, each ligament runs anteriorly and laterally to pass through the inguinal canal and attach within the labia majora.

    d. The **vagina** (Fig. 28.2, 28.3a, 28.7a) is the female organ of copulation. Its fibromuscular wall surrounds the vaginal canal, lined by nonkeratinized stratified squamous epithelium, that extends from the uterus to the labia minora; it is situated between the bladder and urethra anteriorly, and the rectum and anal canal posteriorly (see MODELS).

B. External genital organs, located anteroinferiorly to the pubic symphysis. Identify the following on the FEMALE TORSO, PELVIS, and HALF-PELVIS MODELS (Fig. 28.2, 28.9):

    1. The **mons pubis** is the rounded area in front of the pubic symphysis and is formed by adipose connective tissue and covered with skin and pubic hair.

    2. The **labia majora** (singular: labium major) are two prominent skin folds which extend posteriorly from the mons pubis, ending close to the anus.

    3. The **labia minora** (singular: labium minor) are two small skin folds medial to the labia majora. They extend posteriorly from the clitoris on each side of the vaginal orifice, ending between this orifice and the labia majora.

    4. The **clitoris** (MODELS) contains two columns of erectile tissue and is homologous to the penis. It is located between the anterior ends of the labia minora.

C. Accessory glands. Use the FEMALE TORSO, PELVIS, and MAMMARY GLAND MODELS to identify the following terms:

    1. The greater vestibular glands are the homologues of the bulbourethral glands in the male. They consist of two small, round or oval bodies, one on each side of the vaginal orifice (Clemente, Fig. 368); PELVIS MODEL only.

    2. Each **mammary gland** consists of glandular tissue and its ducts, adipose and dense connective tissue, blood vessels, lymph vessels, and nerves. The glandular tissue produces breastmilk which the ducts carry to release at the nipple. Covered by skin, the mammary gland forms the breast that lies primarily over the pectoralis major muscle. Identify the following on the FEMALE TORSO and MAMMARY GLAND MODELS (Fig. 28.10):

        a. The rounded **areola** with the centrally located and protruding **nipple**, both of which are darkly pigmented.

        b. **Glandular tissue** arranged radially around the nipple. Surrounded by adipose tissue and supported by dense connective tissue bands, the glandular tissue drains onto the nipple through **lactiferous ducts**, each duct with a terminal expanded region called a **lactiferous sinus** (or **ampulla**) where milk is stored before release.

D. Microscopic Anatomy

    1. **OVARY.** Use the VIRTUAL MICROSCOPE SLIDE(S) OF OVARY to identify the following (Fig. 28.4):

a. ovarian follicles are located in the cortex (outer region) of the ovary. Ovarian follicles represent the various stages of the ovarian cycle and also produce the hormones estrogen and progesterone. The following developmental stages of follicles can be identified (Sobotta, Figs. 424–5):

    i. Multiple primordial follicles may be seen. Each consists of a primary oocyte surrounded by a single layer of flattened follicle cells.

    ii. In a **primary follicle**, the follicle cells have become cuboidal-shaped **granulosa cells** surrounding the **oocyte** and proliferate from a single layer early to several layers thick in more developed primary follicles. A pink-staining membrane, the **zona pellucida**, may have developed around the oocyte, separating it from the follicle cells.

    iii. In a **secondary follicle**, a fluid-filled cavity, the **antrum**, has formed between the layers of **granulosa cells**. The **zona pellucida** may be seen immediately around the **oocyte**.

    iv. A vesicular (mature, Graafian) follicle (probably not present on the OVARY slide(s)) is fully developed and may form a bulge on the surface of the ovary. When the follicle reaches this stage, ovulation soon occurs. Typically, only one follicle fully matures and ruptures during the ovarian cycle.

b. A corpus luteum (Sobotta, Fig. 422) is formed from the walls of the vesicular (mature, Graafian) follicle after ovulation; however, a corpus luteum is not seen on the OVARY slide(s). The corpus luteum produces hormones (progesterone and estrogen) that maintain the uterine lining. If fertilization occurs, the corpus luteum remains active through the first trimester of pregnancy. If fertilization does not occur, the corpus luteum degenerates after ten days and is replaced by a white scar called the corpus albicans (Fig. 28.4; Sobotta, Fig. 422).

2. The **UTERUS** has the following layers in its wall. Be able to identify the inner two and their components on the UTERUS slide(s) (Fig. 28.7a, c):

a. The perimetrium, which is an outer serosa, is formed by areolar connective tissue and simple squamous epithelium.

b. The **myometrium** makes up most of the uterine wall and consists of three layers of smooth muscle.

c. The **endometrium** is the innermost layer of the uterine wall. It consists of a thin **basal layer** of primarily connective tissue adjacent to the myometrium, and a thicker **functional layer** adjacent to the uterine cavity. The surface is covered by simple columnar epithelium invaginated to form tubular **uterine glands**. Periodic changes in components of the functional layer occur during the uterine or menstrual cycle (Sobotta, Figs. 435–437).

IV. Study Tips for this Chapter

A. Use the pictures in your text to help you identify reproductive system structures. You can use these text pictures at home to review these structures.

B. Make sure you learn the reproductive structures on both the DONORS and selected MODELS. The model keys at the end of this chapter list most of the structures that you will be responsible for on a particular model.

C. At home, make a list of the reproductive system structures you learned in lab. Writing the names of the structures over and over again will help you remember their names. Also practice pronouncing the terms.

D. Study lab and lecture material at home by doing the following: review text pictures and say the names of the reproductive system structures aloud. Then look in your lecture notes to determine the functions of each structure.

E. In lab, have your lab partner "quiz" you on the VIRTUAL MICROSCOPE SLIDES. Reverse roles: YOU display a microscope slide to quiz your lab partner. Both you and your lab partner will be better able to identify the structures on the slides when it comes time for the exam.

F. List the *cells*, *follicles*, *layers*, and *organs* you need to identify on the slides.

G. Compare the microscopic anatomy of the ductus deferens to the microscopic anatomy of the ureter. Upon first glance, they may seem similar, so make sure you can distinguish the two! Also, make sure you can distinguish the ductus deferens from the duct of the epididymis.

H. Be able to distinguish a primary follicle from a secondary follicle. Be able to list the cells and structures found in each kind of follicle.

I. Remember to use the VIRTUAL MICROSCOPE to review the reproductive system structures when you get home!

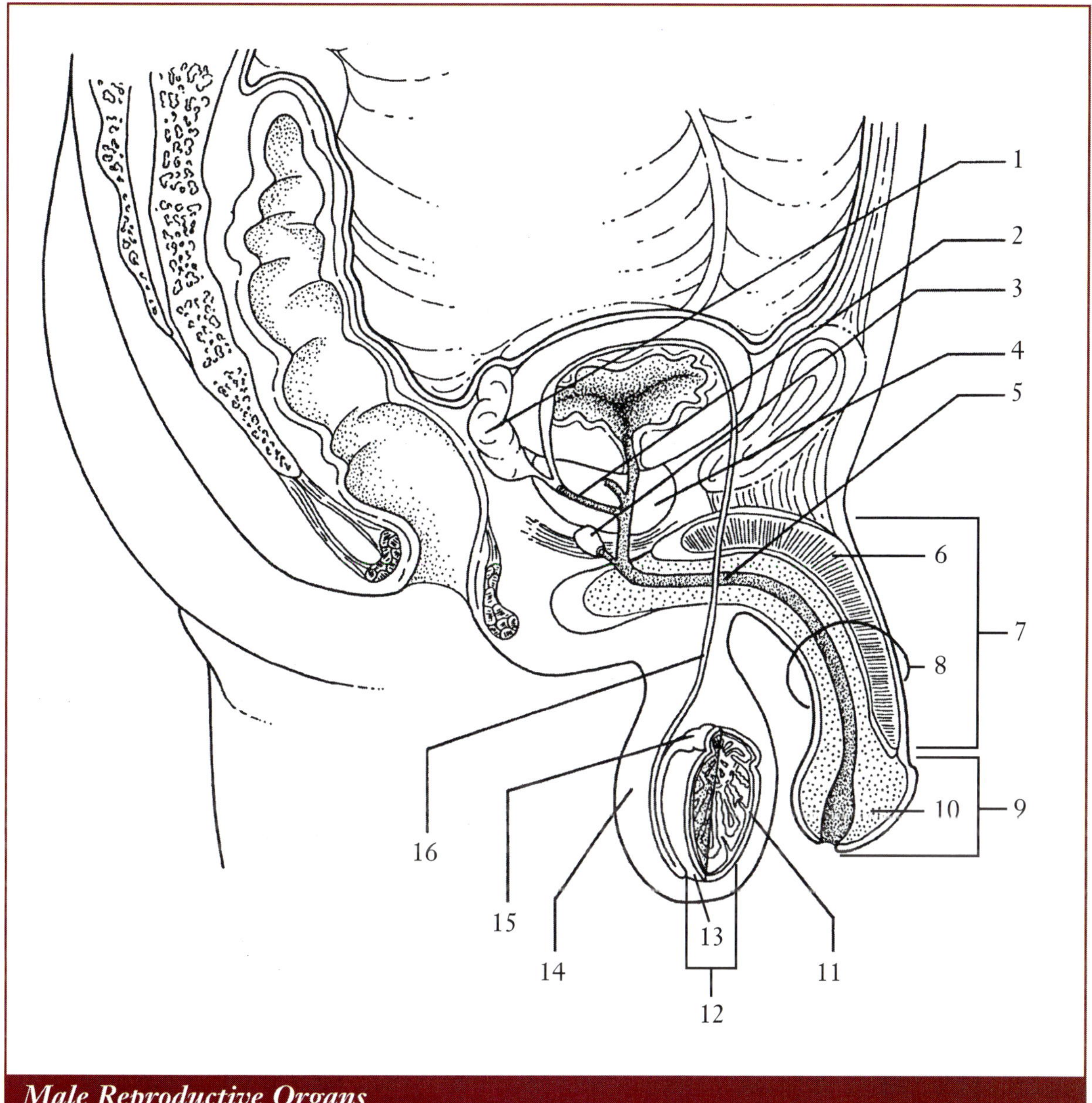

Male Reproductive Organs

1. seminal vesicle
2. ejaculatory duct
3. bulbourethral gland
4. prostate gland
5. spongy (penile) urethra
6. corpus cavernosum
7. body of penis
8. penis

9. glans of penis
10. corpus spongiosum
11. tunica albuginea
12. testis
13. tunica vaginalis
14. scrotum
15. epididymis
16. ductus (vas) deferens

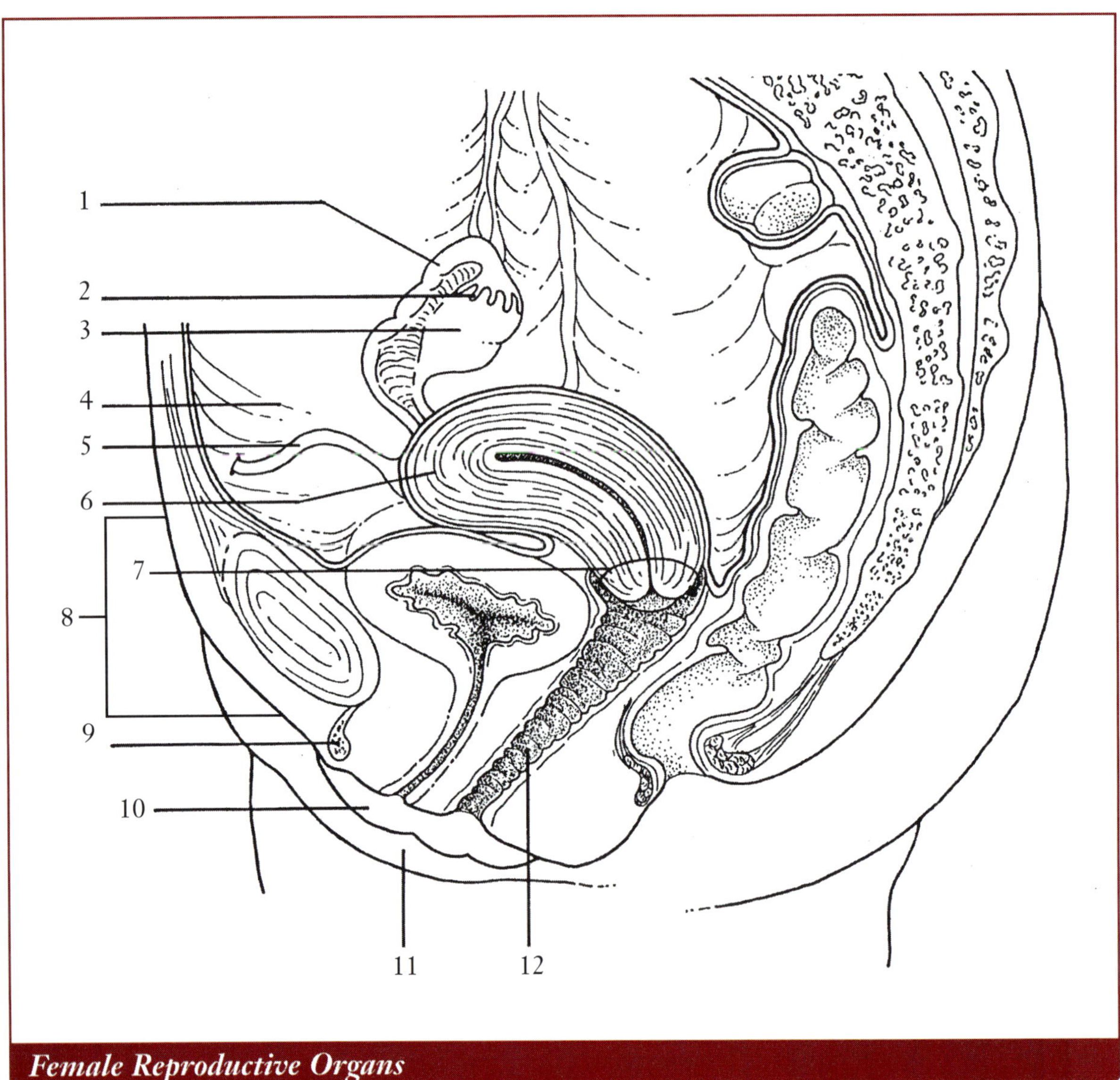

Female Reproductive Organs

1. uterine (Fallopian) tube
2. fimbriae
3. ovary
4. broad ligament
5. round ligament
6. uterus
7. cervix (circled)
8. mons pubis
9. clitoris
10. labium minor (plural: labia minora)
11. labium major (plural: labia majora)
12. vagina

V. Male Reproductive System Model Keys

TORSO MODEL N1

591. scrotum
592. testis
593. epididymis
577, 586. urethra
583. corpus cavernosum

576. ductus deferens
575. prostate gland
574. ejaculatory duct
578. bulbourethral gland

PELVIS MODEL

1. penis
3. scrotum
32. ductus deferens
33. spermatic cord
38. seminal vesicle
40. prostate gland
41. ejaculatory duct
42. bulbourethral gland

44–45. urethra
47. corpus spongiosum
48. corpus cavernosum
49. glans
52. testis
    tunica albuginea
    (septa and lobules)
    mediastinum testis
53. epididymis

HALF-PELVIS MODELS M1–M6

5. prostate gland
    ejaculatory duct (within prostate)
    urethra
        (6 in prostatic segment)
7. seminal vesicle
24, 8. ductus deferens
10. corpus spongiosum

11. body of penis
12. glans of penis
14. corpus cavernosum
15. testis
16. epididymis
17–19. spermatic cord

TORSO MODEL N2 (SEXLESS)

327. gonadal artery
328. (left) gonadal vein
329. (right) gonadal vein

VI. Female Reproductive System Model Keys

TORSO MODELS S1 and S2

37. labium major (plural: labia majora)
38. labium minor (plural: labia minora)
41. vagina
42–45. uterus
44. cervix
46, 47. uterine or Fallopian tube
47. fimbriae

48. ovary
50. round ligament
mammary gland
6. glandular tissue
7. areola
nipple
lactiferous ducts
lactiferous sinuses (ampullae)

PELVIS MODEL

1. mons pubis
labium major (pl: labia majora),
   3 on right side of model, 2 on left
labium minor (pl: labia minora),
   4 on right side of model, 3 on left
16. round ligament
18. broad ligament
20. uterine or Fallopian tube
fimbriae

21. ovary
22. uterus
23. cervix
29. vagina
37. clitoris
40. greater vestibular gland

HALF PELVIS MODELS F1–F6

4. labium major (pl: labia majora)
5. labium minor (pl: labia minora)
6. clitoris
10. vagina
11. uterus

12–13. cervix
14. uterine or Fallopian tube
fimbriae
15. ovary
17. round ligament
mons pubis
right ovarian artery and veins

TORSO MODEL N2 (SEXLESS)

327. gonadal artery
328. (left) gonadal vein
329. (right) gonadal vein

MAMMARY GLAND MODEL

1, 2. (outer edge of) areola
3. (adjacent to) nipple
5. glandular tissue
lactiferous ducts
lactiferous sinuses (ampullae)

References

In addition to the text, the following books or their earlier editions were used in the preparation of laboratory materials or this laboratory guide. They are excellent supplementary references and many (or their more recent editions) are available in the Life Sciences Library or elsewhere in the IU system.

Carr, K.E., and P.G. Toner. *Cell Structure*. New York: Churchill Livingstone, 1982.

*Clemente, C.D. *Anatomy: A Regional Atlas of the Human Body*. 3rd ed. Baltimore: Urban and Schwarzenberg, 1987.

*Hammersen, F. *Sobotta/Hammersen Histology: A Color Atlas of Microscopic Anatomy*. 3rd ed. Baltimore: Urban and Schwarzenberg, 1985.

Stevens, A. and J. Lowe. *Human Histology*. 3rd ed. Elsevier/Mosby, 2005.

*Toner, P.G., and K.E. Carr. *Cell Structure*. Baltimore: Williams and Wilkins, 1968.

Standring, S. (ed.). *Gray's Anatomy*. 40th ed. New York: Churchill Livingstone, 2008.

Young, B., Lowe, J., Stevens, A., and J.W. Heath. *Wheater's Functional Histology: A Text and Colour Atlas*. 5th ed. New York: Churchill Livingstone, 2006 (or its earlier editions).

*Indicates that the book, or material from it, is used in lab.

Notes

Notes

Notes

Notes

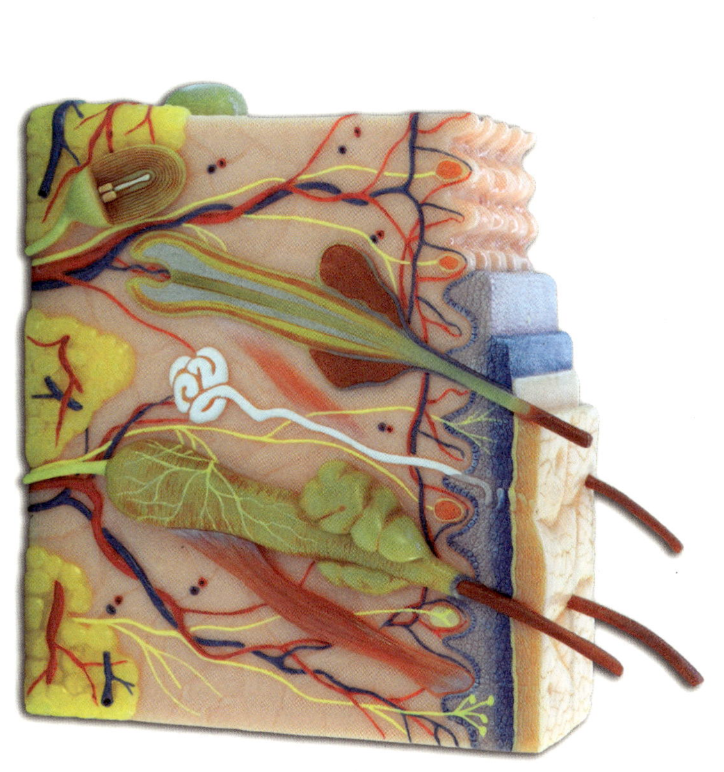

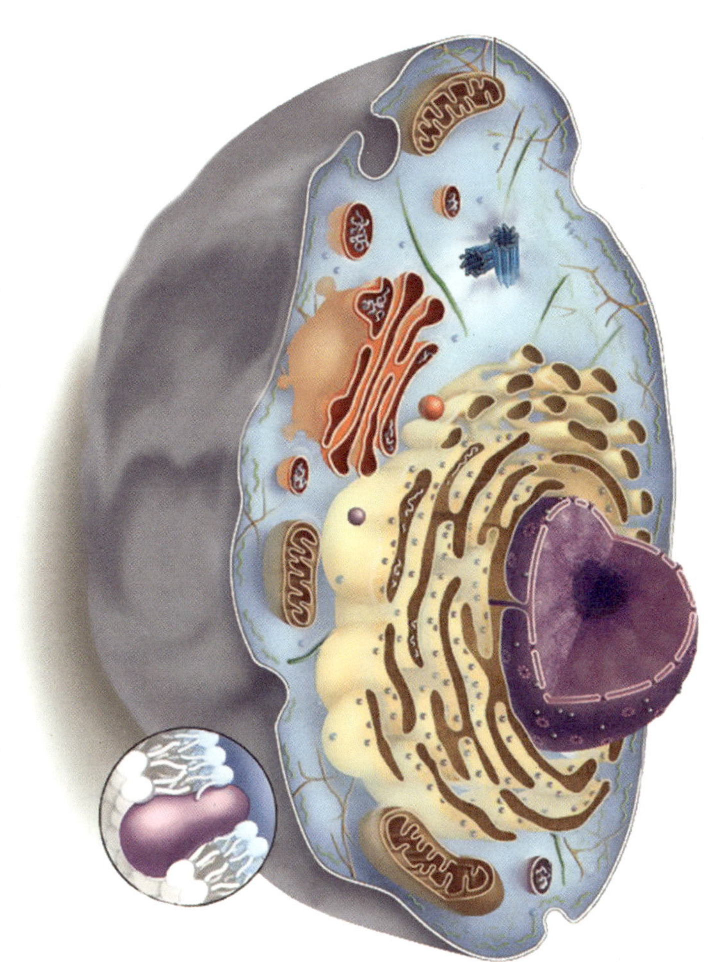

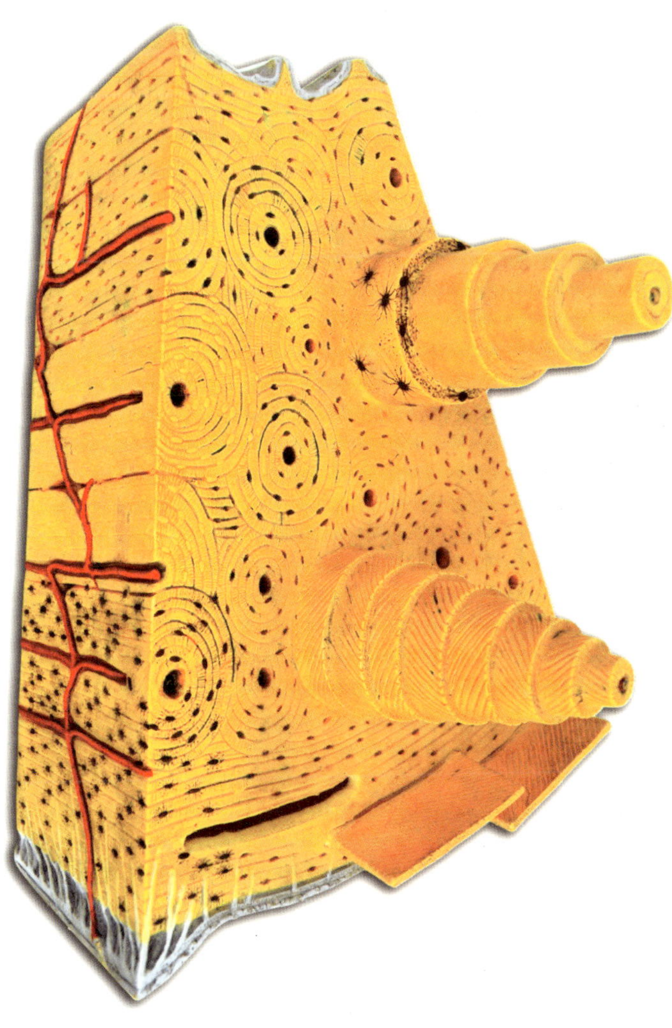

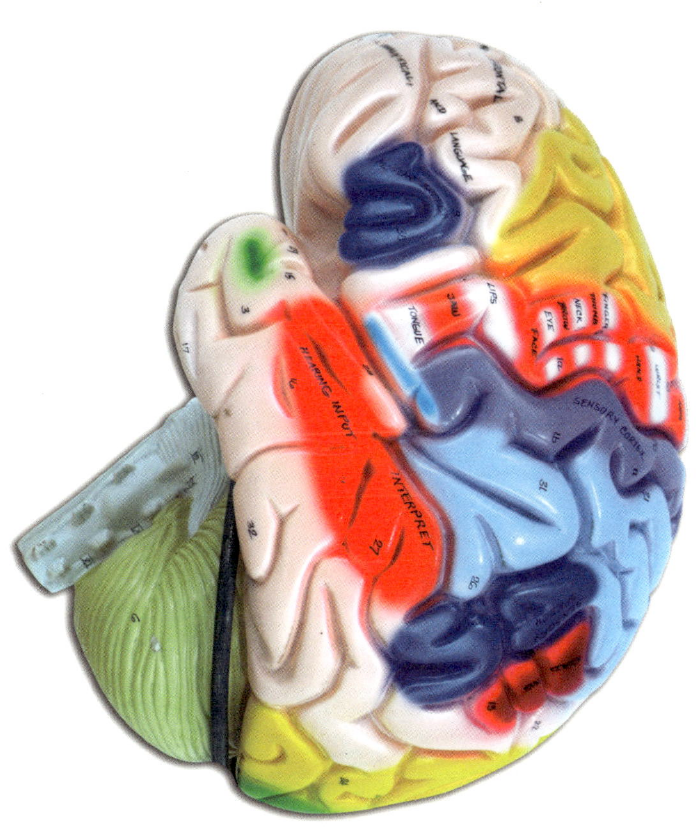

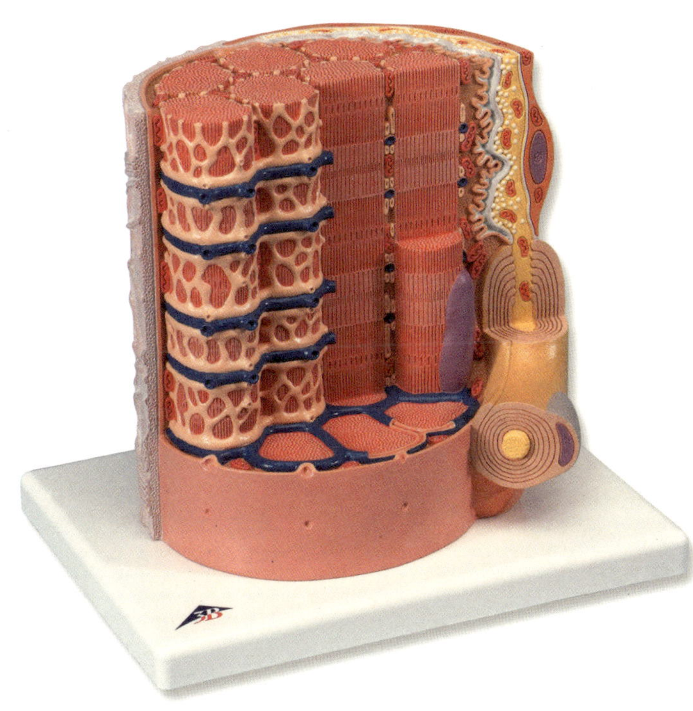

Based on product B60 3B Scientific®

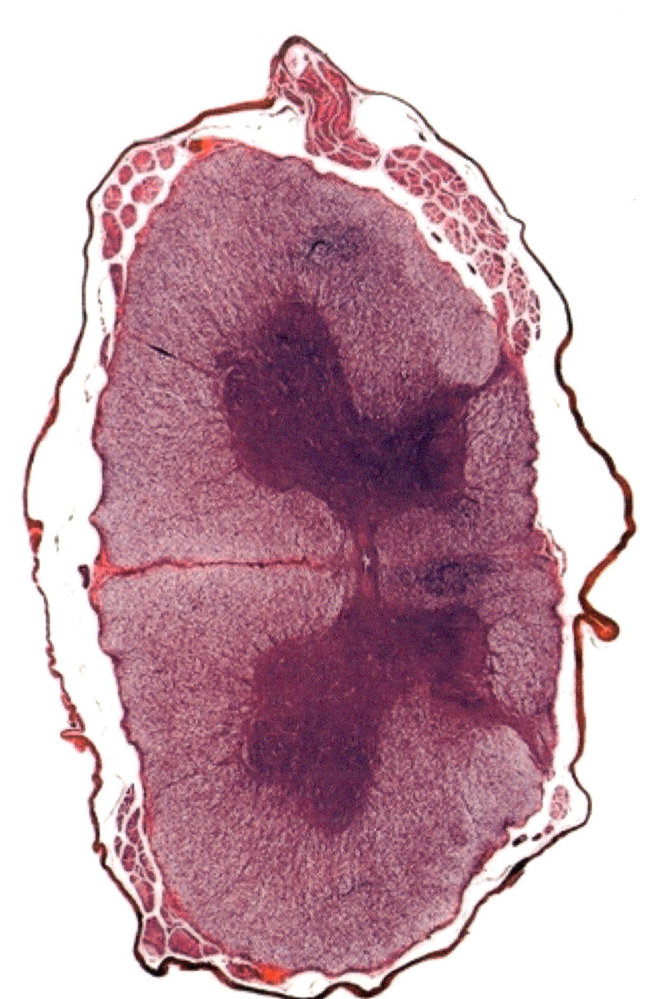

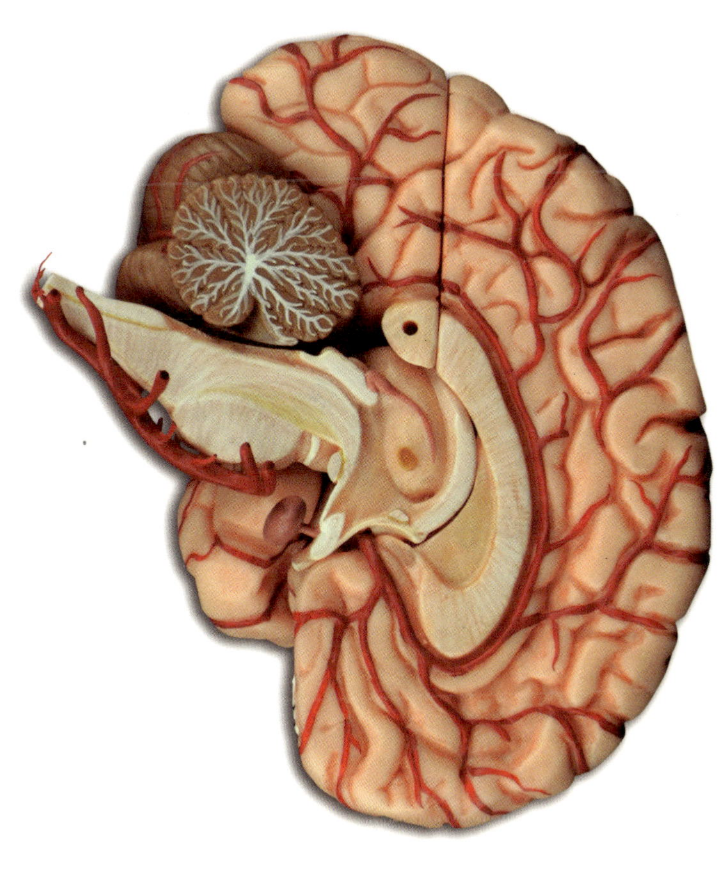

5

6

7

8

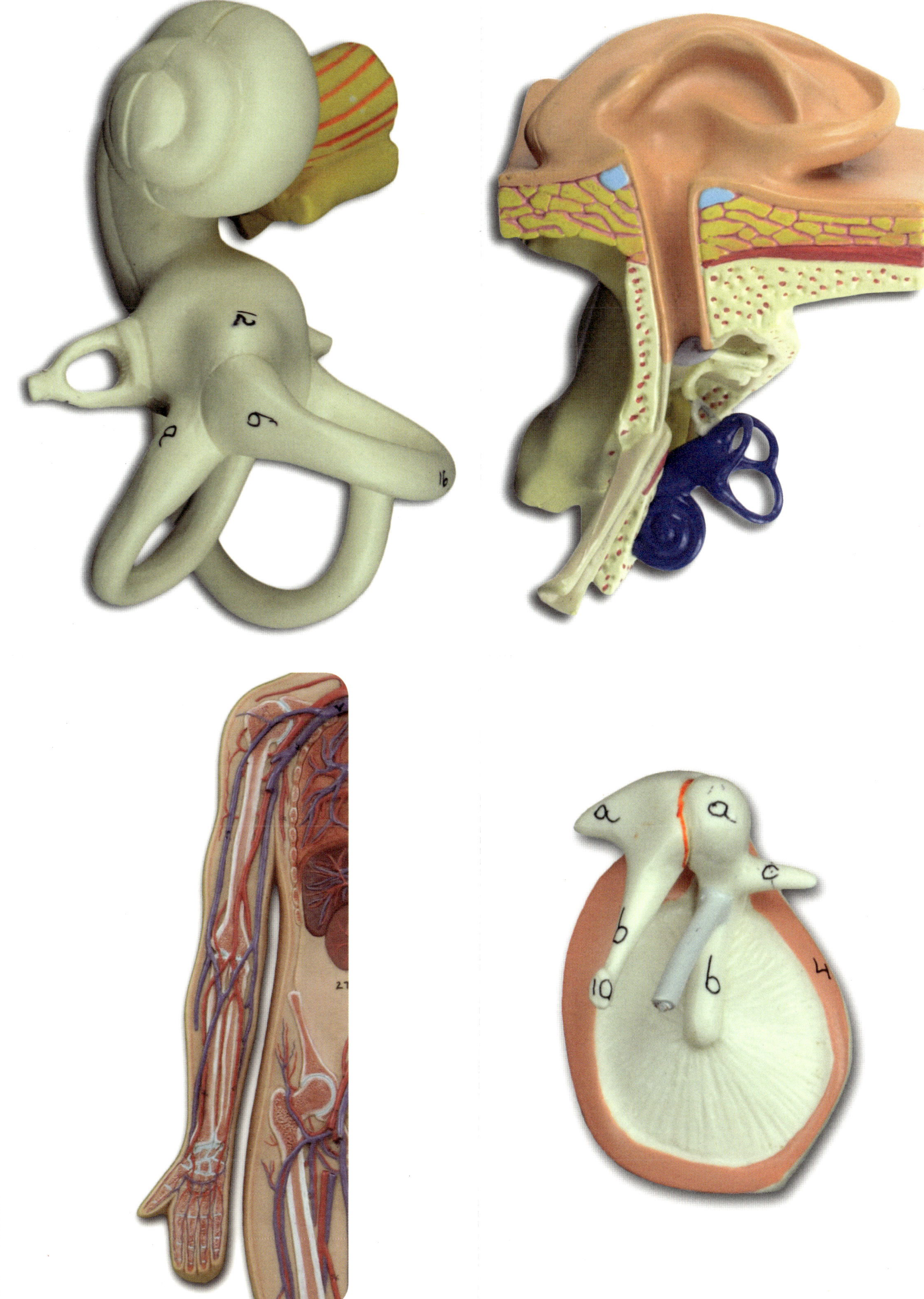

9

10

11

12

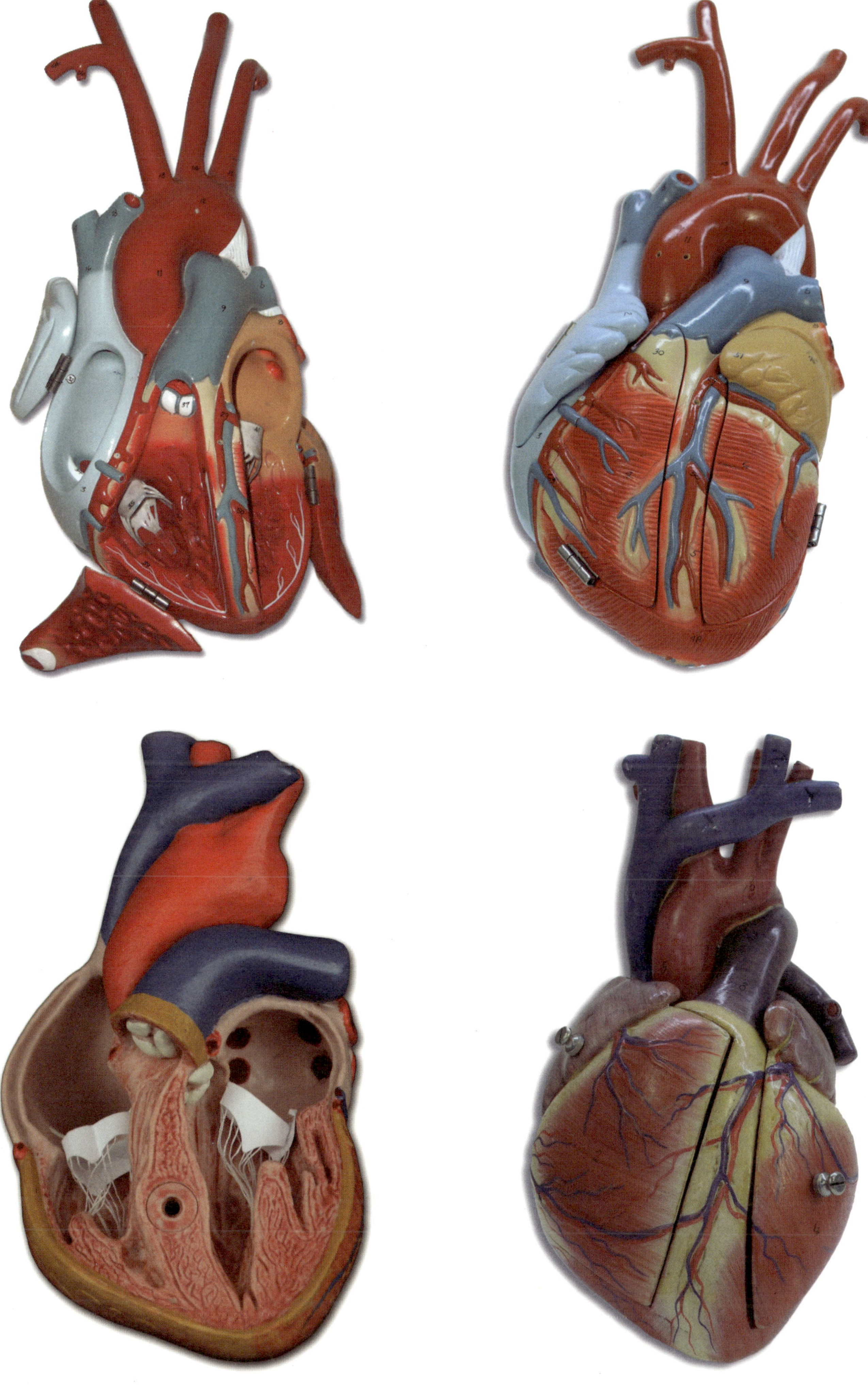

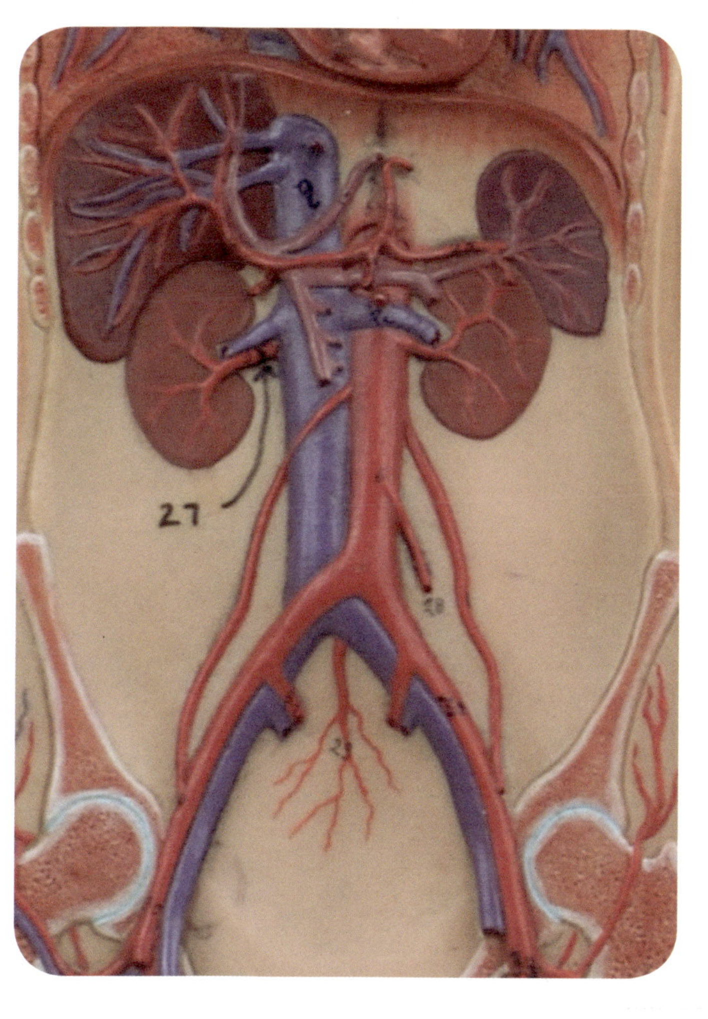
27

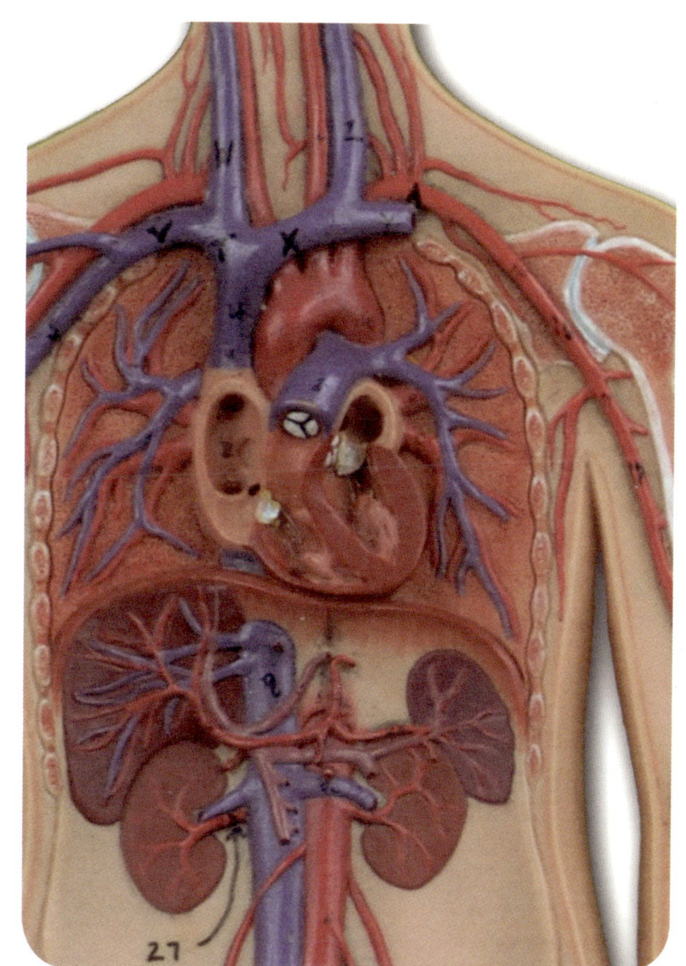
27

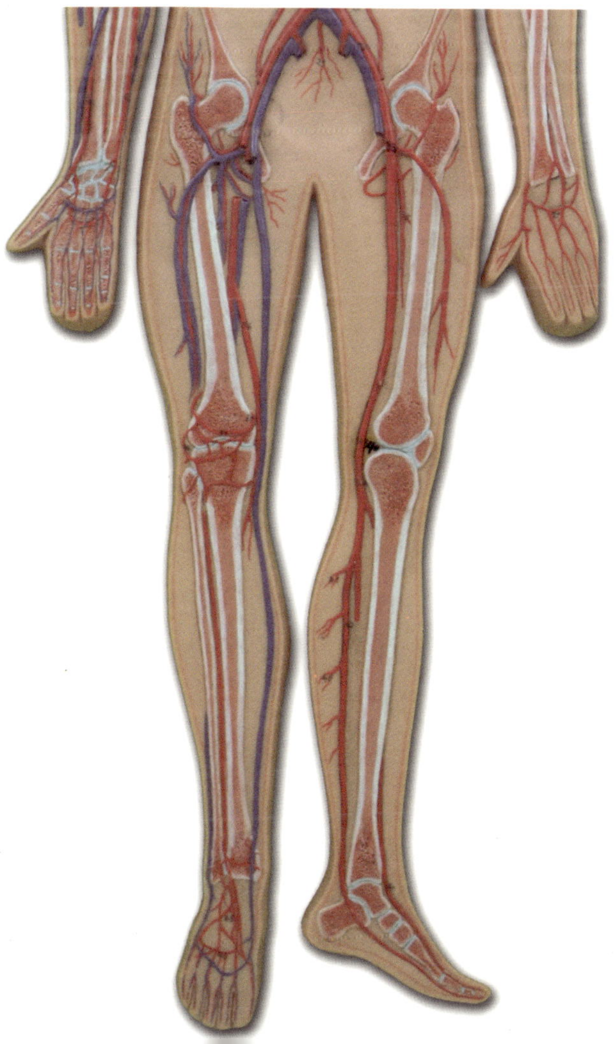

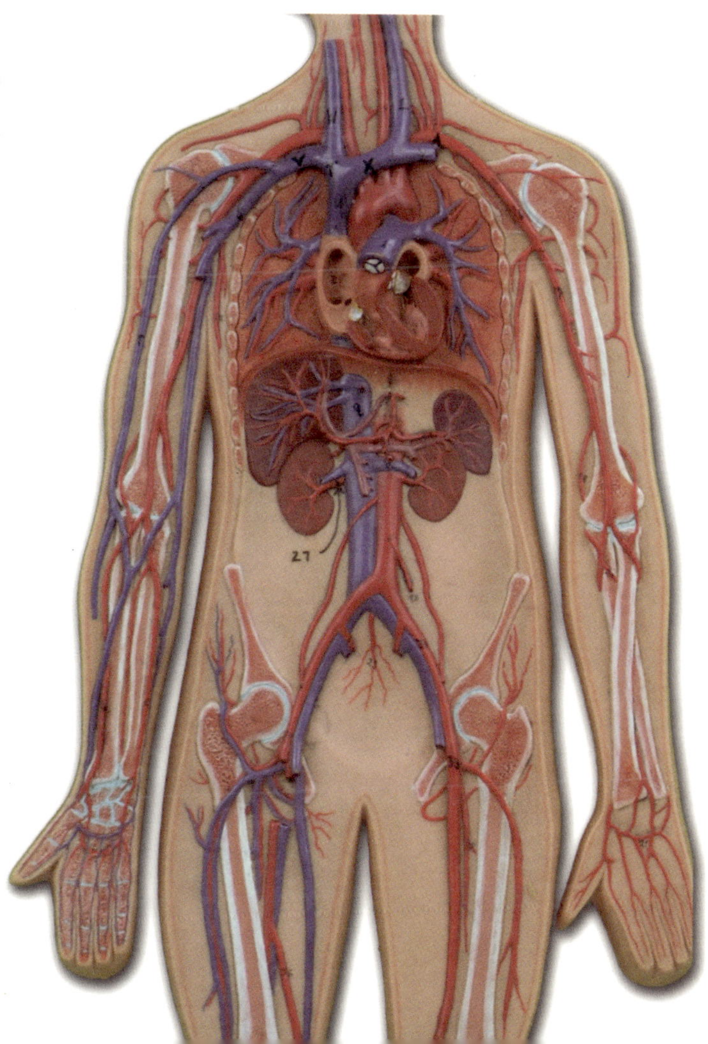
27

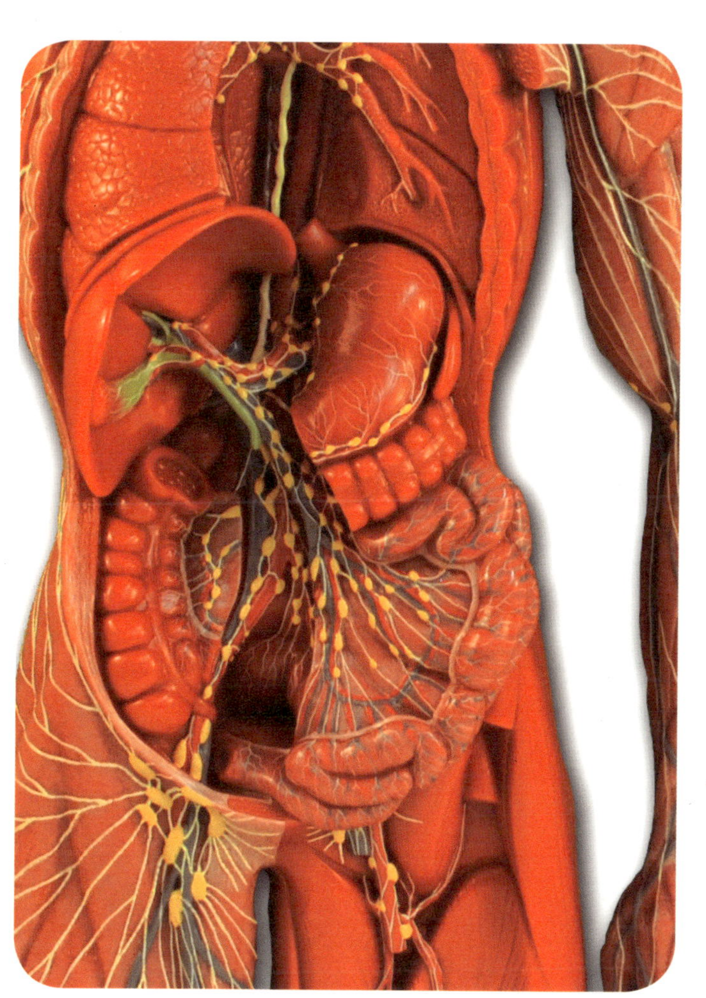
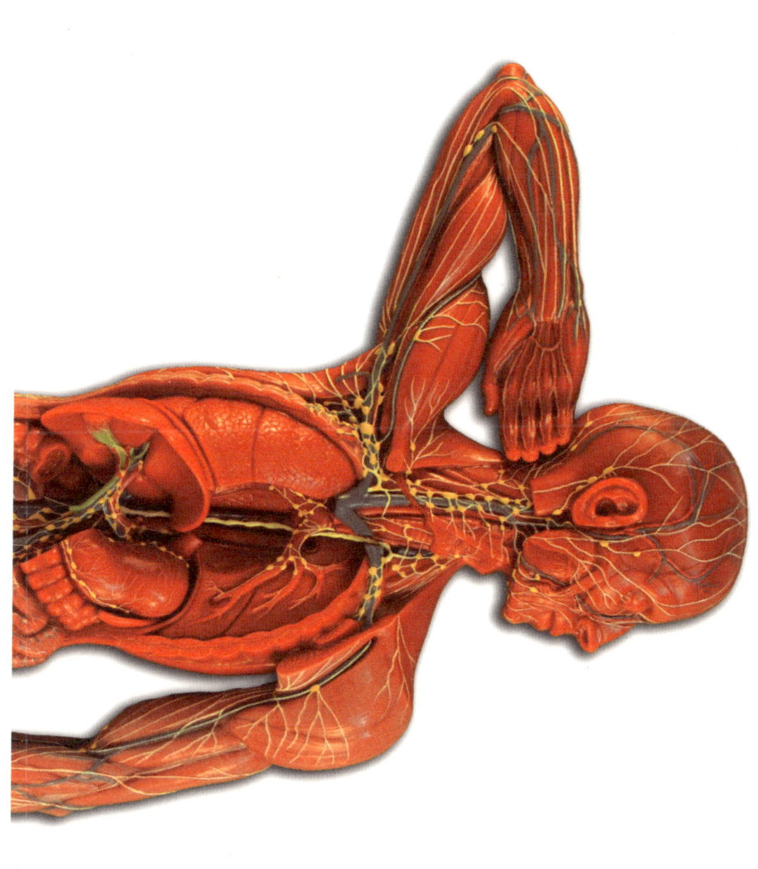
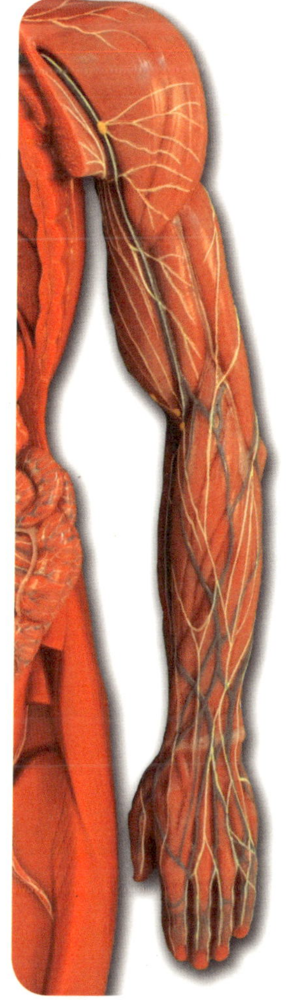
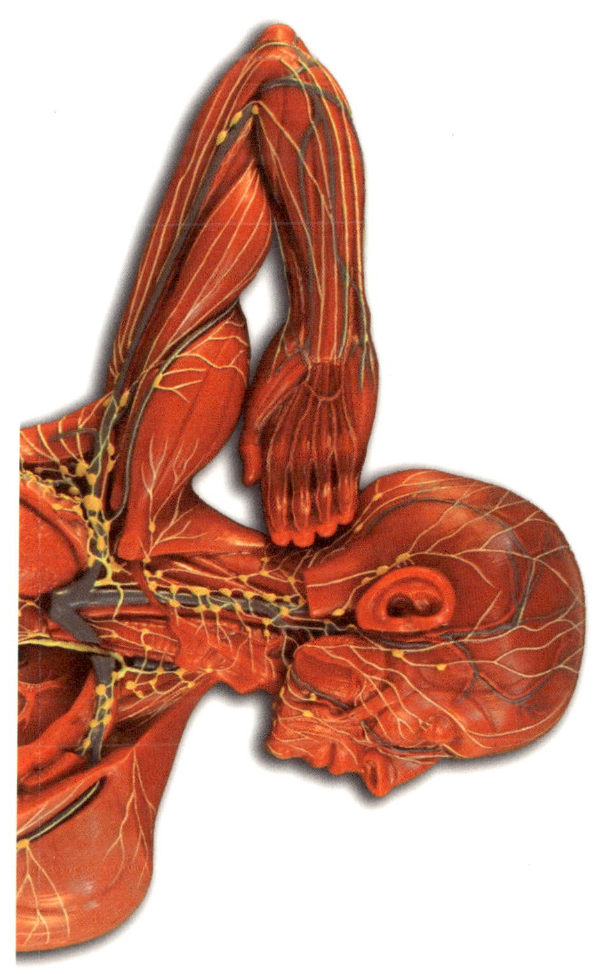

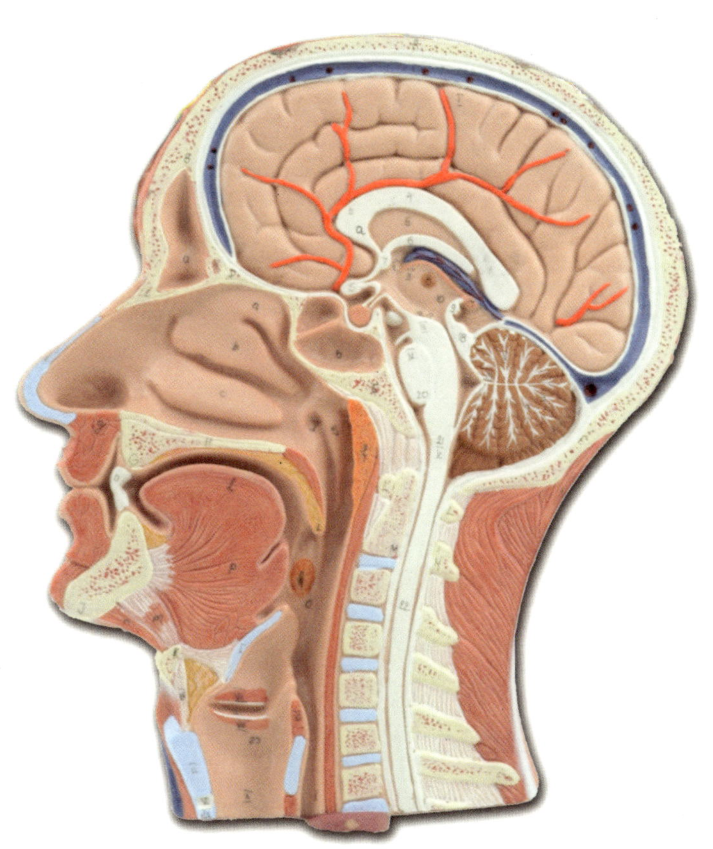
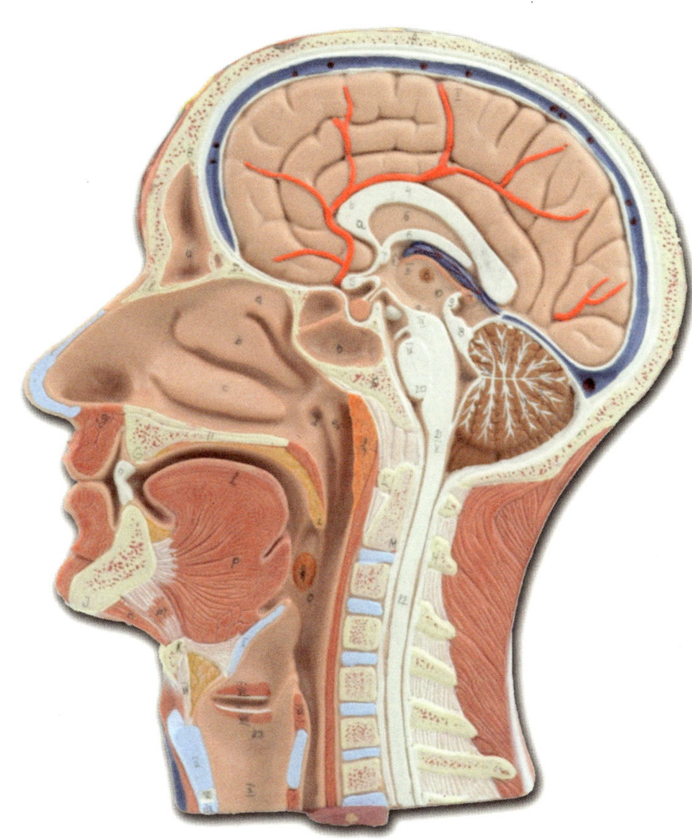
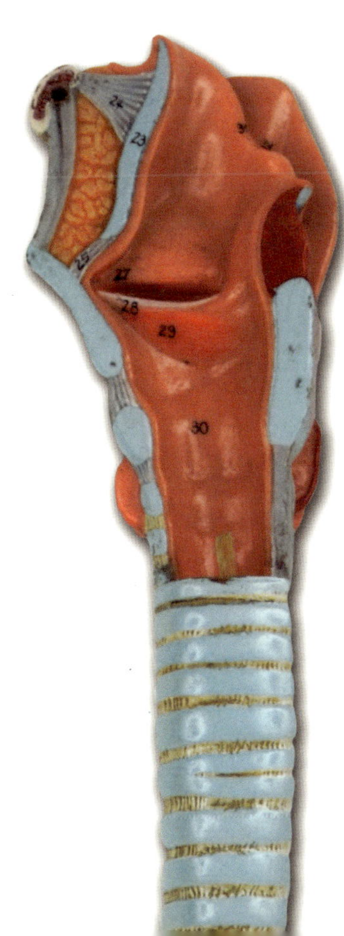
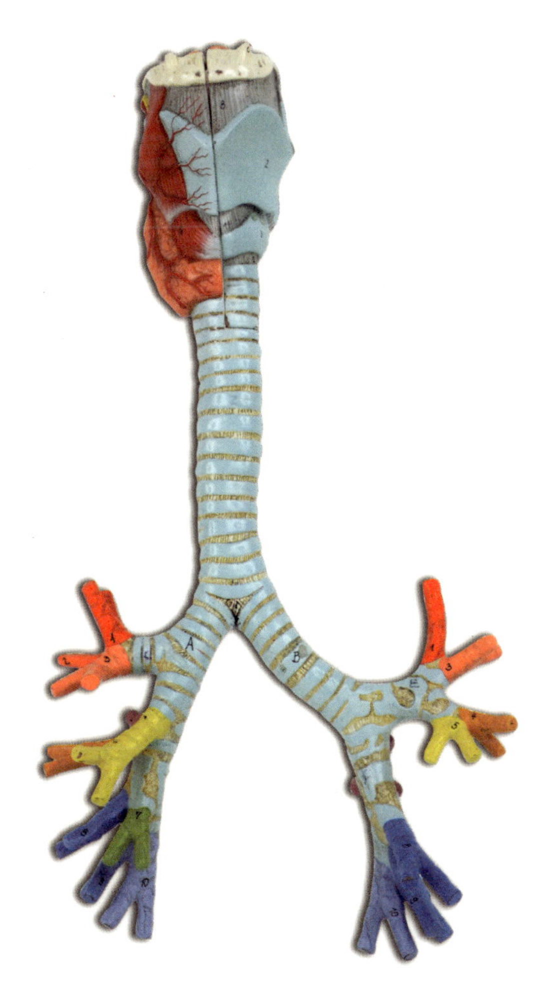

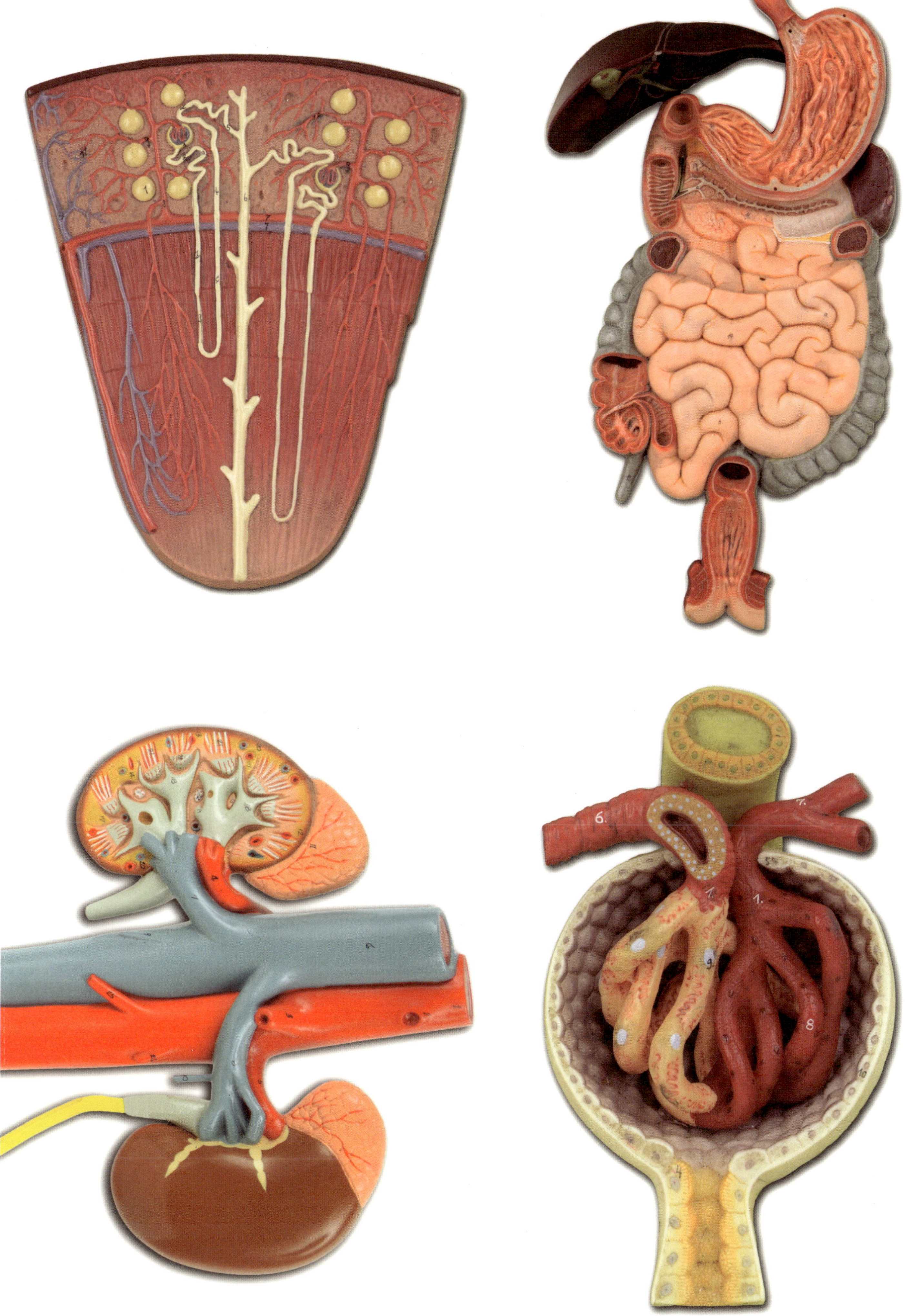

31

29

32

30